THE TOTAL BOOK OF

HOUSE
PLANTS

Additional illustrations by

Dorothea Barlowe
Susan Korner
Enid Kotschnig
Manabu Saito
Elmer Smith
Arthur Singer

THE TOTAL BOOK OF
HOUSE
PLANTS

by RUSSELL C. MOTT

Illustrations by
ALAN SINGER

DELACORTE PRESS
New York

Published by
DELACORTE PRESS, NEW YORK

An original work created and produced by
Vineyard Books, Inc.
159 East 64th Street
New York, N.Y. 10021

Dell TM 681510. Dell Publishing Co., Inc.
ISBN: 0-440-05751-5

Library of Congress Cataloging in Publication Data

Mott, Russell C
  The total book of house plants

    "A Vineyard book."
    Includes index.
    1. House plants. 2. House plants—Pictorial
works. I. Singer, Alan. II. Title.
SB419.M8   635.9'65   75-10735
ISBN 0-440-05751-5
Printed in Hong Kong

CONTENTS

Foreword

Since ancient times, house plants have brightened the homes of people throughout the world. Today, as the outdoor world of trees and shrubs and vines continues to shrink, erased by highways and parking lots and shopping centers, they are more than ever essential to the well-being and inner tranquillity of all plant lovers.

In recent decades ecologists and nurserymen, growers and biologists have worked alongside one another to augment our knowledge of cultivating and breeding indoor plants and foliage. As a result, infinite new varieties and sophisticated new techniques of culture have come into being.

It is the purpose of this volume to set forth this diversified information simply and succinctly. The range of house plants covered is worldwide, extending from orchids to cacti, from begonias to African violets. In each case all relevant information is included in the simplest form possible—mixing soils, how and when to plant, use of fertilizers, repotting and starting new plants. For closely related plants with similar culture needs, such as the many varieties of begonias or geraniums, culture requirements are given in a general article within the relevant section; for all other plants with individual culture needs, the instructions accompany the article on each species of plant. In the case of the palm family, culture requirements for all the species cited are presented in a full-page chart.

Much attention is given to dish gardens and terrariums, tropical bonsai and hanging baskets, year-round care of patio plants and home culture and forcing of flowering bulbs. Included also are formulas for soilless potting mixes and new slow-release fertilizers, along with precise instructions as to light requirements, watering and temperature needs. The botanical name, family name, common name and original habitat of each ornamental plant add to the reader's knowledge of this fascinating and rewarding hobby or avocation.

What makes this book unique in its field, beyond any other factor, is the care and time and patience that have been spent on the illustrations. Seven artists were involved, and I am grateful beyond measure to Alan Singer, who illustrated the major portion of this book. My thanks go as well to Alan's father, Arthur Singer, who illustrated the jacket, to Manabu Saito, who illustrated the cacti section, and to Elmer Smith, who illustrated the orchid section. Credit for special renderings and drawings go to Dorothea Barlowe, Enid Kotschnig and Susan Korner.

Others to whom I am grateful for their help in reading the manuscript or making special contributions to the text include Richard Peterson, editor of the American Orchid Society Bulletin, and Gordon G. Dillon, executive secretary of the American Orchid Society Inc., Botanical Museum, Harvard University, Cambridge, Massachusetts; Dr. H. E. Moore, Jr., and Dr. Wm. J. Dress of the L. H. Bailey Hortorium, Dr. Kenneth Horst, associate professor, Plant Pathology Extension, and Dr. Raymond Fox, Department of Floriculture, all of Cornell University, Ithaca, New York.

Lastly, I am indebted to my good friend on the staff of Vineyard Books, Lucille E. Ogle, whose years of experience in the publishing field gave me guidance and encouragement in putting it all together.

R. C. M.
Ithaca, New York

This book is dedicated to
my wife BETTY,
who shares my love
for all growing things.

8

*Chrysanthemum blossoms
vary in
form and color*

HOLIDAY PLANTS

CHRYSANTHEMUM (*Chrysanthemum morifolium*) from China and *C. indicum* from China and Japan are the parents of most of the plants known to American growers as mums and in Europe and Australia as chrysanths. They are grown as pot plants and used as cut flowers for table arrangements, bridal bouquets and for spectacular flower displays both indoors and out. Flowering can be timed by regulating the day length, making blooms possible every month.

Colors offered are white, bronze, yellow, red, maroon and lavender pink, with pastel shades of each.

Flower form is varied. There are pompons with globe-shaped, compact flowers, some with flat, fluted or quilled ray florets. Disbudded pompons measure up to five inches in diameter. The smallest button pompons in colors mainly white and yellow are less than 1½ inches across.

Single and daisy types come in all sizes and forms.

Cushion types have tiered ray florets. Their dwarf growing habit makes them fine for potting.

Anemone-flowered plants have one or more layers of ray florets and a large raised center disk.

Spider chrysanthemums have curling tubular ray florets with ends shaped like a fishhook.

Fancy are Japanese types, which are rather shaggy in appearance. There are also feathery flowers that are carnationlike with cupped or twisted ray florets.

Hardy varieties sold as pot plants can be set outdoors to give flowers again in the autumn. It is well known that not all varieties sold are hardy. Only a few varieties cultured as florists' chrysanthemums are hardy to northern latitudes (check with your florist). When flowers have faded, cut the foliage back to about four inches and, as soon as the freezing weather is gone, plant outdoors.

Plant in a sunny location with a well-drained, well-prepared bed of garden soil. Addition of a complete garden fertilizer like a 5-10-5 is desirable. In hot climates protection from afternoon sun should be considered. Well-rooted cuttings can be planted directly in the garden bed. Vigorous single-stem sections are made when dividing a clump. Use the outside of the clump, discarding the woody centers. A second and third application of fertilizer during the growing season is beneficial. However, the last application applied two to three weeks before blooming, using a low-nitrogen type, will produce better quality flowers.

Pinch top growth when stems are five to six inches high to promote lateral growth. Select from one to four for continued growth. Continue pinching all shoots reaching five to six inches. In areas of early frost pinching should cease by mid-July.

If large blooms are desired, begin disbudding when buds are large enough to handle. Remove all flower buds except one or two per flower cluster; allow these to develop.

Plants not hardy enough to live over winter can be dug up, potted and moved indoors for late fall flowering. Grow as cool as possible. Give full exposure to sun and keep potting mix moist. Cuttings are made from suckers which sprout from the base of the plant, are rooted in peat, sand or vermiculite. Pot them up, moving to larger pots as needed. The short days of winter will naturally initiate buds, and flowering may take place February or March. Grow in a room about 60° F. Give full sun days but long nights of darkness. Do not expose the plants to any light during the night if you want flowers.

Home care for lasting quality of a potted chrysanthemum is the same as for most florist flowering plants. Provide bright light but not direct sun. Keep the temperature at night at least 10 degrees lower than in the daytime. Water daily, if needed, to keep pot moist.

Lilium longiflorum

EASTER LILY or **NOVEMBER LILY** *(Lilium longiflorum)* This beautiful lily from Japan is a main crop for flower growers all over the warm temperate world, producing its large white flowers in spring. It is often bought just as its first flower is about to open. Other buds will then open in the home. The yellow floral parts, the male anthers, may be removed as each bud opens to prevent pollen staining the white petals.

Before 1940 most of the bulbs were grown for forcing in Bermuda and Japan. Through breeding and selection, researchers in the United States developed varieties which grew successfully in Southern states and in the Northwest. Bulbs treated for forcing are shipped to greenhouse growers by the thousands for Easter sales each year.

After flowering, the plant, which grows from a lily bulb, may be moved to a sunny garden. The survival of forced Easter-lily bulbs in a garden depends on where the bulbs were grown for forcing. Those grown in northern regions, for example, would probably survive in temperate areas, while those from southern regions may survive only in a warmer climate.

Plant outdoors when danger of freezing is past. Carefully remove bulb with soil mass and roots intact. Dig hole large enough so that the bulb will set eight to nine inches below the ground. A couple of handfuls of coarse sand or gravel at the bottom will facilitate good drainage. A tablespoonful of garden fertilizer mixed with the backfill will furnish food for continued growth. Sometimes a forced lily will bloom again in late summer. Normal blooming time is summer, but forced bulbs may need another year to build up strength for flowering. It is inadvisable to plant forced Easter-lily bulbs in the same area with garden lilies because of a chance of virus transmission.

In the home provide bright light, out of direct sun. Keep low temperature at night, check water need daily. If plant is foil-wrapped, punch holes in the foil bottom so excess water drains away.

CYCLAMEN (*Cyclamen persicum*) is a very popular winter pot plant, particularly in Europe, Australia and the United States. Most modern cultivars are sold under the name *Cyclamen persicum grandiflorum*. The typical shuttlecock-shaped flowers come in shades of pink, red, lilac, orchid-purple and white. The leaves of some cultivars are boldly patterned with silver. In table arrangements the flowers are as attractive as sweet peas. Later the same plants are sold as potted plants.

Blooming plants are available from autumn until spring, usually offered with several flowers and buds in all stages of development. The cyclamen is difficult to grow as a house plant because of its low temperature requirement.

This plant must have a cool place to survive. High day temperatures cause flower buds to wither and leaves to yellow.

Check the plant for water daily. If plant dries out, submerge the pot in water for 15 minutes.

Cyclamen persicum

HYDRANGEA (*Hydrangea macrophylla*) is a native of Japan, where it grows as a woody shrub about 12 feet tall. The large flower head is composed of a number of florets that are produced in late spring and early summer. The showy parts are the large sterile florets while the fertile ones are small and inconspicuous. The fertile complete flowers are hidden in the inflorescence. The color range is white, pink, red, lavender, blue and purple.

It is a plant sold in the Northern Hemisphere for Easter and other spring holidays. The flowers will last for at least six weeks.

Care in the home requires much water and as low a temperature as possible. Give bright light and no more than four hours of direct sun.

New plants may be started from cuttings in late summer.

In potting, add lime to the compost for pink varieties only; for the blue flowers the compost must be completely lime free. Use mix formula A.

Hydrangea macrophylla

Primula malacoides

Calceolaria herbeohybrida

FAIRY or **BABY PRIMROSE** (*Primula malacoides*) is a perennial species, but is usually grown as an annual. Flowering plants are usually found in the market early in the year and are available throughout spring. The dainty flowers range from pinks and reds to purple and white and many single and double cultivars have been raised. Since it is produced in a greenhouse, cool home temperatures are required. Keep moist in a bright window with indirect sun.

The variety Rinepearl White is grown commercially and comes in mixed colors of white, rose and carmine.

ENGLISH PRIMROSE (*Primula polyantha*), polyanthus primrose, is in flower markets from winter to spring. Usually potted in five-inch pots with fresh green leaves bearing flowers one to two inches in diameter, it comes in mixed shades of orange, red, yellow and mahogany.

This hardy species may be planted outdoors in a shady spot when frosty weather is gone. An excellent plant to combine with spring-flowering bulbs. A cool, moist climate suits them best, so this one is for northern gardeners to enjoy. Keep moist.

CALCEOLARIA (*Calceolaria herbeohybrida*) is known as "pocketbook plant." It is an old-time florist favorite and one of the most showy and interesting of all potted flowering plants. Calceolarias have coarsely toothed, soft, hairy leaves measuring to six inches long. The flowers are composed of an upper and lower lip; the lower lip is very large and inflated, more or less slipperlike. Some varieties produce flowers that are two inches in diameter and borne close to the foliage. Grown as an Easter plant, it comes in red, pink, maroon and yellow flower colors with orange, red and purple dots.

It is not suitable for areas where minimum temperatures habitually exceed 60°F.

Take care of the plant in the home as you would the primrose. Lots of water, no direct sun and as cool temperatures as possible to help it last. As a biennial, it has finished its flowering when the blooms have faded.

Senecio cruentus

CINERARIA *(Senecio cruentus* syn. *Cineraria cruenta)* is another pot plant which has low temperature culture requirements. It is a biennial and so is discarded when the flowers have faded, and new plants must be bought or grown. An inexpensive flowering pot plant, it is found in shops from late winter to spring. Numerous varieties are grown, with the colors of the daisylike flowers ranging from red and pink through mauves and purples to blue and white. Several bicolored forms are also grown.

One of the most widely grown varieties is Festival. Its compact, well-rounded growth habit combines with larger flower heads of medium-size flowers.

To keep it healthy in the home, grow it as cool as possible. It should not dry out and should be shaded from direct sunlight.

Cinerarias are excellent as container plants for patio decoration. Sow the seed in late fall for plants to set out in March. Seedlings potted in three- to four-inch pots using

mix A should be shifted gradually to avoid becoming pot-bound until they reach desired container size. Feeding every two weeks with a water-soluble fertilizer will produce vigorous flowering plants. Six- or eight-inch size pot specimens are effective when combined with begonias and other foliage plants on a terrace.

A related vine for outdoor culture in mild regions is *Senecio confusus,* or Mexican flame vine. A twining vine, needing the support of a trellis, it reaches 10 to 12 feet. It will die back to ground if subjected to a mild frost but will grow again from roots. The daisylike flowers are produced in large clusters of a startling orange-red color with golden centers. It will flower all winter where the weather is mild.

It can be grown also in a hanging basket and is effective when cascading over a wall.

Easily propagated from cuttings, this flame vine is subject to red spiders and aphids, unfortunately.

14

Euphorbia pulcherrima

POINSETTIA *(Euphorbia pulcherrima)*. Tropical Mexico and Central America are its native habitats. It is the most popular and showy flowering plant of subtropical climates and temperate interiors. Hybridizers have developed beautiful Christmas colors of red, white, pink and even pale yellow floral leaves or bracts. The true yellow and green flowers are inconspicuous at the center of the bracts.

Display in full sun, if possible. Leaves will sometimes drop because of poor light. Temperature can be warm.

Too low humidity can cause leaf drop. Keep moist.

Fresh plants from the florist are a joy to see each Christmas. When properly cared for, they will last for several months. When the colorful bracts have faded, the plant should be discarded in favor of other seasonal flowering plants.

THE LEGEND OF THE POINSETTIA:
On a Christmas Eve long ago Pepita was sad. This little Mexican girl wanted more than anything to give a fine present to the Christ child at the church service that evening. But she was very poor and had no gift. As she walked sorrowfully to church with her cousin, Pedro, he tried to console her. "Pepita," he said, "I am certain that even the most humble gift, given in love, will be acceptable in His eyes." So Pepita gathered a bouquet of common weeds from the roadside and entered the church. As she approached the altar, her spirits lifted. She forgot the humbleness of her gift as she placed it tenderly at the feet of the Christ child . . . and there was a miracle! Pepita's insignificant weeds burst into brilliant bloom. They were called Flores de Noche Buena—*Flowers of the Holy Night. We call them poinsettias.*

Courtesy, Paul Ecke, Encinitas, California.

CHRISTMAS PEPPER or ORNAMENTAL CHILLI (*Capsicum annuum conoides*). This is an attractive plant originating from Central and South America. It has cone-shaped berries which are in fact miniature peppers. The edible, upright cone-shaped fruits are pungent to taste and display red, purple and cream colors. Although a perennial, it is grown as an annual.

Place in full sunshine, if possible. Yellowing or dropping of leaves is caused by low light. This ornamental pepper requires cooler than normal room temperature for lasting quality. Keep soil moist. A dry soil will cause leaves to turn yellow and drop. Water daily, if needed.

The Christmas Pepper is an annual and should be discarded after its beauty is past.

If you wish to grow your own, sow the seed in May or June. Treat the same as Jerusalem cherry seedlings. Plunge the pots in the soil out of doors. A pinch is necessary to shape the plant. A final shift to desired pot size is made in September when the plants are moved inside.

JERUSALEM CHERRY (*Solanum pseudocapsicum*). The Christmas or Cleveland cherry is a Christmas potted plant with shiny green leaves and large orange-scarlet cherrylike fruit. A yellow fruited strain is also grown.

Cherry plants need full sun and a cool room at night. As for all fruit-bearing plants, potting mix should be moist, otherwise leaves and fruit drop.

Plants may be kept after fruit has dropped. For best flowering and fruit set plant outdoors in summer. Some leaf drop occurs due to root disturbance when lifted in fall.

To grow your own, sow seeds early in February. Fluorescent light for a 14-hour day and 50° temperature are desirable. Pot seedlings in peat pots, then four-inch pots, before moving outdoors for summer. Pinch back now and then to encourage bushiness. Do not pinch after July 1. In September lift pots and make final shift to a five- or six-inch pot; move indoors. Fruit will turn bright orange-red for Christmas.

REMARKS: The berries contain toxic substances and should never be eaten.

Capsicum annuum conoides

Solanum pseudo-capsicum

AZALEA. *Rhododendron indicum* and *R. obtusum amoenum* are the two main parents of the hybrid varieties grown as florists' pot plants today. They are the most showy of the spring-flowering pot plants and are available in a wide range of colors from white and yellow to red and violet with both single and double flowers.

A class known as *Kurume* is probably the hardiest for outdoor planting of any of the forcing types. Your florist can tell you the variety name. The plants will winter outdoors in the more temperate regions.

When frosty nights are gone, the *Kurumes* can be planted out. Azaleas planted outdoors grow best in a sunny location or with partial shade and protection from the wind. In dense shade they become spindly and bloom sparsely. A likely location is under oak trees or pines, which have deeply penetrating roots. Shallow tree-root locations such as those under elms or maples are to be avoided.

Azaleas do best planted in straight coarse peat moss as it comes from the bale. Lumpy peat assures good aeration and drainage.

Dig hole larger than the ball of roots. Discard the existing soil and backfill with peat. A layer of sand or gravel in the bottom will afford good drainage. Set the plant only to the depth it was in the pot.

After planting, water heavily and never let dry out thereafter. When plants are set, apply a mulch about two inches deep, using peat moss, pine needles or leaf mold to conserve moisture. Much attention must be given to watering the first year.

If chlorotic foliage appears—*i.e.,* yellow leaves—it may be caused by a lack of iron. Apply iron sulfate or chelated iron according to directions on the package.

All azalea varieties sold by florists are handled alike in the home. Keep the plant in a cool spot while in flower, especially at night. A warm, dry atmosphere will make it bloom quickly; hence the blossoms will last only a short time. Keep the plant in a cool, sunny location and remove the faded flowers as soon as they wilt. Daily watering is necessary.

Unless you live in a mild climate, it is too much trouble to keep it for another year.

Rhododendron hybrids

Kalanchoe blossfeldiana

KALANCHOE *(Kalanchoe blossfeldiana),* an attractive long-lasting plant with showy red flowers, is available for Christmas and for Valentine's Day. 'Tetra Vulcan' is a variety grown most commonly today. It is a natural dwarf and bushy type with large red flower heads.

The average height of most varieties is eight to 12 inches. The plants, popular for their compactness, bear masses of four-petaled flowers ¼ to ½ inch in diameter. Flower colors come in shades of red; one variety is yellow. Named varieties grown are 'Scarlet Gnome,' 'Tom Thumb' and 'Brilliant Star.' 'Yellow Tom Thumb' is a variant of red 'Tom Thumb.' 'Jingle Bells' is a trailing type that is appropriate for hanging baskets. It has large, bell-shaped flowers. Taller-growing varieties known as Swiss Strain are also available to the trade.

To start new plants, make terminal cuttings in the fall or sow seed in the spring.

The plant's low-temperature require-ments for successful flowering limit its use as a flowering house plant. Instead, it may be grown as a foliage plant at room temperature, giving it culture as for any succulent plant.

The plant's water requirements are on the dry side.

A schedule for flowering at different times of the year as used by some commercial flower growers follows:

Temperature of 60° specified.

Shading plants by black-cloth treatment, giving total darkness from 5:00 P.M. to 8:00 A.M.

Seed started from January to July.

Shade applied July 20 to September 20 will produce flowering plants in mid-October.

Shade applied August 15 to October 1 will flower plants by early December.

Shade applied September 1 to October 15 will give flowering plants for Christmas.

Flowering will occur without black-cloth treatment if grown at 50°.

FLOWERING HOUSE PLANTS

Amaryllis *(Hippeastrum* hybrids)

A native to the Peruvian Andes. Bulbs are available at garden stores and florist shops. Hybrid strains have a color mixture ranging from pure white to rose, red, carmine, crimson and candy-striped flowers. "Prepared" bulbs are imported into many areas from Holland and will flower in the Northern Hemisphere for Christmas. Allow about eight weeks to flowering.

Seed pods develop rapidly after pollination. They are mature within four or five weeks. Pods should be picked as soon as they turn yellow and begin to split open. Remove the seed from the pod, allow it to dry for a few days and then plant. Use mix formula D in a flat or shallow container that has good drainage. Provide shade for germination, then increase light to full sunlight for development of seedling bulbs. Transplant to individual pots as soon as seedlings are large enough to handle.

LIGHT: Indirect sun is needed when the bulb starts to flower. Partial shade helps to bring out brilliant color of flowers.

TEMPERATURE: A warm temperature is needed for forcing into flower; cool conditions make flowers last longer.

MOISTURE: Water well after potting, then water on the dry side until root growth is started. Then keep moist while in leaf.

PROPAGATION: Propagate from seed (three years to flowering) or offset bulbs at potting time (two years to flowering).

POTTING: Use a well drained potting mix B, potting the bulb into a five- to seven-inch pot. Allow one inch of mix around the bulb. The bulb is potted to leave the upper third exposed above the mix level.

FERTILIZER: Apply water-soluble fertilizer once a month during growth season.

INSECTS: Amaryllis is subject to spider mites and mealy bugs.

REMARKS: After bulb has flowered, place outdoors in a semishady location for summer growth. In fall, when leaves dry down, store in a cool, dry location until signs of growth appear in late fall or winter.

Hippeastrum vittatum

Kafir Lily *(Clivia miniata)*

A native to South Africa and a member of the amaryllis family. Three species are available: *C. miniata*, salmon red funnel-shaped flowers; *C. cyrtanthiflora*, tubular flowers, orange, red and green; *C. nobilis*, tubular flowers, brilliant orange-red with green tips. In addition, several hybrids have been raised. Flowering period is late winter and early spring. Flowers are followed by ornamental red berries.

Flowering-size plants usually grow best in eight- to ten-inch pots and do best when left undisturbed. When masses of the tuberous thick roots seem to be replacing the potting mix, it is time to repot.

When repotting is needed, the best time to do so is after flowering in the spring; divide the plant, if necessary. Do not cut into more than two sections. The larger the section, the more leaf surface, the better the chance of flowering.

The Kafir lily is a large plant that usually occupies much space; some plants attain 18 to 24 inches in height and are as broad. It is hardly an apartment dweller, but it is an excellent plant to use on the outdoor patio in summer for decoration.

Belgian and Zimmerman hybrids, grown in the United States, offer outstanding foliage and flower characteristics. Plants grown outdoors are planted in borders with plants such as ferns, azaleas and other shade types. Plant in rich soil with top of tuber above soil line. Leave undisturbed for several years to obtain the best bloom.

LIGHT: When grown outdoors they need high light and protection from sun; bright indirect light indoors.

TEMPERATURE: Winter temperature cool, spring warm.

MOISTURE: Keep moist in growing period, water sparsely in winter.

PROPAGATION: By seed or by division.

POTTING: When extremely pot-bound, repot (probably every three or four years). Use mix A.

FERTILIZER: Apply water-soluble fertilizer once a month during growing period.

INSECTS: Mealy bugs.

Clivia miniata

Allamanda
(A. cathartica hendersonii)

Also known as Golden Trumpet, a vinelike shrub, eight to ten feet high, it comes from Brazil. Can be grown as a potted house plant. It produces golden-yellow funnel-shaped flowers. Prospers if grown in a conservatory, greenhouse or on an enclosed sun porch. *A. neriifolia* is more shrublike, having golden-yellow flowers striped inside with reddish-brown.

The plant's small, oleanderlike leaves are arranged in whorls around the stems. This species flowers in late winter and early spring. It is propagated by cuttings and also seeds when produced.

Another variety is *A. williamsi*, which produces smaller blooms in less profusion than *A. cathartica hendersonii*. It is propagated by air layering and also by cuttings.

LIGHT: Very high. Full sunlight is required for best growth and flowering.

TEMPERATURE: Provide warm temperature for growing, cool in winter.

MOISTURE: Keep moist in growing period, dry in winter.

PROPAGATION: Stem cuttings from mature growth in spring; air layering.

POTTING: Mix B.

FERTILIZER: Should be fertilized monthly in spring and summer.

INSECTS: Subject to aphids, red spider mites.

PRUNING: When plants cease flowering in winter, prune back and give less water.

Allamanda cathartica hendersonii

Star Jasmine
(Trachelospermum jasminoides)

Also called Confederate or Chinese star jasmine, it is a twining, vinelike shrub from southern China. It is not a true jasmine, belonging to the dogbane or *Apocynaceae* family. With support it will twine to 20 feet. Without support and with pinching back it makes a spreading shrub or ground cover. The new foliage is glossy green, becoming lustrous dark green as it matures. Leaves measure to three inches long. Flowers are white, star-shaped, one inch across, borne in clusters and fragrantly sweet. Heaviest bloom occurs in late spring to early summer. A popular plant for greenhouses.

It may be trained in any shape or direction desired. Train on columns, walls or balconies by providing a cord tied for direction. For training start with a staked plant or one that has not been tip-pinched to make it bushy. Choose a spot where its fragrance can be enjoyed or where night lighting can pick up its white blossoms.

Train as indoor potted plants by occasionally tip-pinching wiry vine type of growth. Young plants are slow to start and are grown warm until plant matures.

LIGHT: Very high. They do best in direct sunlight in winter and filtered sunlight in summer.

TEMPERATURE: Warm temperatures are needed for seedlings, cool for mature plants.

MOISTURE: Keep moist in summer, dry in winter.

PROPAGATION: Use stem cuttings of half-ripened wood in spring with a hormone rooting aid. Use any rooting medium.

POTTING: Mix B.

FERTILIZER: Fertilize with water-soluble solution monthly in spring and summer. No fertilizer in winter. When blooms fade, withhold water to cause more flowering.

INSECTS: Red spider mites, mealy bugs and scale insects.

REMARKS: Place in cool room for rest period in winter.

Trachelospermum jasminoides

Bougainvillea glabra

Bougainvillea (*B. glabra*)

Is native to South America and a member of the four-o'clock family or *Nyctaginaceae*. They are named after the French navigator Louis A. de Bougainville (1729–1811), who discovered the plants in Rio de Janeiro.

The floral bracts that surround the small inconspicuous flowers are the showy parts. *B. spectabilis*, a species grown in frost-free areas, is less desirable for container culture because of its tall growing habit and thorny stems. Many intermediate botanical varieties and forms have been developed by hybridizers. Bougainvilleas can be grown as potted specimens trimmed for bushy forms, as tree forms and hanging baskets.

Some desirable varieties for container plants grown in many tropical areas are:
B. 'Afterglow'; orange, turning pink, a sport of *B*. 'Crimson Lake'
B. 'Alba'; common white with greenish cast
B. 'Barbara Karst'; bright deep orange, long-blooming season, vigorous
B. 'Bois de Rose'; very good pink, long-blooming season
B. 'Crimson Jewel'; glowing red, adapted to basket culture
B. 'Hugh Evans'; vigorous, good foliage, no fixed season of bloom
B. 'Lady Mary Baring'; golden yellow, bushy
B. 'Mahara'; dark red, double flowers, dwarf, long-lasting bracts
B. 'Manilla Red'; large clusters of double red flowers. Train to trellis
B. 'Scarlet O'Hara'; fast-growing climber, large deep purple bracts, winter bloomer

LIGHT: Very high. Needs bright sunlight.

TEMPERATURE: Warm temperature is necessary.

MOISTURE: Keep moist, although less water required after pruning.

PROPAGATION: Use stem cuttings of pencil thickness, six to eight inches long. Best time is in spring after flowering. Root in sand and peat. Rooting hormone is helpful. Keep moist. Two to three months for roots to develop.

POTTING: Pot in any basic mixture. Grow flowering-size plants in gallon-size containers. Roots do not mesh to form ball, so disturb as little as possible.

FERTILIZER: Apply complete fertilizer solution once a month for young plants. Feed established flowering plants only late spring and summer.

INSECTS: Mealy bugs, aphids, red spider mites.

Passionflower
(Passiflora X alato-caerulea)

Most species came from South America. Natural, fast-growing climbing vines produce edible fruits used in the tropics for flavoring sherbets, juices and jams; some varieties are eaten with sugar directly from the pod with a spoon.

It is best grown by training on a trellis or other supports, or about the casement of a picture window. The flowers open and last for one day only. Florists cement the sepals and petals with a few drops of candle wax to make them last for several days. They can be floated in a bowl of water or can be worn as a corsage.

Other species for home culture are: *P. caerulea* (parent of *X alato-caerulea*), having three- to four-inch pink and blue flowers and gray-green foliage.
P. coriacea, with small green, yellow and purplish flowers and leathery green leaves, curiously formed, appearing to be attached crosswise, with two lateral points.
P. trifasciata, small greenish flowers and leaves with gray and purple coloring along the three veins of the leaf.

LIGHT: High, full sun in winter; responds to fluorescent-light growing.

TEMPERATURE: warm.

MOISTURE: Needs moisture year round.

PROPAGATION: Seeds or terminal cuttings of half-ripened wood, with several nodes to a cutting. Rooting hormone beneficial.

POTTING: Any basic well-drained mix is suitable for potting. Mix B.

FERTILIZER: Feed once a month with water-soluble fertilizer. Omit in winter months after cutting plants back.

INSECTS: Red spider mites and mealy bugs.

REMARKS: Outdoor summer growth on patio gives vigorous healthy plants as well as profuse flowering.

Passiflora X alato-caerulea

Glory Bower or Bleeding Heart Vine
(Clerodendrum thomsoniae)

A vinelike plant named for the wife of W.C. Thomson, a missionary at Old Calabar on the west coast of tropical Africa who in 1861 sent specimens of this plant to Edinburgh, Scotland. May be grown as a vine, a trellis plant or a hanging basket. European growers have produced clerodendrum as a pot plant for many years. Recent research at Cornell University has adapted this plant for crop production in the United States. The colorful white bracts and red flowers provide an unusual and attractive plant for home and office.

LIGHT: Normal short days and high light intensity of full sunlight or fluorescent light promote flowering.

TEMPERATURE: Grow at 70° nights. Lower temperatures inhibit growth. Higher temperatures enhance growth but inhibit flowering.

MOISTURE: Keep moist.

PROPAGATION: Propagate by means of two-node stem cuttings. Keep moist (polyethylene bag). Summer-propagated plants flower in about 12 weeks after cuttings are started. Use any rooting medium.

POTTING: Use potting mix formula B. Plant one to three rooted cuttings per pot, depending on the size of specimen desired, and use a four- to five-inch pot.

FERTILIZER: Water-soluble fertilizer is needed once a month or use slow-release type according to direction.

INSECTS: Susceptible to red spider mites, mealy bugs, aphids and white flies.

PRUNING: If more than one cutting is used in a pot, pinching is not necessary. If a single cutting is used, the new shoots should be pinched when they are one to two inches long. Remove only the top (soft pinch).

REMARKS: High temperature and low light intensity can cause a serious problem with bud and flower drop. High light intensity or low temperature (below 60°) prevents bud drop. Susceptible to leaf spot diseases. Remove infected foliage; avoid splashing water.

Clerodendrum thomsoniae

Glory or Climbing Lily
(*Gloriosa rothschildiana*)

A native to tropical Africa. Walter Rothschild cultivated this lily in England with tubers imported from Uganda, Africa. The generic name *Gloriosa* comes from the Latin *gloriosus*, full of glory. The only climbing bulb, *G. rothschildiana* grows as a vine, reaching six to ten feet with its red and yellow flowers. *G. superba* grows as tall but with smaller flowers that have narrow but crisped green petals turning to yellow and finally orange-red as they mature. *G. superba lutea* is a variety having all-yellow flowers.

Its climbing habit with tendril-like prolongations of leaves needs a trellis or stake for support. The blooming season is summer to late autumn. Tubers normally are started in spring after a dormancy period. In warm, frost-free areas, they can be planted outdoors or in large containers for patio growing. A light shade from direct sun is beneficial.

LIGHT: High.

TEMPERATURE: Grow at cool temperature not to exceed 65°.

MOISTURE: Moist soil is needed.

PROPAGATION: Propagate either by seed or division of tubers when dormant. Its tubers, similar to those of dahlias, are easily separated when dormant. Select larger-sized new tubers with healthy growing tips for starting new plants. Make division when new growth appears.

POTTING: Use mix A or B. Set tubers horizontally four inches deep.

FERTILIZER: Apply water-soluble fertilizer every two weeks until flowers fade.

INSECTS: Red spider mites.

REMARKS: Gloriosa tubers can be started at any time of the year after a couple of months of rest. Two blooming periods a year may be had since the growth cycle is completed within six months. In warm countries, leave in the ground the year round. In colder regions, dig in the autumn before frost. Carefully clean soil from tubers and store in peat moss at 50°–60°.

Gloriosa rothschildiana

Natal Plum *(Carissa macrocarpa)*

C. macrocarpa, a plant species from South Africa, is a shrub with thornlike spines used as a hedge in the south. It is often planted by the seashore because it is unaffected by salt spray and wind.

The varieties *C. macrocarpa* 'Boxwood Beauty,' with glossy dark-green leaves, and *C. macrocarpa nana*, with similar but smaller leaves, are dwarf clones; they make attractive ground-cover plants in the south and desirable potted plants for home culture indoors. Other varieties are *C. macrocarpa* 'Green Carpet,' a dense spreading growth resembling a carpet of green. Also *C. macrocarpa* 'Tomlinson' with dwarf compact growth to 2½ feet high, extending horizontally to three feet. Without thorns, its slow growth makes it a nice tub plant for summer patios. These varieties, available in the United States, do well in terrariums because of their dwarf growth habit.

The fragrant white flowers occur irregularly throughout the year. Fruiting and flowering often occur at the same time. The fruits are eaten as plums and also used for jelly and preserves.

LIGHT: High light; will stand full sun.

TEMPERATURE: Cool nights and warm days.

MOISTURE: Needs moist soil condition.

PROPAGATION: May be propagated at any time from stem cuttings; rooting hormone beneficial.

POTTING: Use mix B in three-quarter-size pots or containers.

FERTILIZER: Fertilize with water-soluble solution monthly.

INSECTS: Mealy bugs.

PRUNING: Prune to shape and keep low or for bonsai effect.

Carissa macrocarpa 'Boxwood Beauty'

Gardenia jasminoides

Gardenia *(Gardenia jasminoides.)*

The gardenias of today which grow in tropical gardens or as potted plants are forms or grafted varieties of *G. jasminoides*; some may be *G. jasminoides veitchii*. Florists grow them as pot plants for spring sales and harvest the cut flowers for corsages. Popularity of this flowering plant is attributed to its large fragrant white flowers. Its dark glossy green foliage makes it attractive as a house plant.

However, when its complexity of culture is understood, it becomes a challenge to grow, and one may decide that it is not a good house plant for today's environment.

It should be understood that the flowering period is largely determined by night temperatures between 62° and 65°. Above 65° will increase vegetation growth but decrease growth of flower buds and increase bud drop.

LIGHT: Gardenias need at least four hours of full sunlight daily.

TEMPERATURE: Night temperature must be a cool 62° to 65°.

MOISTURE: Soil must be moist at all times. Drying causes chlorosis and bud drop.

PROPAGATION: Propagate any time from terminal cuttings. Insert the potted cutting in a plastic bag. Rooting hormone is beneficial.

POTTING: Use mix A without limestone; the gardenia requires pH 4.5–5.5. Add acid fertilizer to mix.

INSECTS: Susceptible to mealy bugs, red spider mites, scale insects and root nematodes.

FERTILIZER: Apply water-soluble type once a month at recommended strength. Iron chlorosis, evidenced by yellow-green leaves toward top of plant, can be corrected by one or two applications of a chelated iron solution.

REMARKS: Culture in the home is further complicated by the plant's susceptibility to disease. Leaf troubles such as tip burn (black tips) are caused by lack of moisture. Leaf spots are caused by fungi; brown leaf margins are caused by nutritional deficiencies; sooty mold is another problem. These are described in the chapter on diseases, pages 202 and 203.

All of these and more may contribute to failure with gardenia culture in the home.

Spathiphyllum
'Mauna Loa'

*Strelitzia
reginae*

*Anthurium
scherzerianum*

Bird-of-Paradise Flower
(Strelitzia reginae)

Dedicated to Queen Charlotte Sophia, of the house of Mecklenburg-Strelitz, wife of George III. A slow-growing plant from Transkei, South Africa, it belongs to the banana family. Potted specimens grow to five feet. The exotic flowers resemble a tropical bird with vivid colors of red, orange and blue. Flowering period occurs usually in early summer and lasts until late autumn. Individual flowers last a few weeks in bloom.

LIGHT: It needs very high light, with full sun in winter and light shade if outdoors.

TEMPERATURE: Warm temperatures suit it well.

MOISTURE: Dry soil conditions.

PROPAGATION: When propagating from seed, allow six to eight years to flowering. If by division of clumps, three to four years to flowering.

POTTING: Use mix A. Grow in large containers and repot only when necessary. Large undisturbed clumps bloom the best.

FERTILIZER: Apply water-soluble fertilizer monthly or top-dress with slow-release fertilizer as recommended on container.

INSECTS: Susceptible to mealy bugs.

REMARKS: Sink pot in ground or set on patio during summer.

Flamingo Flower
(Anthurium scherzerianum)

One of the world's loveliest, most exotic flowers.

A. andraeanum has a variety of colors, larger leaves and flowers and an upright habit of growth. It is a popular cut-flower crop for Christmas in Hawaii. It does best under greenhouse culture, where atmospheric humidity and watering can be better controlled and maintained. *A. scherzerianum* is better suited for house culture because of its habit of low growth. Flowering is continuous under good culture, and the brilliant scarlet flower bracts last a month or more. Flowers are excellent when they are cut for floral arrangements.

LIGHT: Medium light is best.

TEMPERATURE: Warm.

MOISTURE: Soil should be moist.

PROPAGATION: By seed or by separation of root-bearing side shoots from the main stems.

POTTING: Orchid mix D should be used. Or use equal parts of sphagnum moss and fine fir bark or shredded tree fern fiber.

FERTILIZER: Apply water-soluble solution once a month to *A. scherzerianum* and every two weeks to *A. andraeanum*.

INSECTS: Aphids, mealy bugs.

REMARKS: Keep upright growing stems covered with sphagnum moss and keep moist.

White Flag
(Spathiphyllum 'Mauna Loa')

Species of *Spathiphyllum* are found growing from Mexico to Peru and Brazil. For the most part they grow in foothills of mountains, in moist shady places along edges of rivers and streams. *S. clevelandii,* more typically a species, is less robust than *S.* 'Mauna Loa,' which has smaller flowers and leaves. Both types seem tolerant of artificial light and low atmospheric humidity as long as the root ball is constantly moist. Flowering occurs infrequently throughout the year.

LIGHT: Medium light is required; filtered sunlight in winter.

TEMPERATURE: Warm.

MOISTURE: Moist soil conditions are required at all times.

PROPAGATION: By division. It does best when undisturbed. Divide to larger clumps.

POTTING: Use mix A. Shift to larger pots not more than once a year.

FERTILIZER: Feed once a month with water-soluble fertilizer.

INSECTS: Mealy bugs, red spider mites.

REMARKS: Flowers are long-lasting when cut and placed in water.

Acalypha hispida

Justicia brandegeana

Chenille Plant *(Acalypha hispida)*

A native shrub from the East Indies, cultivated as hedges and bedding plants. It is an interesting flowering-foliage plant for the greenhouse and house culture. Its fuzzy minute red flower bracts are long pendant spikes and are often called 'Red-Hot Cat Tail.' Another species, *A. wilkesiana*, possesses striking foliage of red copper and pink color tones. The flowers of this species are less conspicuous.

LIGHT: High. Bright sun is needed in winter.

TEMPERATURE: Warm daytime and cool night temperatures are necessary.

MOISTURE: Soil should be kept moist.

PROPAGATION: Terminal cuttings of summer growth or shoots from cut-back plants in spring.

POTTING: Use mix A. Move to larger pot when root-bound.

FERTILIZER: Apply water-soluble solution once a month.

INSECTS: Red spider mites, mealy bugs and white flies attack it.

REMARKS: Prune severely to rejuvenate old plants in spring. Start new plants for replacement of old from cuttings.

Shrimp Plant

(Justicia brandegeana; Beloperone guttata)

Found growing in Mexico, with its white flowers beneath showy overlapping reddish-brown bracts, it is so named because of its resemblance to that tasty morsel from the sea. A cultivar with yellow bracts instead of copper is *J. brandegeana* 'Yellow Queen.' Flowering seems continuous since the bracts remain attached to the plant after the flowers fade.

LIGHT: It needs good high light.

TEMPERATURE: Warm day and cool night temperatures.

MOISTURE: A moist soil is required.

PROPAGATION: Terminal cuttings.

POTTING: Use mix A.

Amaranthus flowers start out green, but become more colorful as they mature.

Buying Tips

Sow seeds or buy as bedding plants. Make sure the soil in the pot has not dried out and that leaves and stems are healthy and firm.

Lifespan: A summer-flowering annual.

Season: Growth and flowering season from June through October.

Difficulty quotient: Ease is dependent on the summer temperatures.

In Brief

Size and growth rate

Love-Lies-Bleeding is a summer-flowering annual which can reach a height of 3-5 feet, depending on the temperature and general growing conditions. The plants are rather large and should be placed about 12-14 inches apart.

Flowering and fragrance

The long, hanging, red "tassels" bloom from June through September. No scent.

Light and temperature

Love-Lies-Bleeding is frost tender so sow outside in early May or plant out seedlings when the risk for night frost is over. A warm and sunny spot is vital for their well-being.

Watering and feeding

Water when needed according to temperature and weather. Feed with liquid fertilizer once every 3-4 weeks and sprinkle out lime once every 4 weeks if needed. Water with tepid water if possible.

Soil and transplanting

The soil should be light and porous. Improve the soil by adding a little sand before planting out seedlings. No transplanting except to set out indoor-sown seedlings.

Grooming

None.

Propagating

Use seeds, either sown directly in the garden or indoors in pots for later planting out.

Environment

Love-Lies-Bleeding is a decorative and unusual plant which grows best when planted together in a large grouping. Useful as a cut flower for indoor use. Also, try drying it for winter use.

Love-Lies-Bleeding—decorative and different

Love-Lies-Bleeding is one of about 50 species of *Amaranthus,* many weedy, which occur naturally in tropical and subtropical areas. Some are grown for their decorative flowers while others are grown for their brightly colored leaves.

Long-lasting
One of the popular names for this plant, Tassel Flower, refers to the purple flowers which grow tightly together in long tail- or tassel-like clusters. The generic name *Amaranthus* is Greek and means "not fading," a reference to the flowers and their long-lasting qualities.

Plant in groups
The typical height of Love-Lies-Bleeding is about 30 inches, but it can reach a height of about 5 feet in ideal conditions. The long, hanging, purple "tassels" make it easy to recognize. Its height may make it a difficult plant to place in the garden and it looks best with several planted together. It may be necessary to

tie the plants to a support, unless they are growing among other tall plants which can serve the same function.

Fertilizer and lime
Love-Lies-Bleeding needs warmth and sunshine and grows quite well in alkaline soil. It needs frequent

A season with Love-Lies-Bleeding

The growth and flowering season of Love-Lies-Bleeding is from June through October.

Plants will develop best in a warm and sunny position and they should preferably be watered with tepid water.

Feed every 3-4 weeks with a liquid all-around fertilizer and lime every fourth week if the soil in the garden is very acidic. Keep the surrounding area free of weeds.

Sow in the spring

Love-Lies-Bleeding is an annual summer plant and should be re-sown each year. Either sow the seeds directly out in the garden, fairly late in the spring, or sow them in indoor propagating trays and pick them out later.

Sow outdoors in early May in prepared, weed-free soil. Thin out to about 12-14 inches apart once the seedlings are growing well.

Sow indoors in a light and chalky soil in early April. Sow 2-3 seeds in each pot or peat briquette and select only the strongest for planting out.

Plant these seedlings out in early June in soil with a top layer of sand.

Plant Doctor

□ **Aphids** can appear on leaves, stems, and flowers. In addition to the insects themselves, black patches of excre-ment may be visible on the stems or eggs under the leaves. Minor infestations can be fought by spraying with soapy water. Use insecticide if they persist.

□ **Poor growth** is usually due to too low soil pH or damp and cold conditions. Growth may come to a standstill in bad summers.

NOTE: Pesticides not used according to label directions can be harmful to man, animals, and plants. Use only pesticides that have labels with directions for home and garden use. Always read and follow label directions.

feeding. Alternate between all-round fertilizer and lime, if the soil is acid.

Love-Lies-Bleeding
Amaranthus caudatus

Love-Lies-Bleeding is fun to plant in groups where its tassel-like flowers can wave together in the breeze. Plant it with other tall plants which provide support for each other.

FERTILIZER: Use water-soluble solution monthly.

INSECTS: This species is very susceptible to red spider mites, mealy bugs and white flies.

PRUNING: Prune old plants to eliminate straggly growth and maintain bushy character by pinching out tip growth.

Fuchsia *(Fuchsia hybrida)*

A group name for hundreds of cultivated hybrid fuchsias. Each year new varieties too numerous to mention are added to the list. Single- and double-flowered varieties suitable for hanging baskets, pot culture, espalier training, pyramids and standards or tree forms are available.

Additional information regarding fuchsia varieties may be obtained from nursery catalogs. The American Fuchsia Society has its headquarters at 738 22nd Ave., San Francisco, California 94121.

LIGHT: High. Direct sun in winter, light shade in summer.

TEMPERATURE: Cool, especially at night.

MOISTURE: Moist at all times. Daily watering sometimes necessary for hanging baskets.

PROPAGATION: Terminal cuttings of soft wood two to three inches long, in medium of half coarse sand and half vermiculite.

POTTING: Mix A or B is required when potting; good drainage is essential. Repot once a year to larger pot.

FERTILIZER: Fuchsias are heavy feeders, so apply water-soluble solution every two weeks in summer, once a month in winter.

INSECTS: They are susceptible to aphids, mealy bugs, scale insects and white flies.

PRUNING: Pinch tips out occasionally to make bushy growth. Prune back late fall or spring to promote new growth for flowering. Cut off fruits to get more flowers.

REMARKS: Fuchsia flowers best in long warm days following a cool growing period. Put plants outside as soon as danger of frost has passed. Bud drop caused by high temperature and poor light.

F. 'Rose of Castile'

F. 'Display'

F. 'Thalia'

I. 'Starfire'

I. wallerana
var. holstii

I. wallerana var.
sultanii variegata

I. 'Mt. Kum'

I. longifolia

Impatiens or Busy Lizzie

(Impatiens wallerana, also called *I. sultanii)*

A long-time favorite as a window garden plant, it has recently become the most popular bedding plant for shady moist places. Flower breeders have developed new varieties that develop into compact forms without pinching. They are free-flowering and available in a wide range of color and foliage patterns. Popular dwarf varieties in America are the F_1 Elfin series, and also the F_1 Imp series. More recently the United States Department of Agriculture Longwood plant exploration (1970) to New Guinea brought back new species and hybrids. Flower color ranges from pure white through shades of lavender to magenta and from pale orange to dark vermillion and scarlet. Leaf and stem color vary from green to intense dark red and may be beautifully variegated with white, yellow and pink.

LIGHT: Medium light needed; indirect sun in winter.

TEMPERATURE Warm by day and cool by night.

MOISTURE: Moist soil necessary.

PROPAGATION: By seeds or terminal cuttings (fluorescent light—16-hour day). Optimum temperature for germination is 70° F., with continuous light.

POTTING: Use mix A. Plants may be dug in fall and potted for indoor use.

FERTILIZER: Water-soluble fertilizer once a month.

INSECTS: Aphids, mealy bugs and white flies.

REMARKS: New F. strains have dwarf habit of growth; no pinching needed.

Oxalis species

*O. martiana
aureo-reticulata*

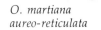

O. ortgiesii

Wood Sorrel *(Oxalis* species)

A large genus of about 400 species found growing throughout the tropics, belonging to the Wood Sorrel family or *Oxalidaceae.* The leaves of the plants resemble clover, having three leaflets. The roots are semibulbous like tubers. Several species are troublesome weeds in gardens and greenhouses, especially in warm climates. Others are grown in hanging baskets or on the windowsill. *O. martiana aureo-reticulata*, known as Sour Clover, produces large leaves and carmine-rose flowers with red lines radiating from a white throat. *O. ortgiesii*, named Tree Oxalis because of its taller growth habit, has large leaves, fish-tailed at the ends, and small yellow flowers borne five to ten in a cluster at the tops of small stems. *O. hedysaroides*, called Firefern, is well named for its fernlike foliage of a glowing satiny-red. Its bright yellow flowers are in sharp contrast to the showy leaves.

LIGHT: High light and full sun required. Flowers open on sunny days, go to "sleep" at night and in dull weather.

TEMPERATURE: Warm day and cool night temperatures suit this plant.

MOISTURE: Soil must be moist for growth. After foliage withers, keep dry until fall.

PROPAGATION: From seeds, divisions or bulblets separated at repotting.

POTTING: Use mix A and repot once a year when growth starts. Pot three to four bulbs in five-inch pan.

FERTILIZER: Feed once a month during the summer with water-soluble fertilizer.

INSECTS: Subject to mealy bugs, red spider mites and white flies.

O. hedysaroides

BEGONIAS

Grown as potted flowering plants, as foliage plants, bedding plants and as hanging baskets. The many species and varieties fall into three groups: fibrous-rooted, tuberous-rooted and rhizomatous.

The fibrous-rooted types, which have a central stalk, are extremely variable in foliage and flowers and include many free-flowering forms.

Tuberous-rooted kinds are mainly summer-flowering, with large camellia-type single and double flowers.

The rhizomatous types are distinguished by creeping rhizomes and large and small, beautifully colored leaves.

RIEGER ELATIOR BEGONIAS of the florist industry are a 1971 introduction to the United States and Canada from Europe. They were brought in by J. C. Mikkelson of Mikkelson's, Inc., the exclusive licensing agency for the Rieger Company of Nürtingen, West Germany.

Many begonias are offered in florist shops and garden stores along with poinsettias, azaleas and chrysanthemums. Their long-lasting spectacular blooms make them highly desirable for home embellishment.

For home culture the requirements are not difficult. High light exclusive of direct sunlight is of first importance. The potting mix must be kept moist. Drying out weakens the plant, making it susceptible to disease. Similarly, good aeration is important. A sun porch or outdoor patio is an excellent location for summer culture. Most varieties will flower continuously with proper care.

Fertilize only at half strength once a month. Too much fertilizer will slow down flower production.

There are two basic types:

'Schwabenland Red' is the predominant variety, with medium-red flowers and a distinct yellow eye. Other varieties have flower-color shades of pink, rose and orange.

Most of the Schwabenland varieties will flower the year round. In Europe, they are used extensively as attractive flowering house plants.

Aphrodite types are useful as hanging baskets because of their habit of growth. A new Aphrodite variety introduced in 1972, 'Amoena,' has a two-tone color effect of pink and yellow double flowers. Other varieties include Aphrodite 'Cherry Red,' 'Red,' 'Rose,' and 'Pink.'

Rieger elatior begonia (Begonia X hiemalis)

BEGONIA SEMPERFLORENS is the fibrous-rooted or wax-leaf type, and hybrids of it are the most widely cultivated of the begonia family. It is offered in the spring by nurseries and garden stores for use as a bedding plant in gardens and in containers. Flowering occurs, regardless of the length of day, thus making it adaptable as a house plant for the sunny window sill.

For many years wax-leaved varieties have been grown as pot plants and only occasionally used for bedding plants. Today, as a result of breeding new varieties both in the United States and Europe, there are many excellent F_1 hybrids. Most garden stores offer them in "packs," as they do for petunias and marigolds.

Two groups of plants are available: dwarf, which averages three to five inches tall when grown in pots, and an intermediate group that grows about four to eight inches high in pots. Each of these groups is further divided into green-leaved plants and bronze-leaved plants. Growing the bronze-leaved plants in full sunlight intensifies the bronze foliar color in some varieties.

A few of the dwarf-class varieties, identified as F_1 hybrids, created by plant breeders are: B. 'Scarlotta,' bright scarlet; B. 'Gin,' bright rose; B. 'Vodka,' bright scarlet; B. 'Viva,' pure white.

Another series of the variety 'Cinderella' is about ten inches tall. It produces about 50 percent extra-large flowers having a bright golden pincushionlike center. The leaves are larger than the regular fibrous type. Colors available are rose, white and a mixture. A fibrous-rooted double-flowering strain is also available. It produces about 50 percent doubles. Australian nurseries offer several varieties of *Begonia semperflorens*, including "Thousand Wonders."

Plants are started from seed, which is very fine and must be sown thinly on a *moist* surface. The seed container is covered with a piece of glass to reduce the need for frequent watering. A light sandy medium with sifted sphagnum moss will help maintain moisture. Seed usually germinates in about two weeks when given 70°. After germination, water the seedlings with a water-soluble fertilizer solution at half strength. When large enough to handle, transplant seedlings to 2½-inch pots.

Terminal cuttings made in the fall will grow into fresh plants for winter.

This group is also suitable for pot-plant culture. It has larger flowers than the regular fibrous group. The flowers are extra large and showy, with large bright golden-yellow centers. Plants are available in white, rose and a mixture of flower colors.

Begonia semperflorens

Begonia tuberhybrida pendula flore pleno

TUBEROUS BEGONIA *(Begonia tuberhybrida)*, sometimes called Camellia-flowered begonia, is a hybrid group derived from several South American species of begonias. The group is mainly summer- and fall-flowering. Plants are used in outdoor beds and containers. If they are grown for more than eight to ten weeks in the dry atmosphere of the home, they become weak and spindly.

Their flowers are remarkable for size, beauty and diversity of color, form and texture. Flowers are mostly double with plain, ruffled and frilled edges.

CULTURE OF TUBEROUS BEGONIAS
Starting dormant tubers
Tubers are started in the spring or whenever the pink vegetative buds start to show. Place them in pots or flats for starting. Use a medium of one third peat moss and two thirds sand or perlite. Peat moss alone holds 90 percent of its weight in water when saturated, thus is not recommended without amendment because it tends to pack and become soggy, excluding air. A coarse hardwood leaf mold or hardwood bark soil amendment may be used as a substitute.

Space tubers to allow for heavy root development. Bury by covering with half an inch of the medium. Water the container of tubers carefully to distribute moisture evenly, avoiding soggy wetness. Place container at a warm temperature of 65° to 75° in high light, but shield from direct sun.

Transplant to pots or outdoor prepared beds when the first two leaves have reached full development. Danger of frost must be past before planting outdoors. Rooting is usually heavy at the two-leaf stage, and the tuber will adjust to transplanting. Begonias are shallow rooting, requiring shallow containers such as an azalea pot rather than a standard-size pot. Choose a pot size that allows two inches between the tuber requiring a six-inch pot and larger tubers requiring an eight- or nine-inch pot. Use potting mix B. Fill pot two thirds full and position tuber; finish filling around root mass with mix. Firm medium and finish by covering root mass lightly with one-quarter inch of potting medium. Water carefully until water seeps from drainage hole in bottom of pot. When danger of frost is past, set pots outdoors on patio or other area where high light prevails but not in direct sun or dense shade.

For transplanting in outdoor beds, the prime considerations are: *perfect drainage* and location of planting area in relation to *sun*. Prepare planting bed to consist of one third peat moss or leaf mold or bark soil amendment, one third coarse sand and one third sandy loam. Well-rotted cow or steer manure can be added but must be mixed well. The bed should be spaded and worked with components a month in advance of planting. Addition of a garden fertilizer during bed preparation is recommended. Dig holes large enough to receive the mass of roots without crowding, replacing soil to barely cover top of tubers. Firm in place and add water carefully. Soil should not be in contact with stem of plant.

Suggested planting areas are north sides of buildings, under trees of light shade or lath houses. The correct degree of light and shade will produce strong compact plants and profuse blooms. They will not perform satisfactorily in complete shade or in a bright sunny spot. If too shaded—no blooms. If excess sun—stunting and burn.

Digging tubers and dormant storage

Potted begonias can be forced into dormancy at any time by gradually withholding water. Growing should be encouraged through November, if possible, to increase size of tubers and storage of food for the next year. Bedded begonias growing in colder regions, where chance of early frost may

injure plants, can be lifted with a large amount of soil and set in a frostless basement or garage, where they will gradually mature and dry down. A first light frost will not harm the tubers.

When bedded plants or pot begonias drop their foliage the stem will dry and break free from the tuber. Wash all soil from tubers and dry in sunshine for a few days until tuber is hard and dry. Be sure to remove all traces of stem tissue from tuber to prevent decay and infestation. Store in open trays or boxes in a cool, dry place until the pink vegetative buds appear. These are usually visible in spring. Then start over again as outlined for starting dormant tubers.

Tuberous begonias are also started from seed.

Begonia tuberhybrida pendula flore pleno is the Basket begonia. It is a very popular plant, taking the lead for summer-flowering baskets on the patio or the porch. Its pendant habit comes from the species *B. boliviensis* and its varieties come with red, rose, salmon, yellow and white flowers. Basket begonia tubers, which do not sprout more than two branches at the beginning of the season, should have the tips pinched off when the first flower bud appears. This will make a fuller basket.

All tuberous begonias need semishade, cool temperature and moisture. An application of water-soluble fertilizer once a month encourages luxuriant growth and flowering.

Begonia tuberhybrida

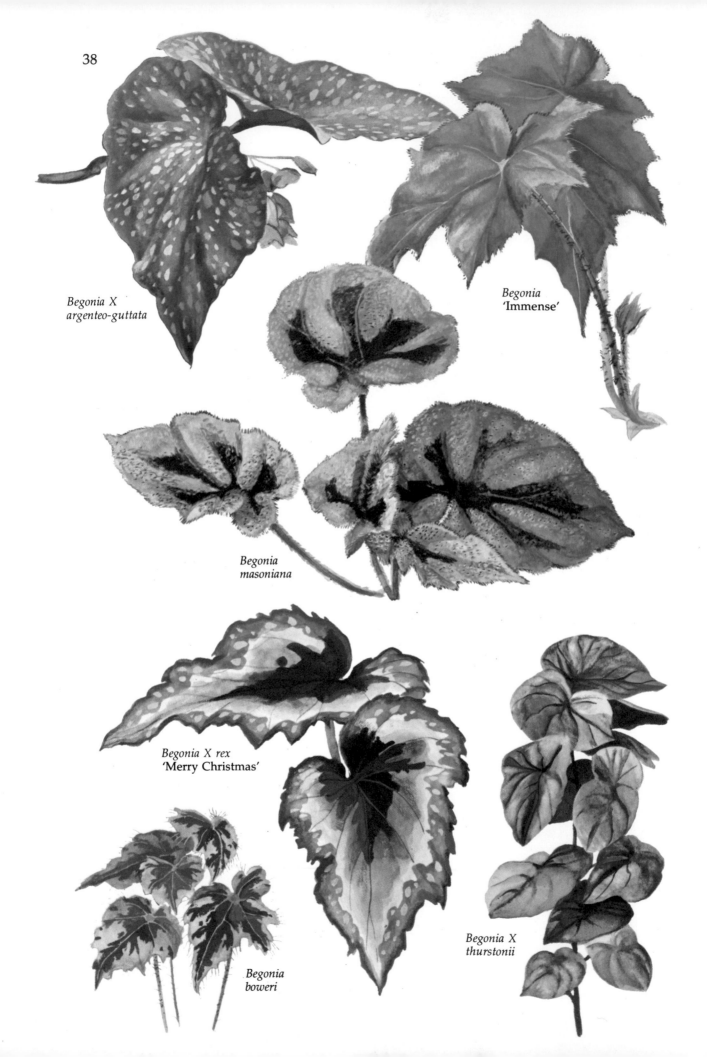

Begonia X
argenteo-guttata

Begonia
'Immense'

Begonia
masoniana

Begonia X *rex*
'Merry Christmas'

Begonia
boweri

Begonia X
thurstonii

BEGONIA X REX is of the rhizomatous group, is the foliage plant of the family and has many hybrids with brightly colored tapestrylike leaves. Some are upright, but most are creeping. *B. X rex* 'Merry Christmas,' as illustrated, is one of the many varieties. Dwarf types of rex are among the miniatures of the begonia family. Most of them are excellent for small pots and terrariums. Rex begonias need shade from direct sun from late winter to late fall. Supplemental fluorescent lighting is beneficial in the winter from early in the morning until late at night. Repotting of rex begonias is necessary when the rhizome outgrows the pot. Use a shallow or azalea-type pot because of the plant's shallow root system. Mix A for potting or a mixture composed of 50 percent peat for moisture-holding capacity. Like other members of the family, rex varieties like a moist mixture. Avoid a potting mixture that remains soggy wet, which may cause the rhizome to rot. Fertilize rex plants once a month, except in winter. Winter is a period of semirest for some varieties, and at that time some leaf drop may occur.

Propagation

Propagation of rex is accomplished in a number of ways. Division of the rhizome can be done at repotting time. Cut the rhizome into pieces one to two inches long and press into the potting mix longitudinally to a depth of one half the diameter of the rhizome. Keep moist and warm until shoot growth appears.

Another method is by leaf and petiole cutting; the new plant sprouts from the base of the stem. Still another is to cut the leaf into pie-shaped wedges, each having one main vein; insert the leaf base a half inch into the potting medium; position at a 45° angle. Another method is to slit the main vein of the leaf at numerous places on the back side. The slit leaf is then laid on the moist rooting media and fastened with a hairpin.

BEGONIA MASONIANA, the Iron Cross Begonia, is considered one of the most beautiful begonias in cultivation. This species was introduced from the gardens of Singapore and is thought by some to be a rex, although it is truly a rhizomatous type. Start new plants by division of the rhizomes and by leaf and petiole cutting.

BEGONIA X ARGENTEO-GUTTATA, called Trout Begonia and often referred to as Angel Wing Begonia, has leaves arranged at an angle resembling angel wings. It is a cane-stem type and becomes bushy when soft-pinched. Propagate by terminal cutting or by sectional cuttings.

BEGONIA BOWERI, is a rhizomatous type native to southern Mexico. Its popular name, Eyelash begonia, comes from the erect white hairs evenly spaced along the margins of the vivid green leaves. The margins of the leaves are spotted with black and purple patches. The flowers appear during the winter and spring months and are of a characteristic pink color. It is in the dwarf section of begonias, useful for dish gardens and terrariums. New plants can be started in the spring by division of the rhizomes. Cut off the old leaves and let the new ones develop.

BEGONIA 'IMMENSE' is a seedling offspring of *B. x ricinifolia* and is a robust plant with large, starlike, light-green waxy leaves. The upper surface of the leaf is covered with very short bristlelike hairs; the margins of the leaves and the leaf petioles are covered with short red hairs. The flowers are pink, and new plants are started by division, as are *B. rex* and other rhizomatous types.

BEGONIA X THURSTONII is a fibrous-rooted type, a hybrid between *B. metallica* and *B. sanguinea*. Pinching out the terminal growth makes it a desirable, bushy house plant. Red-colored petioles are covered with white hairs. Its leaves have a glossy bronze-green color on the top surface, with the red color of the stems on the under surface. Its flowers are light red. Start new plants by stem cuttings and by division of the larger plant at repotting time in the spring.

GERANIUMS

A native plant species, **Pelargonium hortorum,** *from South Africa. The geranium has been popular for over a century and ranks worldwide as the most important and useful plant today. As a sun-loving plant it is excellent for the greenhouse, yet it grows in the home with full sun exposure or under fluorescent lights for a 16-hour day. A popular pot plant, it is sold by florists and garden stores for Easter and Mother's Day. It is used in porch boxes, in containers for patios and in cemetery urns. In the United States, Canada, Alaska and in northern Europe it is planted in gardens as a bedding plant. It is ever-blooming throughout the entire season. It is seldom found in southern climates where temperatures exceed 85°, yet it will tolerate temperatures as low as 28°.*

Varieties of P. hortorum *are used by growers as the main crops for indoor-outdoor plants. The matter of varieties changes considerably with demands of the consumers and markets in different parts of the world. Red, pink and white with shades of dark and light colors are offered. Hundreds of cultivars have been created and it is best to consult the catalogs of local nurserymen before buying.*

Some varieties available in America are:

Red—'Red Perfection,' dark red
'Irene,' an excellent bright scarlet-red
'Sincerity,' a dark orange-red
'Cardinal,' a robust dark red
'Imp. Ricard,' a dependable large-flowered brick-red

Pink—'Skylark,' a large medium-pink
'Genie,' a free-flowering rose-pink
'Enchantress Fiat,' an excellent light salmon-pink
'Penny,' a semidouble neon-pink
'Salmon Irene,' an excellent medium salmon

White—'Snow Mass,' one of the better whites
'Modesty,' a white 'Irene'

A few noteworthy cultivars grown in Great Britain are:

Crimson—'Distinction,' rounded leaf marked with a dark brown zone close to margin of the leaf

Coral—'Fiat,' a semidouble flower

Pink—'Gazelle,' salmon pink flower, a dark purple zone near the center of the leaf

Culture of geraniums

TEMPERATURE: For the production of geraniums in greenhouses a temperature of 60°–65° Fahrenheit is recommended. In the home, maintain a warm temperature during the day but keep plants cool at night.

MOISTURE: Geraniums are kept moist but not excessively wet, which is contrary to an early concept of growing on the dry side. Withholding water may cause yellowing and dropping of the leaves. Pots or planters must have drain holes to allow excess water to flow out.

PROPAGATION: Use terminal cuttings 2½ to four inches long and leave as many leaves attached as possible. A good medium for rooting is a coarse sand or a peat and perlite combination. Water the pots or flats of cuttings on the dry side for the first two weeks to encourage callus formation. Thereafter, more moisture added to the medium will encourage rooting. Enclosure within a polyethylene bag is beneficial to prevent cuttings from wilting. The use of a rooting hormone will hasten rooting, though it is not essential.

SEED (new strains): A major development in geranium culture is growing from seed. Carefree is a well-known strain that comes in red, scarlet, white and shades of pink. An American strain, Nittany Lion, and the Moreton hybrids show colors similar to the Carefree series. Commercial growers grow a four-inch potted flowering plant in 120 days from seed.

POTTING: Mix A or well-aerated soilless mix is used for potting cuttings and growing. The well-rooted cutting may be potted directly into a four-inch pot.

FERTILIZER: Application to growing geranium plants once every two weeks in summer and once a month in winter will produce a healthy plant and encourage subsequent flowering. Use of a complete water-soluble fertilizer solution is recommended. A slow-release type incorporated into potting mixture or top-dressings may also be used.

INSECTS AND DISEASE: These often cause problems with geraniums. White flies, mealy bugs and aphids are the troublesome insects. Geraniums are very susceptible to bacterial stem and leaf rots. Fungous infection by pythium produces blackened stems near base of young plants. It can be avoided by using sterilized mixes and by not overwatering. Sanitation is the best method of control. For home gardeners, it is better to discard old diseased plants and grow new plants.

IVY-LEAVED GERANIUMS A recent craze for hanging-basket plants has brought new interest in the vining ivy-leaved geranium for home culture and greenhouse. Known botanically as *Pelargonium peltatum*, a species with many varieties; differs from *P. hortorum* in its trailing, drooping or somewhat climbing habit. Its leaves and stems are somewhat succulent and smooth. An old favorite, Sunset Ivy geranium, *P.* 'L'Elegante,' has green-and-white variegated leaves which take on pink color when grown dry.

Pelargonium 'L'Elegante'

P. X hortorum
'Mrs. Henry Cox'

P. X hortorum
'Maréchal MacMahon'

P. X hortorum
'Distinction'

P. X hortorum
'Cherry Sundae'

Some other outstanding varieties are:
P. 'Charles Turner,' a profusely blooming large flower of deep pink.
P. 'Barbary Coast,' with extra-large lavender flowers, a new variety.
P. 'Intensity,' with bright orange-scarlet flowers.
P. 'Mexican Beauty,' a long trailing variety with large dark-red flowers.
P. 'Queen of Hearts,' sturdy arching stems bearing double white flowers, each petal having a red spot.

SCENTED-LEAF GERANIUMS Some of the scented-leaved types of pelargoniums were among the first discovered in cultivation centuries ago and are still grown today. A light pressure on the leaf between the thumb and forefinger releases the plant's fragrance.

Some of these are:
P. graveolens, with rose-scented leaves, used in cookery and perfume.
P. crispum, mildly scented, used in finger bowls or hung in closets.
P. X fragrans, the "nutmeg geranium."
P. tomentosum, the "peppermint geranium," strongly scented, of sprawling habit.

Other more recent introductions are *P. X* 'Clorinda,' eucalyptus-scented with oak-shaped leaves, and *P.* 'Old Spice,' with strong apple and nutmeg fragrance.

FANCY-LEAVED GERANIUMS: These include geraniums with green and white foliage, also some with bronze and gold and others with multicolors.
P. X hortorum 'Flowers of Spring' has glistening bright-green leaves with wide cream-colored border and red blooms.
P. X hortorum 'Lady Esther,' with double red flowers and mottled foliage. Varieties have bronze and gold foliage; for instance, *P. X hortorum* 'Alpha,' a small bushy habit of growth, bearing single scarlet flowers in profusion.
P. X hortorum 'Contrast' has leaves bordered bright yellow, splashed scarlet and brown; scarlet flowers.
P. X hortorum 'Filigree' produces lobed, sil-

very green leaves bearing a wide cream border and zoned with pink and brown; deep salmon flowers.

P. X hortorum 'Golden Oriole' bears small shiny yellow-green leaves with rust-red zones; salmon flowers.

P. X hortorum 'Happy Thought,' an old English variety, bright-green leaves with a large cream-yellow butterfly marking, bearing single flowers of red and scarlet.

P. X hortorum 'Skies of Italy,' a dwarf with maplelike leaves, green and creamy margins, brown zones tinted with orange, red and crimson; single scarlet flowers.

DWARF AND CACTUS-FLOWERED GERANIUMS Dwarf varieties grow nine to ten inches tall in pots and are available in a variety of colors. Some have double blooms and some single.

P. X hortorum 'Robin Hood' is a semidwarf compact with zoned foliage and produces a profusion of cherry-red double flowers.

P. X hortorum 'Gina,' a heavy bloomer with double white flowers.

P. X hortorum 'Cherry Time' has double orange-red flowers borne above a dense growth of yellow-green leaves with faint bronze zonings. The cactus-flowered types, often called poinsettia geraniums, have narrow flat petals, sometimes twisted or rolled in an interesting variation of flower form.

This series includes:

P. X hortorum 'Poinsettia,' with dense double globular flowers and narrow rolled and twisted petals of bright scarlet.

P. X hortorum 'Noel,' with double white flowers, rolled and twisted.

P. X hortorum 'Southern Cross,' with double coral-red flowers, characteristic of the poinsettia geranium.

Other dwarf varieties offered have intriguing names such as 'Fairy Tales,' a tricolor variety; 'Doc,' a red; 'Dopey,' pink and white; 'Sneezy,' red and white; 'Grumpy,' dark red. There also are the light salmon 'Tweedledee' and the dark salmon 'Tweedledum.'

P. X hortorum
'Pompeii'

P. X hortorum
'Pink Poinsettia'

P. 'Prince
of Orange'

P. graveolens
'Lady Plymouth'

AFRICAN VIOLETS AND RELATIVES

African Violet
(Saintpaulia ionantha)

The African violet has been a popular and easy-to-grow house plant since its introduction into cultivation. It is a member of a large, interesting and diversified family; botanically *Gesneriaceae,* referred to by the gardeners who grow any of the related genera as Gesneriads. Saintpaulia cultivars numbering several hundreds have originated from crossing the many different wild forms native to tropical East Africa. In recent years related genera developed in America have become as popular as the violet, and genera such as gloxinia, *Columnea Episcia* and others are cultivated by specialists and offered to the trade.

Gesneriads are recognized by their wheel-shaped, tubular or bell-shaped flowers, some of which are brightly colored, some speckled and others even bicolored. Leaf surfaces are often velvety or hairy and some are thick and succulent. Their habitat is greatly varied, from tree-dwelling epiphytic kinds to those that thrive alongside tropical waterfalls and mountainous streams. One is reported to withstand frost.

LIGHT: A main requirement. A light intensity of about one-tenth of summer sun or an intensity equal to that of direct winter sun is best for flowering in the home. Young plants will grow at less than that but need more light for flowering. Plants growing on windowsills must be protected from direct sun. A combination of cool white and warm white fluorescent lights located six to eight inches above the plants, giving illumination for 16 hours a day, is recommended

'Paul Bunyan'   'Wintergreen'   'Blue Nocturne'

'Blue Canoe'   'Firebird'   'Blue Warrior'

for growing without daylight. Plant-growing lights may also be used.

TEMPERATURE: Warm. 60° to 75° is required for growth. Lower than 60° causes the foliage to become pale green and curl at the margins. Cold drafts or contact with a cold windowpane causes yellow blotches to appear on the leaves.

WATER: As important as light. Overwatering can be fatal to African violets. The potting mix should be kept just moist at all times. Water can be applied on the surface or as capillary water from below. If watered from below, set pot in a pan of water but remove as soon as moisture appears at mix surface. Tepid water (65° to 70°) is best, because colder water causes permanent discoloration and spotting on contact with foliage.

PROPAGATION:

Step 1. Select a large, healthy leaf and cut from plant with a one-inch-long petiole attached. Use a razor blade or sharp knife.

Step 2. For rooting use a 2½-inch-size plastic pot filled with a medium consisting of one half peat moss and one half sand or perlite. Another medium that is just as good is vermiculite. Moisten medium and press firm. Using a dowel, dibber or pencil, make a hole in the center to receive the petiole. Insert petiole to leaf blade. Place pot in polyethylene (polythene) bag. Remove the polyethylene bag as soon as shoot growth appears.

Forsythe pot method is a convenient way to root several cuttings. Place a smaller pot (2¼") with a corked drainage hole inside a large pan of clay or plastic that is filled with a propagation medium. Fill the small pot with water. The water will seep through, keeping the propagation material continually moist.

Step 3. When the cutting has rooted, a cluster of plants will form at the base of stem. When large enough to handle, remove and pot into a small pot, using mix A for growing on.

Step 4. When plants are four or five months old, divide the crown into single plants. A later shift will bring the plants to a finishing four-inch pot.

'Norlina'

'Lili Belle'

'Fury'

'Wild White'

'Blue Boy-in-the-Snow'

'Plum Tipped'

Saintpaulia ionantha 'Hot Drops'

POTTING: Mixture A is recommended because of its high moisture capacity. Mixtures containing leaf mold and soil must be steam-sterilized at 160° for 30 minutes before use.

FERTILIZER: Fertilize African violets only when they are established in the pot. They are not heavy feeders. Use a water-soluble fertilizer once a month according to the manufacturer's directions.

INSECTS: Mainly mealy bugs and aphids.

DISEASE: Several diseases occur, such as mildew, crown and root rot. Most diseases can be avoided by using care in watering. A well-drained aerated potting mix will prevent excess water from standing about the crown of the plant. Using a sterilized potting mix also helps to prevent disease problems. Spraying plants with a sink spray, using tepid water, cleans and refreshes.

BREEDING: Breeding violets for new forms and color is a challenge and can develop into an exciting new hobby. It has been learned that the progeny of a single cross often show several characteristics that were not apparent in either parent plant. Sometimes several generations are required to find the answer.

Since the period of time from sown seed to a flowering plant is about the same as that from cutting to mature plant, no time is lost. A cutting produces only one plant, whereas seeds from a single pod produce many.

For breeding, choose a well-developed, not faded, flower for both parents. Remove the flower from the plant chosen as a male parent and with a razor blade open or slit the anthers, thus releasing the yellow pollen grains. The anthers are then carefully rubbed over the stigma of a flower on the plant selected as the seed-bearing or female plant until it is covered with pollen. A sticky substance on the stigma holds the pollen grains until the flower is fertilized. If the "cross" takes, although not every one will, a tiny seed pod will begin to form about two weeks after pollination. Six to nine months are required for the seed pod to mature fully. After the pod has developed fully, the seed either can be stored (60° to 65°) in a dry place or sown immediately. Mature seed pods are ready for harvest when they shrivel, dry and turn brown on the plant.

Sowing seeds requires special care, as the seeds are fine as dust. A clean sterilized plastic or clay pot covered with a glass plate or polyethylene bag is satisfactory for germinating seed. Use the seed-sowing mix D as suggested in the chapter on soilless potting mixes. Seeds are sprinkled very thinly over the surface of mix and placed in a tray of water for subirrigation.

Fluorescent lighting or curtain-shaded sunlight will fulfill the light requirement. Seedlings will appear in about three weeks. When the seedlings are a half inch or so high they should be transplanted singly to individual pots of two-inch size.

MINIATURE AFRICAN VIOLETS. Breeders and hybridizers have developed miniature or dwarf cultivars and semidwarf varieties as well as some trailing types. A variety of flower colors are offered and a variation of leaves. Growers have learned that the miniature violets respond to higher light intensity than regulars and also use more fertilizer. The development of suckers is prolific, and it is desirable to thin these out regularly every two or three weeks. Tweezers are handy tools for this operation.

Cultural requirements such as temperature, moisture, potting materials and insect control are the same as for large violets. When to repot is a question. A 2½-inch pot is generally used. A shift to a large pot is considered when the diameter of the plant becomes two-thirds larger than the pot.

To facilitate watering these small pots, it is suggested that pots be plunged into trays of moist sand, providing the plants with a constant supply of moisture through the sub-irrigation method.

The Magic Flower
(Achimenes—Species and hybrids)

A very popular, flowering-sized house plant growing naturally in the Caribbean, Mexico and Central America. *Achimenes,* which is summer-flowering, makes wonderful hanging baskets as well as potted specimens. Flowers vary in size from one-half to three inches across and usually cover the plant with cascades of blooms. The flowers are very colorful in pastel shades of orange, red, lavender and some white.

For hanging baskets there are *A.* 'Wetterlow's Triumph,' bright pink; *A.* 'Margarita,' pure white; *A. puchella,* orange-red; and many others. There are varieties with dwarf tendencies that are good as table plants—for example, *A.* 'Adele Delhaute,' large,

A. 'Paul Arnold'

A. 'Ambroise Verscheffelt'

purple-violet; *A.* 'Charm,' pink; *A.* 'Little Beauty,' large pink flowers. There are tall, upright varieties, some of which require staking, and many others that are bushy types.

LIGHT: High; partial shade outdoors in summer.

TEMPERATURE: Warm. Storage in winter at 55°.

MOISTURE: Moist. Drying causes dormancy. Use warm water to prevent leaf spotting.

PROPAGATION: Scaly rhizomes, cuttings, seed. Start seed in late winter.

POTTING: Formula B. Plant rhizomes five to six in a four- or five-inch shallow pot. Set one-half to one inch apart and cover one inch deep.

FERTILIZER: Apply water-soluble fertilizer once every two weeks when growing in soilless mix.

INSECTS: Mealy bugs, spider mites.

PRUNING: On taller varieties pinch out tips when three to four inches tall.

REMARKS: *Achimenes* go dormant for the winter. Gradually stop watering in late fall. Cut off wilted foliage to ground. Store in pots at 55°. Repot in spring when new shoots appear.

Aeschynanthus pulcher

Lipstick Plant or Royal Red Bugler

(Aeschynanthus pulcher)

A climbing epiphytic plant producing roots at the nodes, clinging to trunks and branches of trees in the jungles of Java. Produces brilliant-scarlet tubular flowers in clusters at the tips of the branches in the spring. The trailing habit of growth makes it a good basket plant.

Other varieties worthy of growing are *A. x splendidus*, *A.* 'Black Pagoda' and *A. pullobia*.

LIGHT: High, but no direct sun in the summer.

TEMPERATURE: Warm.

MOISTURE: Dry; moist atmosphere in summer.

PROPAGATION: Stem or terminal cuttings, division.

POTTING: Mix B or a well-drained and aerated mix as for other epiphytes.

INSECTS: Mealy bugs, red spider mites, white flies.

PRUNING: Thinning out of old flowered branches encourages new growth.

Gloxinia *(Sinningia speciosa)*

The florist gloxinia and species; easy to grow under home conditions; native to Brazil. Woody tuberous-rooted; most species are rosette-type plants ranging in size from two inches to two feet across. Flowers are small to large, slipper-shaped and bell types in many color patterns as well as various pastel shades. Tubers are purchased from garden stores in early spring for summer bloom. *S. barbata*, *S. eumorpha* and *S. regina* are species types worthy of growing for the plant collector. The miniature species *S. concinna* and *S. pusilla* (the world's smallest gloxinia) have been hybridized to produce many interesting varieties. All are identified by trumpet- or slipper-shaped flowers. Plants measure from two to three inches across to not more than one to three inches high. They are ever-blooming and grow well in terrariums. Some better known are *S.* 'Bright Eyes,' *S.* 'Cindy,' *S.* 'Doll Baby,' *S.* 'Freckles' and *S.* 'White Sprite.'

Sinningia speciosa

Columnea rubra 'Morton'

Columnea gloriosa

Columnea crassifolia

LIGHT: Medium to high; no direct sun.

TEMPERATURE: Warm, with ventilation.

MOISTURE: Moist (high humidity of terrarium).

PROPAGATION: Seeds, division of tubers, leaf cuttings.

POTTING: Mix B. Plant miniatures in 1¼- to three-inch pots. Florist type in five- to six-inch size.

INSECTS: White flies, mealy bugs, aphids.

REMARKS: Rest periods, few days to several weeks, but 14 to 16 hours of fluorescent light prolongs flowering.

Goldfish Plant *(Columnea)*

Fibrous-rooted gesneriads with showy scarlet, orange or yellow flowers from the rain forests of Central and South America. Many are wild species, but hybrids have been created that are tolerant of the adverse conditions of the home. Two types: slender stem vines for hanging baskets and those with stiff upright growth for pot culture. Some of the better basket types, raised chiefly in America, are hybrids of *C. gloriosa:* *C.* 'Cascadilla,' *C.* 'Yellow Gold' and *C.* 'Early Bird.' Upright types include *C.* 'Cornellian,' *C.* 'Cayugan' and *C.* 'Yellow Dragon.' These plants are more tolerant of home culture. Most are seasonal in blooming habits, but through selection of hybrids or species, plants can be in bloom all year.

LIGHT: Bright; indirect sun.

TEMPERATURE: Warm, with exceptions: *C.* 'Stravanger,' *C. hirta* and *C. microphylla,* which require 50° to 59° for bud formation.

MOISTURE: Dry, with atmospheric moisture if possible.

PROPAGATION: Seeds, stem and terminal cuttings, division.

POTTING: Mix B, loose epiphytic type.

INSECTS: Mealy bugs.

REMARKS: Cut off old flower stems to stimulate formation of new shoots.

Kohleria amabilis

Temple Bells
(*Smithiantha zebrina* syn. *Naegelia zebrina*)

A native to the mountains of Mexico. Another species, *S. cinnabarina*, has heavily spotted contrasting red and yellow flowers with dark-green heart-shaped leaves. Also available are crosses between *Smithiantha* and *Achimenes* resulting in a hybrid labeled *X Eucodonopsis*. Crosses between *S. fulgida*, *S. cinnabarina*, and *S. zebrina* have produced cultivars noted for their unusual large flowers and colors ranging from pale peach to deep red. *Smithiantha* flowering period is from late summer to winter.

LIGHT: Indirect sunlight. Fluorescent lighting for 12 to 14 hours a day.

TEMPERATURE: Warm.

MOISTURE: Moist; high humidity if possible.

PROPAGATION: Division of scaly rhizome. Leaf-petiole cutting.

Kohleria (*Kohleria amabilis*)

A native to the mountains of tropical America. A plant easy to grow in the home or greenhouse. Tubular flowers appearing along the stem are showy, speckled with deeper contrasting color. Can be grown as trailing or upright with support. *K. amabilis* has pink flowers with reddish-purple dots, black veins and is dwarf in habit of growth. Hybrids of *amabilis* include *K. 'Rongo,'* which is almost ever-blooming. *K.*

LIGHT: High; no direct sun. Flowering under long-day conditions: 16 hours under artificial light.

TEMPERATURE: Warm.

MOISTURE: Moist.

PROPAGATION: Terminal cuttings, division of scaly rhizomes.

POTTING: Mix B.

INSECTS: Mealy bugs, white flies.

REMARKS: Cut back after flowering. Sprouts will grow from scaly rhizomes without rest period.

Smithiantha zebrina

Rechsteineria cardinalis

POTTING: Repotting and dividing, put one rhizome to a four- to five-inch pot. Mix A.

FERTILIZER: Apply water-soluble type once a month during spring and summer when plants are in active growth.

INSECTS: Mealy bugs, white flies.

REMARKS: After flowering, gradually withhold water to give semirest period until new growth commences.

Cardinal Flower
(*Rechsteineria cardinalis*)

It is closely related to the gloxinias in the family *Gesneriaceae*. The native habitat of the genus ranges from Brazil to Central America and into Mexico. Flowers are less showy than gloxinia, being rather slender, tubular, of red and orange colors, one to 2½ inches long. Low-growing species like *R. cardinalis*, *R. macropoda* and *R. leucotricha* are the best species for indoor culture. *R. macropoda* differs from *R. cardinalis* in that it has large, less velvety leaves and orange-red flowers, but it lacks the hood characteristic of *R. cardinalis*. *R. leucotricha* resembles *R. cardinalis* except that sometimes it produces long center stems with leaves and flowers at the end. Its leaves are unusual, being covered with dense silvery wool which also covers stems and flowers.

The color of the flowers is bright salmon-red. Flowering of *R. cardinalis* takes place from late fall to Christmas, making it a good gift plant.

LIGHT: High; indirect sunlight or 14 to 16 hours of fluorescent lighting.

TEMPERATURE: Warm.

MOISTURE: Dry, but followed by a thorough soaking.

PROPAGATION: Leaf-petiole cuttings at any time. Seeds.

POTTING: Mix B. Repot when new shoots start to grow.

FERTILIZER: Apply water-soluble fertilizer during summer and fall once a month.

INSECTS: Mealy bugs and white flies.

PRUNING: Cut off old stems after flowers have faded. New shoots will grow after a short rest period.

REMARKS: Tubers grow larger each year and need repotting when new shoots develop.

E. 'Bronze Queen'

E. 'Acajou'

E. 'Ember Lace'

Flame Violet

(Episcia cupreata var. *cupreata)*

Grows wild in Colombia and Venezuela. Foliage patterns are variable due to variants and mutants. Veins of leaves are often pale green or silvery, but all flower colors of *E. cupreata* are orange-scarlet. A species, *E. dianthiflora*, has small velvety green leaves and large heavily fringed white flowers.

Most episcias have trailing habit, but some grow erect, such as: *E. punctata* with magenta-spotted flowers; *E. melittifolia* has purple-pink flowers; *E. decurrens* has white flowers. *E.* 'Cygnet,' introduced by Cornell University, is a cross between *E. dianthiflora* and *E. punctata.*

Many excellent commercial cultivars are available. Those with orange and red flowers seem to be the best-flowering. Among the many are *E.* 'Acajou,' *E.* 'Chocolate Soldier,' *E.* 'Cameo,' *E.* 'Filigree,' *E.* 'Jean Bee,' *E.* 'Moss Agate.' *E.* 'Ember Lace' has pink flowers and variegated foliage. *E.* 'Tropical Topaz' has bright green leaves and yellow flowers.

LIGHT: High; give more intensity than for African violets.

TEMPERATURE: Warm. Below 55° injures foliage as if frozen.

MOISTURE: Moist. Never let stand in a saucer of water.

PROPAGATION: Stem cuttings, runners.

POTTING: Mix B. Best grown in hanging baskets or raised pots.

INSECTS: Mealy bugs, white flies.

REMARKS: Removal of stolons or runners encourages flowering.

Cape Primrose

(Streptocarpus X hybridus)

From moist wooded mountain gorges of tropical Africa. The genus comprises numerous species with variable growth habits. The many colors and hybrids of *Streptocarpus* have made it a favorite among plant people. It is used not only as a potted plant, but its cut flowers are used in making flower arrangements and are made up as corsages.

Streptocarpus is not hardy like true primroses and is usually grown indoors or in greenhouses. In temperate regions they are sometimes set in an outdoor flower border in a shady spot and grown like annual bedding plants.

The common hybrid varieties are easily raised from seed. Seed sown in early spring will flower by early winter. Successive sowings will give a succession of blooms throughout the year. Seed is very fine and is counted at an estimated 1,500,000 to the ounce. Refer to the section on page 197, Starting Plants from Seed, for instructions about sowing fine seed. Those best suited for home culture are hybrids from parentage with *S. rexii*. Flowers are large, nodding trumpet-shaped of purple, light to dark blue, deep crimson to white. *S.* 'Constant Nymph' with blue flowers and *S.* 'Massen's White' with pure white flowers are extremely floriferous. *S. saxorum*, a branching stem type, has fleshy medium-green leaves with nodding light lavender-blue flowers; it blooms for six months at a time.

LIGHT: High, exclusive of direct sun. Fluorescent lights are beneficial.

TEMPERATURE: Warm.

MOISTURE: Moist; never let dry.

PROPAGATION: Seed, division of crown, leaf cuttings by nicking the midrib in one or two places and setting the leaf on moist medium, or cutting in three-inch sections. (*S. saxorum:* seed and stem cuttings.)

POTTING: Use mix B.

FERTILIZER: Feed water-soluble, type once a month at half strength. Responds to foliar application at the above rate.

INSECTS: White flies, mealy bugs, aphids.

REMARKS: An "easy-to-grow" house plant.

S. 'Constant Nymph'

P. 'Red Emerald'

FOLIAGE PLANTS

Philodendrons are the favorites of all foliage plants. Their popularity exists because of their tolerance to indoor growing conditions of low light, dryness and warm temperature. Their tough, leathery, glossy green leaves exhibit a most attractive live appearance. A variety of species and hybrids offers many different kinds of leaf shapes and sizes.

The decorator is offered two types to choose from: vining and self-heading.

Vining types such as P. 'Florida,' P. hastatum and P. 'Red Emerald' really do not climb but when given support will conform to it. The support can be anything decorative that is water absorbent. Sections of tree fern are excellent as supports; wire and sphagnum-moss totem poles or slabs of redwood bark that will furnish the plant's stem with moisture also help the plant to grow better.

Philodendron 'Red Emerald'

Another fine hybrid of the philodendron group. Its climbing habit of growth requires support in the way of a trellis. Its leaves are large. The stem and leaf petioles are red, with light-green, arrow-shaped leaves.

LIGHT: Medium.

TEMPERATURE: Warm.

MOISTURE: Moist.

PROPAGATION: Stem cuttings, air layering.

POTTING: Mix B. Repot at least once a year.

FERTILIZER: Apply water-soluble type once every two to three months.

INSECTS: Mealy bugs, red spider mites.

PRUNING: Air-layer top to start new plants. Cut back to ground if losing lower leaves.

P. scandens
subsp. *oxycardium*

Panda Plant
(Philodendron bipennifolium)

Often referred to as "Fiddle-leaf philodendron." A climbing type with large rich green leaves, it is a long-time favorite as a house plant. Climbing types in the home do not really attach to support but must be tied to it.

A water-holding column of sphagmun moss packed in wire or plastic mesh, tree-fern stem totem or slabs of redwood bark that hold moisture make the plants grow better.

LIGHT: Medium to high. High light exclusive of direct sun is best.

TEMPERATURE: Warm.

MOISTURE: Moist.

PROPAGATION: Air layering of leafy tops; sectional cuttings.

POTTING: Mix B.

FERTILIZER: Feed water-soluble type once a month; controlled-release type twice a year.

INSECTS: Mealy bugs.

PRUNING: It is natural for most philodendrons to drop older leaves occasionally in the home. Air-layer tops or cut back to short stub to grow again.

REMARKS: Wash foliage once a month.

Heart-Leaved Philodendron
(Philodendron scandens subsp. *oxycardium)*

The most common and popular of all the philodendrons. It is used in combination with other plants for dish gardens, as a ground cover for large planters, trained upright on totems and in hanging baskets.

LIGHT: Low to medium.

TEMPERATURE: Warm, but will survive short cool spells.

MOISTURE: Moist.

PROPAGATION: Terminal cuttings, leaf-petiole cuttings.

POTTING: Mix B. Repot when plants are rootbound or appear too large for the container.

FERTILIZER: Feed water-soluble type once a month.

INSECTS: Red spider mites, mealy bugs.

P. bipennifolium

P. selloum

Philodendron

(Philodendron selloum)

Sometimes called "Saddle-leaved philodendron," it is a member of the large aroid
family *Araceae*. Philodendrons, favorite indoor ornamentals, are available in many different sizes and leaf shapes. Some are
climbers and some are erect and self-
supporting. An exceptional cultural note:
Some varieties of *P. selloum* are susceptible
to a bacterial leaf-spot disease brought on by
moist potting soil and high atmospheric
moisture. Therefore, it should be cultured
on the extreme dry side. *P. selloum*, a self-
heading type, is much used as an interior-
decoration plant. Another self-supporting
type is *P. wendlandii* and its hybrids. It grows
a rosette of thick, waxy green, broad leaves
with a thickened midrib and a short bulblike
petiole. It looks much like a bizarre bird nest.

LIGHT: Medium to high. Grows best in high light,
but not direct sun.

TEMPERATURE: Warm.

MOISTURE: Dry. Plants can become conditioned
to less frequent watering where light intensity is
low.

PROPAGATION: Air layering of tops of old plants
and sectional cuttings.

POTTING: Mix B. Repot only when root-bound.

FERTILIZER: Feed water-soluble type once a
month or apply controlled-release type every
four months.

INSECTS: Red spider mites, mealy bugs.

REMARKS: Dust or wash foliage once a month to
restore luster of leaves.

Elephant's Ear

(Philodendron hastatum syn. *P. domesticum)*

A species climber from Brazil, a long-time favorite as a house plant. Its popularity has given way to many fine hybrids. It is a lush grower with fleshy, green, arrow-shaped leaves. As an adult form, the leaf shape changes to more broadly arrow-shaped with more wavy appearance. It has an outstanding inflorescence, consisting of a pale-green spathe suffused with red inside. Flowering occurs on mature plants. This is usually not experienced indoors, because they are seldom allowed to grow over four feet tall.

P. hastatum variegatum is a striking mutant of *P. hastatum*. Its fleshy, light- to dark-green leaves are irregularly variegated and splashed with nile green, yellow and creamy white.

This is one of the many desirable characteristics of the philodendron group. A variety of sizes, shapes and textures offers the decorator much style to choose from.

Culture as for Heart-Leaved Philodendron.

Self-heading varieties such as *P. selloum, P. wendlandii, P. squamiferum* and hybrids of these make short, broad sets of leaves that radiate from a central crown.

An exciting experience takes place when a philodendron flowers. Older plants will reach an adult stage when grown on tall totems—provided that heat, light and moisture are at optimum levels. The flowers look somewhat like calla lilies, with a boat-shaped bract surrounding a club-shaped, spikelike structure. The bracts are sometimes colored greenish white or reddish.

In spite of the very best growing conditions, philodendrons naturally drop lower leaves in time, exposing the bare stem. To remedy this, one can either air-layer, rooting the stem and cutting it off to pot up, or cut plant back to a stub and start over again. Best advice is to toss the plant out and buy a fresh new one to take its place.

When aerial roots form, train them to travel down the totem and into the potting mix. They function by taking up water and nutrients to supply the tops.

P. hastatum

Caladium hortulanum

Fancy-Leaved Caladium
(Caladium hybrids*)*

Members of the popular ornamental family *Araceae,* they are native to the hot humid Amazon basin of Brazil.

Tubers are raised commercially for forcing as potted foliage plants and for bedding out of doors in warm climates. Tubers are available in grades, expressed in inches of diameter. A ''No. 3 size,'' measuring three quarters to one inch, is the smallest; a ''Mammoth'' measures 3½ inches or more. Some specialists store tubers under controlled conditions, making them available at any time of the year.

The tubers may be started directly in flowering-size pots at home by following the simple rules of culture.

In America several hundred cultivars have been produced by plantsmen with leaves in shades of red, green and white, often overlain with red or white markings. The most popular grown is 'Candidum'— white with green veins.

A few of many fine varieties are:
'Carolyn Whorton': Fine for pots. Rose, darker veins, green hue.
'Edna': Excellent pot plant. Large glossy leaves. Brilliant red.
'Frieda Hemple': Dwarf, all-purpose red.
'Mrs. Arno Nehrling': Bronze turning white, pink hue, red mid-ribs.
'Fanny Munson': Excellent, brilliant pink with deeper veins.

A variety of caladium leaves, showing different colors and patterns

'Lord Derby': Transparent rose with dark ribs. Bushy.

A distinct class differing from the regular fancy-leaved varieties in leaf appearance is that of the lance-leaf or strap-leaf varieties. Leaves are narrower and the plants grow shorter. They are better adapted for outside beds or in pots for patio growing.

LIGHT: Medium. Avoid direct sun. Leaf burn will occur if exposed to direct sun.

TEMPERATURE: Warm. Temperatures below 70° should be avoided.

MOISTURE: Moist at all times. Excessive moisture and poor drainage may induce root rot. Leaf burn will result from direct sun.

PROPAGATION: Division of tubers at potting time.

POTTING: 100 percent sphagnum peat moss for starting and growing on. Plant in pots or flats (boxes), covering about one inch deep. One tuber will need a four- to five-inch pot.

FERTILIZER: Water-soluble feeding once a month will increase tuber size for next year.

INSECTS: Slugs, in outdoor beds.

REMARKS: When leaves begin to wither, water less frequently until tuber is dormant. Store in pots at 65° to 70° in a heated, well-ventilated area for about four months. Remove from pot, clean off medium and start in spring. Bottom heat of 80°-85° will hasten development of shoot growth.

P. griseo-argentea

P. argyreia

Peperomia

A genus of succulent and semisucculent plants from the subtropics, and mainly of South America. A popular plant because it is one of the exceptions to the rule—"always moist." Its compact, dwarflike growth makes it useful for dish gardens and as a foliage pot plant for the coffee table or windowsill. Foliage plant specialists are constantly selecting new and better peperomia varieties.

Ivy peperomia in America is *Peperomia griseo-argentea*. In Brazil it was known as *P. hederaefolia* and has been introduced in Europe under the same name. A plant of bushy habit with shieldlike, quilted leaves, blotched with glossy silver; the veins of the leaf are purplish olive. A cultivar found in California is *P. griseo-argentea* 'Blackie' with metallic olive-green to blackish, coppery leaves.

Peperomia scandens variegata a semierect, creeping plant suitable for table display. It is fast-growing, filling a four-inch pot in four months from a rooted cutting under fluorescent lighting. An all-green leaf form is *P. scandens*, which resembles a miniature philodendron with its heart-shaped leaves.

P. argyreia, watermelon peperomia, from Brazil, with long, upright flower spikes is very attractive and tolerant of dryness.

P. caperata 'Emerald Ripple,' a natural cultivar from Brazil, is very popular with its heart-shaped, rippled leaves and upright flower stalks of tiny, greenish-white flowers.

P. obtusifolia variegata, a variegated-leaf type similar in growth and description to *P. obtusifolia*, is now identified by taxonomists as *P. floridana*; *P. obtusifolia variegata* is general terminology referring to variegated-leaf

P. scandens variegata

P. caperata
'Emerald Ripple'

*P. obtusifolia
variegata*

forms with similar characteristics. Among the cultivars listed are *P. obtusifolia alba*; *P. albo-marginata*; *P.* 'Gold Tip,' an American introduction; also *P. lougenii*, a miniature version and another miniature, *P. minima*.

P. floridana (*P. obtusifolia*) today is still a popular dish-garden plant propagated by the thousands in Florida nurseries.

P. rotundifolia, formerly called *P. nummularifolia*, was introduced from Puerto Rico and Jamaica. It is a common ground-cover plant found in the Luquillo rain forest of Puerto Rico. It is a ground-cover creeper with threadlike green stems rooting at each node with tiny, succulent, round, thick leaves measuring only one-third of an inch. It is an excellent plant for terrarium landscapes and for miniature gardens of all kinds.

P. metallica is an attractive, erect, bushy type, low-growing with red stems bearing narrow, waxy leaves of a metallic luster. The underside of the leaf is silvery.

LIGHT: Medium; indirect sun in winter.

TEMPERATURE: Warm.

MOISTURE: Dry. Allow mix to become moderately dry before watering.

PROPAGATION: Terminal cuttings from branching types. Leaf-petiole cuttings for stemless varieties. Rooting medium of coarse sand to provide good drainage. Division of crown of older plants.

POTTING: Mix B for good aeration and drainage.

FERTILIZER: Feed large established plants once every three months with water-soluble fertilizer.

INSECTS: Mealy bugs.

PRUNING: Pinch out tips of stem varieties to encourage branching for compact growth.

P. rotundifolia

Helxine soleirolii

*Pilea
cadierei*

*Pilea
involucrata*

Mind Your Own Business or Baby's Tears *(Helxine soleirolii)*

A plant native to Corsica and Sardinia belonging to the nettle family. A very popular plant for home culture because of its matlike creeping habit.

LIGHT: High. Medium light causes elongation of stems, giving a trailing habit of growth.

TEMPERATURE: Warm. Cool nights beneficial.

MOISTURE: Moist at all times. Leaves readily injured if allowed to dry.

PROPAGATION: Division of clump. A small piece spreads rapidly.

POTTING: Mix A.

FERTILIZER: Apply water-soluble type at half strength every two weeks.

INSECTS: White flies, mealy bugs, slugs.

Aluminum Plant

(Pilea cadierei)

Pilea is another genus of the nettle family with several species in cultivation; used as table plants in the home and office or combined with other plants in dish gardens. The outstanding leaf characteristic is its pretty silver patterning. The average height is around 12 inches.

P. 'Moon Valley,' probably a natural hybrid from the wild, is popular; has a rough textured leaf surface. The center portion of the leaf is blotched brownish with the margin diffused with tawny gold.

Other species available are *P. involucrata* or 'Panamiga,' the friendship plant, and *P. microphylla*, the artillery plant.

LIGHT: High. Fluorescent light for 16-hour day.

TEMPERATURE: Warm.

MOISTURE: Dry but not completely.

PROPAGATION: Stem cuttings and division.

POTTING: Mix B.

FERTILIZER: Feed with water-soluble type at half strength once a month.

INSECTS: Mealy bugs, aphids and white flies.

PRUNING: Soft-pinch to maintain bushiness.

Piggyback Plant
(Tolmiea menziesii)

A hardy outdoor plant native to the West Coast of the United States, where marine influences bring about mild winter weather. For the home or office it makes an excellent table plant, surviving under the most adverse conditions. However, it requires a cooler temperature than most living environments to do really well.

LIGHT: High. Light shade from direct sun in summer.

TEMPERATURE: Cool. A windowsill or cool entrance hall is best.

MOISTURE: Moist at all times.

PROPAGATION: Leaf and petiole cuttings, using leaves on which a plantlet has formed. Insert so base of leaf rests on medium.

POTTING: Mix A.

FERTILIZER: Feed water-soluble type monthly during summer to established plants.

INSECTS: Mealy bugs and white flies.

Tolmiea menziesii

Sensitive Plant (Mimosa pudica)

A member of the pea family, *Leguminosae*, this plant comes from continental tropical America. A fascinating plant attraction for children and adults. The leaves and branches droop and fold up quickly when touched or otherwise disturbed. Following collapse, recovery to fully expanded leaves occurs in from several minutes to a half hour, depending on temperature.

LIGHT: High. Sunny window sill for best results.

TEMPERATURE: Warm.

MOISTURE: Moist. Dryness causes leaf drop.

PROPAGATION: Seeds sown annually.

POTTING: Mix B. Transplant seedlings to a four-inch pot.

FERTILIZER: Feed water-soluble type every three weeks when plant appears pot-bound.

INSECTS: Mealy bugs and red spider mites.

REMARKS: Sow seeds in early spring. Save seeds produced by the plant.

Mimosa pudica

Rhoeo spathacea

Moses-in-the-Cradle

(Rhoeo spathacea)

A single-species plant of the spiderwort family *Commelinaceae*, found growing in Mexico and the West Indies. So named because of the appearance of small, white flowers in a boat-shaped bract at the base of the overlapping leaves, resembling a baby in a cradle. Equally attractive is *R. spathacea variegata*, a variegated form which has leaves longitudinally striped with yellow. Use as a single table plant or in a hanging container.

LIGHT: Medium to high. Direct sun will intensify purple coloration of under-leaves. Filtered sunlight in summer.

TEMPERATURE: Warm. Sensitive to cold and drafts. Lower night temperatures beneficial.

MOISTURE: Dry.

PROPAGATION: Division of clump. Oldest stalks discarded in favor of new shoots. Also by seeds.

POTTING: Mix B. Repot once a year.

FERTILIZER: Feed established plants once a month with water-soluble type.

INSECTS: Mealy bugs.

Classic Myrtle

(Myrtus communis microphylla)

A compact bushy plant with dark-green foliage grown by European plantsmen for wedding embellishment. It is sheared into globe shapes on short or tall treelike stems. Also used in dish gardens and as potted foliage plant specimens. Fragrant, tiny white flowers and aromatic foliage.

LIGHT: High.

TEMPERATURE: Cool to warm.

MOISTURE: Moist soil conditions are needed.

PROPAGATION: By terminal cuttings at any time.

POTTING: Use Mix A, repot in spring. Use three-quarter-size containers or shallow pots for appearance.

FERTILIZER: Apply water-soluble fertilizer solution spring, summer and fall.

INSECTS: Susceptible to red spider mites, mealy bugs and scale insects.

PRUNING: Shear in early spring to maintain shape. Occasionally remove sprouting lower branches on stem.

REMARKS: Susceptible to *Botrytis* (gray mold). Needs good aeration.

Myrtus communis microphylla

Maranta leuconeura kerchoveana

Maranta leuconeura massangeana

Prayer Plant
(Maranta leuconeura kerchoveana)

Of the arrowroot family *Marantaceae*, native to tropical America. A table plant often used in combination with other foliage for planters. Also useful in terrariums. The name "prayer plant" comes from the movement of the plant's leaves in darkness to a vertical position that makes them resemble hands in prayer. During the day they assume the normal horizontal position. This reaction to darkness can be created artificially by turning a table light off and on at intervals.

Another attractive variety, *M. leuconeura massangeana*, has leaves of satiny bluish green with fishbone pattern of pink veins radiating off the center rib of the leaf to the margin.

Calathea makoyana, the "peacock plant," a related genus to *Maranta*, requires similar culture and is interestingly different enough to be in demand. Its oval leaves are surfaced with a feathery design of opaque olive-green lines and ovals in a translucent field of pale green-yellow with purplish coloration beneath. "As beautiful as a peacock's feathers" rightly describes its markings and coloration. Its cultural requirements are warm temperature, a moist atmosphere (like ferns), medium light intensity and a moist potting mix.

Other Marantas are *M. leuconeura erythroneura*, similar to *massangeana* except with bright red veins instead of silver, and *M.* 'Bi-color,' with leaves of gray feathered design, fading to grayish green at edge, purple beneath. *M. repens* is a low plant similar to *M. leuconeua kerchoveana* with smaller leaves.

LIGHT: Medium. High in winter, exclusive of direct sun.

TEMPERATURE: Warm.

MOISTURE: Moist.

PROPAGATION: Division of clump in spring. Terminal cuttings of new shoot growth.

POTTING: Mix B when new growth appears in spring, after a semirest period.

FERTILIZER: Once a month with water-soluble type from spring to fall, after root system is established.

INSECTS: Red spider mites, mealy bugs.

REMARKS: *M. leuconeura kerchoveana* does best after a semirest period in winter. Water less frequently so that leaves turn yellow. Do not dry out completely.

Cyperus alternifolius

Umbrella Plant
(Cyperus alternifolius)

A bog plant of the sedge family *Cyperaceae*; from Africa, but grows also in West Indies and South America. These rush or grasslike plants differ from true grasses because of their three-angled solid stem and differing floral structure. It grows planted in aquariums, yet will survive as a pot plant when kept constantly moist. Valued for its striking form and interesting Oriental silhouette pattern, it makes an attractive addition to the water-lily pool in summer. When given ample pot room it will grow three to four feet in height.

C. *alternifolius gracilis* is similar, but with very slender stalks and leaves; grows about 18 inches tall. C. *alternifolius nanus* is a dwarf form.

C. *papyrus* is the papyrus plant used by Egyptians for paper-making since 2750 B.C. Its tall growing habit prohibits its use in most homes, but it is attractive in indoor shopping precincts or malls.

LIGHT: High; full sun in winter.

TEMPERATURE: Cool to warm.

MOISTURE: Moist. Drying out will cause the tips of leaves to turn brown.

PROPAGATION: Division of the roots, leaf-petiole cuttings, seeds.

POTTING: Mix A. Divide and repot the vigorous sections when clump becomes too large. Use the smaller outside divisions and discard the overgrown centers. If plants have been outside for summer, repot in the fall before moving in for the winter.

FERTILIZER: Feed water-soluble type at half strength every two weeks in summer or use slow-release type as manufacturer directs.

INSECTS: Red spider mites, mealy bugs.

PRUNING: Cut off dead or broken stalks from the base of plant to make room for the new shoots to develop.

REMARKS: The papyrus plant as well as C. *alternifolius* are much used by flowing arrangers; also for bottle and water gardens.

Aglaonema commutatum 'White Rajah'

Aglaonema modestum

Chinese Evergreen
(Aglaonema modestum)

From China and the Philippines, it is a member of the aroid family *Araceae*. Several fine varieties comprise the group, all of which make excellent house plants. Their adaptability to survive low light intensity in the home and their ability to grow in water without soil make them useful for many arrangements. Used in floral decoration, for offices and foyers, for water gardens, even for planters and containers in shopping malls or precincts. Generally classified as a table plant.

A. crispum, formerly known as *A. roebelinii*, is a large-leaved robust species with gray blotches on either side of a darker green midrib. Useful in larger planters, it grows to a height of three feet.

A. commutatum is a slow-growing small-leaved species, its leaves lightly marked with gray. Much in demand for dish gardens and terrariums.

A. commutatum 'White Rajah' is a very attractive cultivar; its narrower leaves, heavily marked with white, resemble a *dieffenbachia*.

A. commutatum 'The Queen' is a cultivar selected from hundreds of seedlings possessing narrow pointed leaves. The stems are green, with leaf petioles flecked with cream color. It is a choice specimen.

A. commutatum 'The King' is similar to 'The Queen' but with cream-colored stems and leaf petioles flecked with green.

LIGHT: Low; excellent for dark corners. North window light.

TEMPERATURE: Warm.

MOISTURE: Moist at all times.

PROPAGATION: Seeds, cane layering, terminal cuttings, division of crown, air layering.

POTTING: Mix B. Repot once a year and only when pot-bound.

FERTILIZER: Apply fertilizer once a month to established plants.

INSECTS: Mealy bugs.

Podocarpus macrophyllus maki

Southern Yew

(Podocarpus macrophyllus maki)

It is also called Chinese podocarpus, Japanese yew or Buddhist pine; family *Podocarpaceae*. It is cultivated as an evergreen shrub for hedges in warmer climates and is used extensively as a container plant indoors in colder areas. Its apparent ability to withstand cool drafts makes it useful for embellishment of entrances to hotels, shopping malls and even the hallway of the home. It is usually grown to six feet as a floor plant; it can be pruned and sheared to maintain a desired height and shape. Seedling plants are used in dish gardens and even in terrariums. *P. gracillior*, whose habit is more pendulous, will vary with culture. Seedlings are more upright in growth pattern.

LIGHT: High; some direct sunlight.

TEMPERATURE: Cool to warm. Maintains best at cooler temperatures.

MOISTURE: Moist. May be adjusted to dry situation at cooler temperatures.

PROPAGATION: Terminal cuttings. Chemical hormone rooting aid beneficial.

POTTING: Mix A. Repot only when root-bound; once every two years probably sufficient.

FERTILIZER: Apply water-soluble type once every two months from spring to autumn; controlled-release type once every four months.

INSECTS: Mealy bugs, scale insects.

PRUNING: Prune and shear in spring of year, if desired.

Variegated Mock Orange

(Pittosporum tobira variegata)

Evergreen shrub from Japan; family *Pittosporaceae*, grown as favored ornamentals and useful as container plants and in planters. Like *Podocarpus*, these plants will withstand dry, cool and drafty conditions.

P. tobira with all-green leaves grows to be a little larger and more robust than the *variegata* form. Clusters of creamy-white flowers are not uncommon on the plants, appearing in spring with the fragrance of orange blossoms.

Both sorts are adaptable to full sun and useful for outdoor summer growing on the patio or penthouse terrace. Display as floor plants.

LIGHT: High; some direct sunlight.

TEMPERATURE: Cool to warm. Can tolerate slight frost.

MOISTURE: Moist to dry. Will acclimate to dry condition.

PROPAGATION: Terminal cuttings with chemical rooting aid.

POTTING: Mix A. Repot only when root-bound.

FERTILIZER: Apply water-soluble type once every two months from spring to autumn. Controlled-release type every four to five months.

INSECTS: Mealy bugs, aphids, scale insects.

PRUNING: Usually not necessary. Plant can be trimmed to maintain height of five to six feet.

Pittosporum tobira variegata

Cordyline terminalis

Ti Plant *(Cordyline terminalis)*

An economic type of plant in its native habitat of Polynesia, where it is used for roof thatching and hula skirts. Another plant of the agave family *Agavaceae*. Many commercial forms are available, with variegated foliage ranging from mahogany red to pink and coppery tones. *C. terminalis* 'Firebrand' is an excellent red-leaved type. *C. terminalis* var. 'Ti' from Hawaii, used for growing grass skirts, is much merchandised as "Ti logs" from stem-sprouting new plants.

Artificial lighting of high intensity will provide necessary illumination for fairly successful indoor culture.

LIGHT: Very high.

TEMPERATURE: Warm.

MOISTURE: Moist. *Never let dry.*

PROPAGATION: Terminal cuttings, cane cuttings, seed. Layer "logs" or canes to half an inch deep in peat and sand or sphagnum moss. When shoots develop three to four leaves, cut off, root and pot.

POTTING: Mix B. Repot only when pot-bound.

FERTILIZER: Feed once every three to four months when plants are established.

INSECTS: Red spider mites.

Aphelandra squarrosa dania

Zebra Plant
(Aphelandra squarrosa dania)

The original species of this very attractive best seller of novelty plants comes from Brazil. The family is *Acanthaceae*. It thrives on moisture and medium light. The zebra plant has proven to be an excellent house plant when its culture is understood. Just don't let it dry out! The hybrid *dania* is a stocky, compact form with very showy white-veined, glossy deep-green leaves. It was selected from a cross between *A. squarrosa leopoldii* and *A. squarrosa louisae*.

LIGHT: Medium to indirect bright light.

TEMPERATURE: Warm.

MOISTURE: Moist at all times.

PROPAGATION: Grows from single-eye cuttings —that is, a leaf and bud with half a stem section attached. Keep moist in propagation medium.

POTTING: Mix A.

FERTILIZER: Feed once a month with water-soluble fertilizer when in good growth.

INSECTS: Mealy bugs.

PRUNING: Pinching will encourage flower buds to develop.

Aspidistra elatior variegata

Cast-Iron Plant

(Aspidistra elatior variegata)

A member of the lily family, *Liliaceae,* native to China. So called because of its ability to withstand neglect, low light and dryness. It is another plant species ranking with *Sansevieria* for toughness. It was used for many years as decoration in barbershops, in the old saloons and in restaurants. Probably it is less used today because of its slow habit of growth when compared with philodendron and other ornamentals.

A. elatior, the all-green leaf, is not as attractive as *variegata,* but its dark-green broad leaves are excellent for contrast in combination with other ornamentals.

LIGHT: Low.

TEMPERATURE: Cool to warm.

MOISTURE: Moist. Will condition to dry category.

PROPAGATION: Division of the clump.

POTTING: Mix A. Repot only when pot-bound; probably every two to three years.

FERTILIZER: Water-soluble type every two months or controlled-release type every three to four months.

INSECTS: Mealy bugs, scale insects.

REMARKS: Occasional washing of the broad leaves enhances the beauty of the dark-green or variegated leaf.

Variegated Screw-Pine
(Pandanus veitchii)

A genus of the *Pandanaceae* or screw-pine family. So called because of the twisted arrangement of the densely borne narrow leaves, which resemble those of a pineapple but are glossy and white-edged. The fruit of mature plants is cone-shaped but rarely borne on pot-grown plants. It is native to the Pacific islands. Plants are often considered undesirable as house plants because of the spines on the leaf edges. Growing to a height of three to four feet, it is used as a floor plant.

When growing on the beaches of the South Pacific the plants produce stout stilt (aerial) roots that serve to anchor the plants against the force of the winds.

LIGHT: Medium to high. Direct sun in winter is beneficial.

TEMPERATURE: Warm.

MOISTURE: Dry. Drench with water and let dry completely before wetting again.

PROPAGATION: Suckers which grow from the base of the plant.

POTTING: Mix B. Repot when crowded in pot every two or three years.

FERTILIZER: Apply water-soluble type to established plants every two months except in winter. Use controlled-release type twice a year—early spring and late summer.

INSECTS: Mealy bugs.

REMARKS: Stilt roots developing on larger plants may be directed back into the pot.

Pandanus veitchii

Fatshedera lizei

Tree Ivy *(Fatshedera lizei)*

An excellent house plant because it is tolerant of almost any environment, withstanding even temperatures to 35° without injury.

An unusual bigeneric cross first noticed in a nursery in France half a century ago between Irish ivy *Hedera helix hibernica* and Moser's Japanese fatsia *Fatsia japonica moserii*, it climbs like an ivy yet grows as a shrub by pruning.

Fatshedera lizei variegata is offered by some nurseries as possessing white-bordered leaves.

Fatsia japonica, Japanese aralia, the related species of *F. japonica moserii*, is a bold, attractive plant with a tropical appearance. Its large, glossy, dark-green leaves measure up to 18 inches across. Deeply lobed and fan-shaped, they are borne on long stalks or petioles. The plant, not of branching habit, will grow up to eight feet tall. Its culture is simple. It requires a moist potting condition, responds to monthly applications of water-soluble fertilizer and tolerates a cool to warm temperature and a medium to high light intensity.

Older plants will flower with good culture, but it is advisable to remove flowers to promote normal leaf growth.

Its habit of growing suckers at the base offers opportunity to start new plants. It is also propagated from seed.

F. japonica moserii is a much slower, more compact cultivar.

LIGHT: High. Takes direct sun in winter.

TEMPERATURE: Cool to warm.

MOISTURE: Moist.

PROPAGATION: Terminal cuttings, sectional cuttings. Chemical rooting aid beneficial.

POTTING: Mix A.

FERTILIZER: Feed water-soluble fertilizer once a month.

INSECTS: Aphids, scale insects, mealy bugs.

PRUNING: Tall plants tend to become leafless on lower stems. Can be trimmed back to start again. Pinch tip growth to control height.

REMARKS: Needs support. A good indoor-outdoor plant for summer patio growing.

Dizygotheca elegantissima

False or Spider Aralia

(Dizygotheca elegantissima)

Native to the Pacific islands, an attractive plant, three to eight feet tall. It is used in large planters or as a house plant in its juvenile stage when its lacy leaves are divided, fanlike, into narrow leaflets about three-eighths of an inch wide and four to nine inches long, with notched edges. The top surface of the leaf is dark, shiny green and reddish-brown beneath. Mature plants are useful in shopping enclosures because they have much larger leaves—to 12 inches in length and three inches in width.

It combines well with broad-leaf foliage plants. It is most attractive as a specimen with three plants potted together. It suggests a decorative Oriental motif.

LIGHT: High; indirect sunlight.

TEMPERATURE: Warm.

MOISTURE: Moist. Water-logged or dry soil will cause leaf drop.

PROPAGATION: Terminal and sectional stem cuttings. Chemical rooting aid beneficial. Air layering of large specimens.

POTTING: Mix B. Shift to larger pot once a year in spring. Provide large container with drainage.

FERTILIZER: Water-soluble type once a month, every two months in winter.

INSECTS: Red spider mites, mealy bugs and scale insects. Weekly spraying of foliage with tap water controls insects and cleans foliage.

PRUNING: Pinch out tips or prune to maintain shape.

Monstera deliciosa

Hurricane *(Monstera deliciosa)*

One of many climbing plants of the *Araceae* family, originates in Mexico and Central America. It is widely used as an indoor decorating plant, but many home gardeners and florists in America misname it as "split-leaf philodendron."

Monstera is distinctly different from philodendron in appearance, particularly its leaf. During the young stage, this plant develops leaves that are solid or have slight indentations. .When mature, the indentations deepen and holes appear in the leaves, as in a slice of Swiss cheese.

How can one tell the difference? *Monstera* has an easily identifiable plant structure called "geniculum" at the junction of the leaf stem and the leaf blade. The geniculum is described as bent like a knee. Such a struc-

ture is never present in philodendron, which has smooth and straight petioles or leaf stems.

LIGHT: High to medium. Low light is the main cause of the topmost leaves reverting to the juvenile form.

TEMPERATURE: Warm.

MOISTURE: Moist; may be conditioned to dry category.

PROPAGATION: Leaf-bud cuttings, cane layering, air layering, seeds.

POTTING: Mix B. Use two or three stems in a pot for nice specimens.

FERTILIZER: Feed water-soluble type once a month or slow-release type every four months.

INSECTS: Mealy bugs.

PRUNING: A climbing plant; should be pruned from time to time to limit growth and maintain desired height and shape.

Java Fig *(Ficus benjamina)*

An excellent indoor plant for home or office from India, Malaysia and the Philippines. A member of the fig family *Moraceae*.

Ficus microcarpa (retuṣa nitida), or Laurel fig, is the more common species in cultivation but not as graceful as *F. benjamina exotica*. Its growth habit is upright branching that will eventually form a crown, becoming semiweeping in habit.

Plants react to pruning in spring by sprouting new growth. They may be trained as "espaliers" or "standards."

In contrast to either species here described is *F. pumila*, creeping fig. Having a most unfiglike habit of growth, this creeping, climbing plant fastens itself to wood, masonry and even metal. It is most useful in its juvenile stages. The delicate tracery of branches bearing tiny heart-shaped leaves, up to half an inch across, will soon cover an inside masonry wall or brick chimney, if desired. In milder climates it is used on the outside for the same landscape value. It is an excellent ground cover for the top of tree-sized containers or for planting pockets. It makes a good hanging basket and helps, in the form of small, rooted cuttings, to landscape terrariums.

If allowed to grow to adult stage, its neat little leaves develop into large leathery oblong leaves, two to four inches long, bearing large oblong fruits on its stubby branches.

LIGHT: Medium. Semishaded location outdoors in summer.

TEMPERATURE: Warm.

MOISTURE: Moist. Drying out causes leaves to turn yellow and drop.

PROPAGATION: Terminal cuttings; rooting hormones beneficial. Air layering.

POTTING: Mix A.

FERTILIZER: Feed every three months with water-soluble type for established plants.

INSECTS: Usually insect-free. Possibly mealy bugs.

PRUNING: Prune occasionally to maintain shape and create bushy form.

Ficus benjamina

Rubber Plant
(Ficus elastica decora)

A member of the fig family *Moraceae* (not a relative of the commercial rubber-producing plant *Hevea brasiliensis*). The less frequently seen true species, *F. elastica*, is a forest tree in Malaysia and India. *F. elastica decora* is a seedling sport and a great improvement over the old-fashioned rubber plant of Grandmother's day. The dark-green, leathery leaves grow in a wide spiral formation from the main trunk. Each leaf is attached by a small petiole or stalk about two inches long. The leaves measure nine to 12 inches in length and five to seven inches wide. While growing, a new leaf is enveloped in a bright red sheath. Later, as the leaf expands, the sheath turns brown and drops off.

F. elastica doescheri is the only large-leaved variegated ficus. Its looks are similar to *F. decora*, but the leaves are narrower and longer. The young leaves are attractive, having broad, irregular cream-colored markings near the edges that narrow as the leaf matures. The center of the leaf is two shades of green in irregular patches. The midrib of the leaf is pink. Although a truly handsome and decorative plant, it is, however, more delicate than *F. decora* in that it requires a warm temperature and must never become dry.

LIGHT: High for best growth. Will condition to medium.

TEMPERATURE: Warm.

MOISTURE: Moist. Drying of root ball causes lower leaves to drop.

PROPAGATION: Air-layering method. Rooting in several weeks. Cut off just below roots and pot, sphagnum and all. See instructions on air layering in the chapter on starting plants, page 196.

POTTING: Mix A. Repot only when pot-bound. Avoid severe root pruning.

FERTILIZER: Feed monthly.

INSECTS: Mealy bugs.

PRUNING: Soft pinch of terminal growth will limit top growth and encourage side branching.

REMARKS: Sponge with water and detergent once a month to remove dust.

Fiddle-Leaf Fig *(Ficus lyrata)*

Another plant of the fig family from tropical Africa. Its large, bold, thick, violin-shaped leaves measure to 15 inches long and ten inches wide, with prominent veins and a glossy surface. Its large-sized leaves and shrubby habit of growth make it desirable as an accent plant in planters. To promote branching and to restrain top growth, pinch young top growth. An excellent large specimen plant when two or three stalks are planted together. When cultural conditions are right, plants will grow upright. Sometimes stakes and tying are needed to keep them vertical.

Another species not mentioned elsewhere is worth some space here. It is called the mistletoe fig, *Ficus diversifolia*, which is a slow-growing, small, shrublike plant making a good house plant. Also a fine subject for training as an indoor tropical bonsai. Its leaf shape is interestingly variable; some are round, some are pointed. A gray overcast webbing effect gives the appearance of dust accumulation on the leaves, but it is normal. Fruits are produced on small plants. They are borne on short stems at the axil of leaf petiole and stem. The early stage is green, turning dull yellow or reddish at maturity.

LIGHT: Medium. A light shade from sun, if used on patio in summer.

TEMPERATURE: Warm

MOISTURE: Moist.

PROPAGATION; Air layering. Difficult from terminal cuttings. Refer to the chapter on starting new plants, page 196.

POTTING: Mix A. Shift to larger pots when rooting indicates; necessary to support large top growth.

FERTILIZER: Apply water-soluble type once every three to four months.

INSECTS: Mealy bugs. Otherwise insect-free.

PRUNING: To encourage branching, make soft pinch when plants are young.

REMARKS: Sponge leaves occasionally with mild soapy water to remove dust and help prevent insect infestations.

Ficus elastica decora

Ficus lyrata

Dieffenbachia picta superba

Dieffenbachia amoena

Dumb Cane
(*Dieffenbachia amoena*)

There are various species and varieties, known as mutants of *dieffenbachia*, belonging to the *Araceae* or arum family and native to South America. Growers have selected desirable varieties for indoor culture.

Many other kinds are available for indoor culture from the species known as either *D. maculata* or *D. picta*. *D. m. exotica* is more compact than *D. amoena*, with smaller leaves. Edges of leaves are dark green with much creamy variegation; midrib of leaf is creamy white.

Another *D. maculata*, 'Rudolph Roehrs,' is a large-leaved, tall grower with leaves of pale chartreuse blotched with ivory and edged with green.

D. maculata superba has a stout trunk with large, thick leaves growing close to the stalk measuring three times as long as they are broad. Leaves heavily blotched with cream.

It is an ideal plant for the patio in summer. Protection from sun and wind must be provided with roof and lattice work.

LIGHT: Medium.

TEMPERATURE: Warm.

MOISTURE: Dry, but not extremely so. Water as soon as surface looks dry.

PROPAGATION: Air layering, cane cuttings, terminal cuttings. Use sphagnum moss as medium.

POTTING: Mix B. Will grow very well in pure sphagnum moss. Some varieties produce offsets and may be separated at repotting time. Repot when root mass tends to push plant upward from the pot.

FERTILIZER: Feed every three to four months. Plants cultured in sphagnum moss will need a water-soluble fertilizer solution once a month.

INSECTS: Red spider mites, mealy bugs.

PRUNING: Overgrown leggy plants, cut back almost to the base, will sprout and grow into a bushy plant.

REMARKS: The common name Dumb Cane refers to the fact that if parts of the plant are eaten, the acrid sap will injure the delicate tissues of the mouth and throat and cause painful swelling.

Striped Dracaena
(Dracaena deremensis warneckei)

A member of the agave family, *Agavaceae*, and native to tropical Africa. Grown in tropical regions for use in the horticulture trade.

A slow-growing plant with palmlike leaves, adaptable to areas of low light intensity. Used as a small pot plant for the end table or larger plants in tubs used as floor specimens. Also used as an accent plant for planters in combination with other plants.

LIGHT: Medium.

TEMPERATURE: Warm.

MOISTURE: Moist.

PROPAGATION: Cane, air layering.

POTTING: Mix A. Repot only when root-bound and plant has become too large for pot.

FERTILIZER: Apply water-soluble type once every three to four months to established, well-rooted plants.

INSECTS: Mealy bugs and red spider mites.

PRUNING: Tall leafless stalks can be cut back after air layering, and new shoots will develop.

Dracaena deremensis warneckei

Malaysian Dracaena
(Pleomele reflexa)

A fine indoor plant recently attaining popularity, belongs to the agave family, comes from Madagascar (Malagasy Republic). Its rosettes of dark-green leaves arranged along the main stem make it an excellent decorator plant. *Dracaena thalioides* is also an attractive indoor type.

LIGHT: Medium.

TEMPERATURE: Warm.

MOISTURE: Moist. *Never let it dry out.*

PROPAGATION: Air layering, terminal cuttings. Chemical rooting aid beneficial.

POTTING: Mix A.

FERTILIZER: Water-soluble feed once every three to four months.

INSECTS: Apparently free.

PRUNING: May be cut back to maintain size; trimmings rooted as cuttings.

Pleomele reflexa

Dracaena fragrans massangeana

Dracaena godseffiana

Corn Plant
(Dracaena fragrans massangeana)

An old-fashioned house plant from Upper Guinea and a member of the agave family, *Agavaceae*. An attractive decorator item can be created by rooting canes of large diameter and placing two or three in a container. A variation in height, with a rosette of leaves at the top, makes an interesting modern plant specimen. *D.f. massangeana* has green leaves with a gold center.

D. deremensis 'Janet Craig' is offered as a green form.

LIGHT: Low to medium.

TEMPERATURE: Warm.

MOISTURE: Moist.

PROPAGATION: Cane cuttings or air layering. Woody cane rooted directly in pots.

POTTING: Mix A.

FERTILIZER: Feed water-soluble type every three to four months.

INSECTS: Spider mites, mealy bugs.

PRUNING: May be cut back if too tall; will sprout new shoots.

Gold-Dust Dracaena
(Dracaena godseffiana)

This is a small dracaena compared with the rest of the genus. Excellent for home culture in planters for table or desk. With its cream-spotted leaves, it combines well with English ivy, philodendron or other green vines. A member of the agave family, or *Agavaceae,* it comes from Upper Guinea.

LIGHT: Medium.

TEMPERATURE: Warm.

MOISTURE: Moist.

PROPAGATION: Stem cuttings. Chemical rooting aid beneficial.

POTTING: Mix A. Repot only when extensive root system develops.

FERTILIZER: Apply water-soluble type once every three months.

INSECTS: Usually free, but red spider mites can be a pest.

PRUNING: Not necessary to prune or cut back.

Madagascar Dragon Tree
(Dracaena marginata)

From Madagascar (Malagasy Republic), it is another plant of the agave family, *Agavaceae*. Older plants with branching habit are both exotic in appearance and decoratively useful. It is a slow grower, yet very durable when grown under good cultural conditions.

LIGHT: Medium bright light, exclusive of direct sun, is best.

TEMPERATURE: Warm.

MOISTURE: Moist. Must have good drainage.

PROPAGATION: Terminal stem cuttings best.

POTTING: Mix B.

FERTILIZER: Water-soluble feeding once in three to four months.

INSECTS: Red spider mites, mealy bugs.

PRUNING: May be pruned, if necessary. Will make new shoot growth when cut back.

REMARKS: Plant stems may be trained to shape by using stiff wire and tying, as in bonsai culture.

Sander's Dracaena or Ribbon Plant
(Dracaena sanderiana)

Another small planter-type plant of the family *Agavaceae* from the Cameroons.

Plants offered today are mostly cultivated forms which have been selected for their more striking variegation and intense coloring of foliage. This plant's growth habit of producing stately upright stems or stalks makes it a good accent plant.

LIGHT: Medium.

TEMPERATURE: Warm.

MOISTURE: Moist (a characteristic of all species and varieties of this group).

PROPAGATION: Stem cuttings and cane cuttings.

POTTING: Mix A. Repot only when pot-bound.

FERTILIZER: Feed once in two to three months when roots are abundant.

INSECTS: Fairly clean of pests. Check for red spider mites occasionally.

PRUNING: Trim tall plants to limit upright growth.

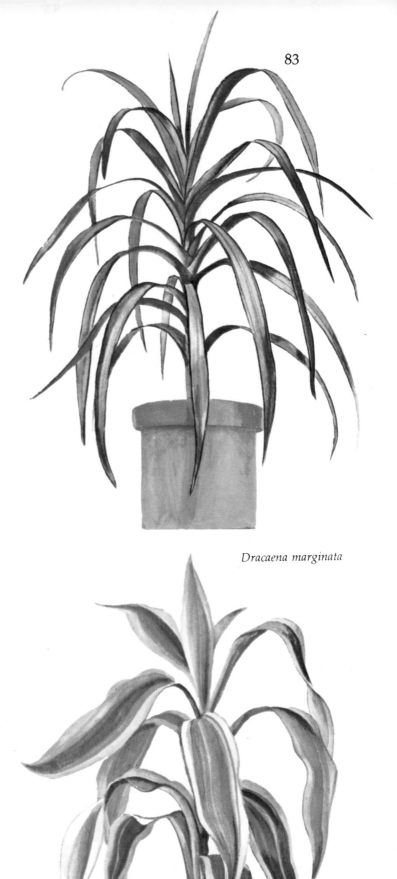

Dracaena marginata

Dracaena sanderiana

Umbrella Tree
(Schefflera actinophylla)

Commonly known as Australian umbrella tree, it is a member of the aralia family. It is a native plant of Queensland, Australia, and is widely cultivated as a large shrub or small landscape tree in Hawaii, southern Florida and California.

As an indoor plant, it can be trained to grow as a bonsai, a dwarf pot plant or a large tub specimen for shopping enclosures.

LIGHT: High, exclusive of sunlight for best maintenance. Will condition to survive with low light.

TEMPERATURE: Warm; will tolerate cool.

MOISTURE: Dry for slow normal growth. Moist with high light for rapid growth.

PROPAGATION: Seeds, air layering, and terminal cuttings.

POTTING: Mix B.

FERTILIZER: For fast growth, use moist category, high light, and fertilize once a month. For slow growth, use dry category, low light, and fertilize once in four months.

INSECTS: Make sure you are buying insect-free plants. Red spider mites and scale are often found on these plants.

PRUNING: Growing tips may be pruned back to encourage side growth.

Schefflera actinophylla

Araucaria heterophylla

Norfolk Island Pine

(Araucaria heterophylla)

An evergreen tree and a member of the *Araucaria* family from the Norfolk Islands in the South Pacific. It is an excellent plant for hotel foyers, shopping malls and interior home environments. They make excellent potted Christmas trees for the table or floor plants in the home and in public places.

Its selection as an indoor plant depends on its adaptability, but you must strive to provide the best environment.

LIGHT: High, exclusive of direct sun for best quality.

TEMPERATURE: Cool. Will tolerate warm. A subtropical plant, it will not take temperatures for long below 40° without showing damage.

MOISTURE: Moist. Ball of roots must not dry out at any time.

PROPAGATION: Seeds. Cuttings are made only by trained nurserymen.

POTTING: Plants received from growers can remain in the same pot for approximately a year. Mix B.

FERTILIZER: Water-soluble feeding every six weeks.

INSECTS: Scale sometimes found.

PRUNING: Removing the leader growth will maintain size, if necessary.

REMARKS: Sponging foliage at feeding time will improve plant's appearance. Use warm water with a few drops of dish-washing detergent.

86

Ivy *(Hedera helix)*

The ivy plant is an evergreen, clinging vine native to Europe and Asia. In ancient Greece it was called cissos *because, according to a mythological legend, it was named after the nymph Cissos, who, at a feast of the gods, danced with such joy and abandon before Dionysus that she fell dead from exhaustion at his feet. Dionysus was so moved by her performance and untimely death that he turned her body into the ivy, a plant which graciously and joyfully entwines and embraces everything near it. The ivy, dedicated to the wine god Dionysus, is hung even today in wreaths over the doors of taverns and wine shops.**

The English ivy (*H. helix*) is one of the most useful house plants.

LIGHT: High. Very high in winter with full sun. Shade in summer.

TEMPERATURE: Cool.

MOISTURE: Moist, with good drainage.

PROPAGATION: Terminal and sectional cuttings.

POTTING: Formula B.

FERTILIZER: Feed water-soluble type once a month.

INSECTS: Aphids, red spider mites, mealy bugs and scale.

PRUNING: Soft-pinch tips of branches to encourage branching.

REMARKS: An excellent ground cover in temperate climates.

Cape Ivy
(Senecio macroglossus variegatus)

Sometimes called the variegated wax vine, which describes its waxy, succulent leaves. This species comes from Cape Province, and it is of the family *Compositae*. It has proven to be a good house plant for dry interiors.

LIGHT: Medium.

TEMPERATURE: Warm.

MOISTURE: Dry.

PROPAGATION: Terminal cuttings.

POTTING: Mix A.

FERTILIZER: Once every two to three months.

INSECTS: Mealy bugs.

PRUNING: Prune off trailers to make plant compact.

Swedish Ivy
(Plectranthus australis)

Probably the fastest-growing of all house plants, it is ideal for hanging baskets. The species comes from Africa and Australia and botanically is of the mint family, *Labiatae*.

LIGHT: Medium to high.

TEMPERATURE: Warm, but growth is slower at cooler temperatures

MOISTURE: Moist.

PROPAGATION: Terminal and sectional stem cuttings. Will root in water.

POTTING: Mix A. Shift to a larger-sized pot when plant becomes root-bound.

FERTILIZER: Feed once in two to three months with water-soluble fertilizer.

INSECTS: Mealy bugs, white flies.

PRUNING: Pruning from time to time will keep plants bushy.

German Ivy *(Senecio mikanioides)*

A fast-growing, ivylike plant from South Africa, it belongs to one of the largest families of plants, *Compositae*. In contrast to German Ivy, other plants of the same genus exhibit thick succulent stems and leaves. *Senecio crassissimum* looks much more like a crassula than its counterpart, the German Ivy.

Cuttings from the plant may be started in water and placed in attractive bottlelike containers to grow as water plants.

LIGHT: Medium.

TEMPERATURE: Warm.

MOISTURE: Moist.

PROPAGATION: Terminal cuttings.

POTTING: Mix B.

FERTILIZER: Feed with water-soluble type once a month.

INSECTS: Mealy bug and red spider.

PRUNING: A soft pinching from time to time will encourage bushiness.

* Lehner, Ernst and Johanna, *Folklore and Symbolism of Flowers, Plants, and Trees,* published by Tudor Publishing Company, New York, N.Y., 1960. "Ivy," John Gerard's *The herball generall historie of plantes,* Adam Islip, London, 1633.

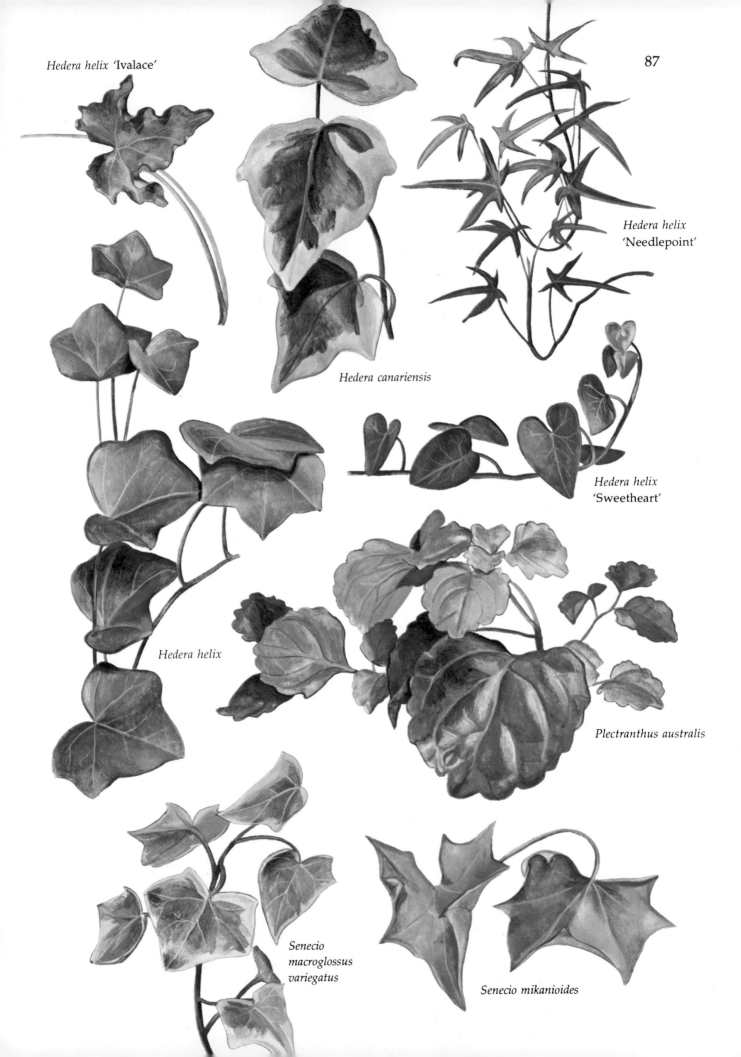

Hedera helix 'Ivalace'

Hedera helix 'Needlepoint'

Hedera canariensis

Hedera helix 'Sweetheart'

Hedera helix

Plectranthus australis

Senecio macroglossus variegatus

Senecio mikanioides

*Chlorophytum
comosum mandaianum*

Spider Plant
(Chlorophytum comosum mandaianum)

A longtime favorite house plant because of its cascading stems producing small white flowers, followed by small plantlets. Its native habitat is South Africa, and it is a member of the lily family, *Liliaceae*. The popularity of spider plants today has increased with the use of hanging baskets, which create a natural environment for its habit of growth.

A cultivar relative, *C. comosum variegatum*, is a more vigorous plant with leaves measuring ten to 15 inches long and about one inch wide, with margins edged with white.

LIGHT: Medium to high.

TEMPERATURE: Warm.

MOISTURE: Moist.

PROPAGATION: Take plantlets forming roots and pot up.

POTTING: Mix A. Repot only when root-bound condition exists.

FERTILIZER: Feed water-soluble type once in three to four months to established plants.

INSECTS: Mealy bugs.

PRUNING: Older leaves tend to brown at tip end and become unsightly. May be removed at the base. New leaves will develop from the rosette-like growth of the crown.

Grape Ivy *(Cissus rhombifolia)*

A table plant sometimes grown in hanging baskets. It is native to northern South America and is of the grape or vine family *Vitaceae*; thus its name "Grape Ivy."

A very attractive plant for any indoor location. It is sometimes used as a ground cover for large floor planters. A sport, *C. rhombifolia mandaiana,* is more compact, with darker green leaves of a waxed appearance.

LIGHT: Medium.

Zebrina pendula

Tradescantia albiflora albovittata   *Gibasis geniculata*   *Tradescantia purpusii*

TEMPERATURE: Cool, but will grow at warm temperature with high light.

MOISTURE: Moist.

PROPAGATION: Terminal cuttings, slow to root. Hormone rooting aid beneficial.

POTTING: Mix A.

FERTILIZER: Feed established plants once a month.

INSECTS: Mealy bugs.

PRUNING: Long tendril-like stems can be cut back to make plant more bushy.

See illustration on page 166.

Wandering Jew
(*Tradescantia albiflora albovittata*)

A creeping type of plant used as a ground cover in warm countries and under benches in greenhouses. Probably best grown as a hanging-basket plant. A native of South America, it belongs to the family *Com-* *melinaceae*. Its many related species differ in minor botanical characteristics. *Zebrina pendula*, also called Wandering Jew, is worthy of mention. Its leaves are of similar shape, deep green to purple, with two broad vertical bands of silver above and purple suffused beneath.

Both species will adapt to growing in water. They will last for several months by changing water once a month and adding a few drops of fertilizer solution.

LIGHT: Medium.

TEMPERATURE: Warm.

MOISTURE: Moist.

PROPAGATION: Terminal or sectional stem cuttings.

POTTING: Mix B.

FERTILIZER: Apply liquid-soluble fertilizer once a month.

INSECTS: Red spider mites.

PRUNING: Trim back to encourage bushiness.

Fittonia verschaffeltii

Fittonia verschaffeltii argyroneura

Mosaic Plant *(Fittonia verschaffeltii)*

A ground-cover type plant coming from South America, and a member of the *Acanthaceae* family. The plant's requirements for much moisture and humid atmosphere make *Fittonia* a desirable plant for terrarium planters. The variety *F. verschaffeltii argyroneura* is more commonly seen, with a lighter green leaf having white veins and midrib. *F. verschaffeltii* has a thicker leaf and is better adapted to growth as a table plant in open containers.

LIGHT: Low to medium.

TEMPERATURE: Warm.

MOISTURE: Moist.

PROPAGATION: Terminal cuttings mostly easily rooted in peat moss in closed containers of polyethylene (polythene) bags. Cuttings wilt quickly after being cut and exposed to air.

POTTING: Mix B or sphagnum moss with liquid fertilizer feeding.

FERTILIZER: Feed established plants once in three to four months with water-soluble fertilizer.

INSECTS: Relatively free. Mealy bugs and slugs, if grown as greenhouse ground cover.

PRUNING: Overgrown plants may be cut back to main creeping stems to sprout new growth.

REMARKS: Grow several plants on a vertical plaquelike support. Construct a simple frame of wood or three-inch-wide material and stuff with sphagnum moss. Seal moss into the frame with half-inch wire mesh. Plant cuttings directly into moss through the wire. Suspend in a polyethylene bag until established. Feed with half-strength water-soluble fertilizer every two weeks.

Coleus *(Coleus blumei)*

One of the most common and easily grown foliage types of plants, coleus belongs to the square-stemmed mint family, *Labiatae.* The original species comes from Java. Plantsmen have selected many cultivars that offer plants in groups with similar size and foliage characteristics.

In America three forms are grown. A "small-leaved class" is popular for house culture and is easily propagated by cuttings. The "rainbow class" offers plants of medium size, free-branching and bushy. This group is easily propagated from seed with selected color range, the most popular being shades of red. A third class, known as "Exhibition," is distinguished by extra large leaves, but is really not suited for home cul-ture. A new strain, "Carefree," grown from seed, comes almost 90 percent true to type. Its foliage is fringed and lobed like an oak leaf. The plants are grown basically for their foliage, which comes in shades of jade, gold, bronze, yellow, red and white.

LIGHT: High for indoor culture.

TEMPERATURE: Warm.

MOISTURE: Moist

PROPAGATION: Terminal cuttings; seed germinates in ten to 15 days at 65° with artificial light.

POTTING: Mix A.

FERTILIZER: Water-soluble feeding once a month.

INSECTS: Mealy bugs, red spider mites, white flies.

PRUNING: Soft-pinch from time to time to make compact growth and to prevent legginess.

Coleus blumei varieties

Hoya carnosa compacta

Hoya carnosa variegata

Wax Plant *(Hoya carnosa)*

Wax plants are native to an area extending from East Asia to Australia. A characteristic of milky sap places it in the milkweed family, *Asclepiadaceae*. Most of its species are climbing vines with leathery leaves bearing white to pink flowers.

They are most effectively displayed growing on supports of trellis, stiff wire loop or totems. The peduncles or stalks that bear the flower cluster should not be removed when picking the flowers, because more blooms will form here year after year.

H. carnosa variegata is an attractive type with blue-green leaves broadly edged with creamy white or, often, pink coloration. *H. carnosa compacta*, known as "Hindu Rope," with twisted leaves resembling braided rope, is a curiosity. *H. bella*, a dwarf with upright to drooping growth patterns, produces small waxy-white parachute clusters of white flowers with purple centers.

LIGHT: High.

TEMPERATURE: Cool to warm.

MOISTURE: Dry. More water given in summer.

PROPAGATION: Terminal and leaf-bud sectional cuttings. Rooting best in coarse peat and perlite medium, not too moist.

POTTING: Mix B.

FERTILIZER: Apply water-soluble solution once a month in summer only.

INSECTS: Mealy bugs.

Rosary Vine *(Ceropegia woodii)*

One of a hundred species cultivated as house plants. A plant belonging to the same family as *hoya*, of the milkweed family, *Asclepiadaceae*. It is often referred to as the "string of hearts" because of the trailing threadlike stems.

It is a small vine with leaves in pairs on short petioles rising from a tuberous base. Its leaves are heart-shaped, thick and succulent, about two-thirds of an inch long. The surface of the leaf is dark green, with whitish veins. The little tubers that form from the trailing stems are used to start new plants. Flowers are small, dull pink or purplish in color; not showy, but of very interesting structure. It grows best in pots. Thrives in low light intensity with atmospheric moisture.

Other species less interesting and better suited for a greenhouse but with intriguing flowers are: *C. debilis* from Nyasaland, a threadlike vine with cordlike roots and linear leaves. The flowers are greenish, marked with purple; *C. dichotoma*, an erect form that comes from the Canary Islands. It is a succulent with jointed forked green stems and scattered linear leaves. Its yellow flowers are interesting and attractive.

Rosary Vine can be displayed attractively with its drooping, trailing growth in small exotic containers on a shelf or as a hanging basket.

C. fusca from the Canary Islands also is an upright, succulent shrub similar to *C. dichotoma*. Its forked, cylindrical columns appearing restricted at joints are gray to purplish in color. The flowers are brown and yellow.

C. barkleyi from Cape Province is a slender vine with cormlike roots similar in growth habit to *C. woodii*. Succulent leaves with silver-white veins and flowers greenish veined with purple.

C. elegans is a trailing vinelike plant from India. Its leaves are oval-shaped, not succulent. Flowers are tubelike or expanded funnel shape. Color is whitish blotched with purple; top lobes are united in the center and edged with long, dark hairs.

LIGHT: Medium.

TEMPERATURE: Warm.

MOISTURE: Dry. Follow with a thorough drenching. In winter, water only occasionally to keep the leaves from shriveling.

PROPAGATION: Sectional stem cuttings with tuberlike roots attached. Pot them up for growing on in regular potting mix.

POTTING: Mix B. Use shallow pots of large proportion because of its surface rooting habit.

FERTILIZER: Water-soluble fertilizer solution applied once in three to four months. Do not feed in winter.

INSECTS: Apparently free.

PRUNING: Seldom needs pruning. Trimmings having tubers attached can be used to start new plants.

Ceropegia woodii

Syngonium podophyllum

Syngonium
(Syngonium podophyllum)

Native to the American tropics, of the family *Araceae*. They are climbing plants with arrow-shaped leaves. The juvenile or young plants are cultivated and grown in planters as small pot specimens for end tables, desks or bookshelves. When the plants become older, they enter an adult phase of growth and require support. The leaves then change from arrow-shaped to fan-shaped leaves about ten inches in size; they also lose their white leaf markings and become all green.

    S. podophyllum 'Emerald Gem' is a more compact-growing cultivar, more of a creeper with all-green leaves. Other cultivars are offered by the trade.

    S. podophyllum albolineatum 'Ruth Fraser' is a horticultural selection, available in America, and showing a distinct improvement in variegation.

    S. podophyllum 'Imperial White' is more compact, with broad, glistening, arrow-head-shaped leaves in the juvenile stage. Margins of leaves have a greenish border and are greenish-white inside.

LIGHT: Medium.

TEMPERATURE: Warm.

MOISTURE: Moist.

PROPAGATION: Terminal cuttings, seed and division.

POTTING: Repot, using mix B, when plants become crowded. Divide at this time, if necessary.

FERTILIZER: Apply water-soluble fertilizer every three to four months.

INSECTS: Mealy bugs and red spider mites.

PRUNING: Pruning off climbing growth will retain juvenile form.

Devil's Ivy
(Epipremnum aureum—Pothos aureus)

A member of the *Araceae* family. Authorities on nomenclature differ in their opinions regarding the name of this genus. Sometimes listed as *Scindapsus aureus*, *Raphidophora aurea* and recently as *Epipremnum aureum*. The devil's ivy is one of the most popular of the climbing or vining foliage plants. In its native habitat, adult plants produce leaves about two feet in length, while leaves of the juvenile plants used for interiors are two to three inches in length. Offered by nurserymen are *E. aureum (P. aureus) wilcoxi*, which has leaves marked with yellow blotches or streaks of color. Another strain is *E. aureum (P. aureus)* 'Marble Queen' with foliage marked with white instead of yellow splashes. The plant is very versatile. It is a favorite as a small pot specimen for end table or desk, used as a filler plant in planters, as well as for small and large totem specimens from 12 to 48 inches tall.

LIGHT: Medium.

TEMPERATURE: Warm.

MOISTURE: Dry.

PROPAGATION: Leaf-bud cuttings, stem cuttings. Propagation medium is kept slightly dry at start to promote callus before rooting. When roots form, add more moisture.

POTTING: Mix B.

FERTILIZER: Feed established plants once every three to four months.

INSECTS: Red spider mites and mealy bugs.

PRUNING: Pinch tips or cut back to control growth when necessary.

REMARKS: Totems of sphagnum moss enclosed in wire or plastic mesh encourage climbers to develop roots.

Epipremnum aureum

Epipremnum aureum 'Marble Queen'

Gynura 'Purple Passion'

Purple Passion Plant

(Gynura 'Purple Passion')

A member of the large family *Compositae*, it is a cultivar of uncertain origin. It has recently become a popular plant because of its velvety purple leaves. The orange composite flowers contrast vividly with the purple color of the foliage.

Unfortunately the fragrance of the flowers is objectionable to most people, and they are usually trimmed out as soon as they open.

It may be used as a specimen pot plant for a table, desk or window sill.

LIGHT: High.

TEMPERATURE: Warm.

MOISTURE: Dry.

PROPAGATION: Terminal cuttings.

POTTING: Mix B.

FERTILIZER: Feed once a month; established plants only.

INSECTS: Red spider mites and white flies.

PRUNING: Pinch occasionally to encourage development of new growth that produces best purple coloration.

Kangaroo Vine

(Cissus antarctica minima)

Originating from New South Wales, Australia, hence its name, this plant is a member of the vine family, *Vitaceae*.

C. antarctica minima, a compact dwarf *Cissus*, has small leaves, is a slow grower with free-branching habit, making it very desirable as a house plant.

C. antarctica, a better-known species, is very similar, but with long shrublike growth of coarse, leathery leaves.

LIGHT: Medium to high.

TEMPERATURE: Cool to warm.

MOISTURE: Moist.

PROPAGATION: Terminal and sectional stem cuttings. Chemical rooting aid is beneficial.

POTTING: Mix B. Repot about once a year.

FERTILIZER: Apply water-soluble fertilizer once every two to three months.

Cissus antarctica minima

Saxifraga sarmentosa tricolor

Saxifraga sarmentosa

INSECTS: Relatively free. Occasionally mealy bugs.

PRUNING: *C. antarctica* needs occasional cutting back of long tendril-like stems.

Strawberry Geranium
(Saxifraga sarmentosa, S. tricolor)

A common name that to some is misleading yet descriptive. It belongs to neither the strawberry family nor the geranium family. Botanically it belongs to the Saxifrage family, *Saxifragaceae*. Its region of origin is East Asia. Its running, plant-producing strawberry habit and bicolor foliage have sustained its popularity through the years. The plant *S. sarmentosa*, with an upper-leaf surface of gray-green with white veins and under-leaf surface of reddish color, is more vigorous than *tricolor*. Both types are used as table plants, in planters and in small hanging containers.

The culture of *tricolor* requires attention because certain phases are critical to its behavior as a healthy plant. It must have a cool, humid atmosphere; a soil or potting mixture of low nutrition. It takes less water than its relative. Grow it on the dry side. A summary of culture follows.

In cool areas with milder winters *S. sarmentosa* is grown as an outdoor ground cover and is attractive in the rock garden.

LIGHT: Medium. *S. sarmentosa* will take full sun.

TEMPERATURE: Cool.

MOISTURE: Moist to dry. *S. sarmentosa* needs more moist conditions than *S. tricolor*.

PROPAGATION: Runners and division of the crown. To increase runner production, set plants in large tray or greenhouse flat to encourage more plantlets to form. When rooting, cut off and pot up.

POTTING: Mix B. Both varieties make attractive additions to old-fashioned strawberry pots.

FERTILIZER: Feed established plants only once in three to four months.

INSECTS: Mealy bugs.

PALMS

Palms, the aristocrats of the foliage plants, are only really successful in centrally heated homes where there is plenty of room. The variety of shapes, sizes and textures available makes palms very useful for decorating the interiors of homes, modern office buildings, shopping malls and outdoor patios in summer.

The price of a palm may seem high in comparison to the price of other plants, but when one knows its durability and longer life, it is a good investment.

PARLOR PALM (*Chamaedorea elegans*). A native of Mexico and of the family *Palmae*, it is grown commercially by the tens of thousands in warm climates. A small dwarf with thin, dark-green feathery leaves, this single-stem palm is used in every kind of container from terrariums to dish gardens to single specimens. Also used with three in a pot as a table or desk plant. A curiosity that is surprising to many is that this palm produces flowers when only one foot tall; since these resemble buds rather than flowers, they are sometimes mistaken for insects.

Flowers are borne in yellow clusters and often extend on stalks above the foliage.

Chamaedorea elegans

Chamaedorea elegans is a dioecious palm. Each sex is confined to separate plants and will not produce viable seeds unless both sexes are found in flower at the same time. Seeds are available, but one must be sure one is purchasing fresh seed.

It is reported that *Chamaedorea elegans* can be propagated by air layering. Sphagnum moss is wrapped about the stem near the top in the form of a ball and kept moist. After several months roots will develop, the top cut from the lower trunk and potted in soil. It is probable that this method could be duplicated for any of the *Chamaedorea* species which have the habit of sending out adventitious roots from the stem.

Many nurserymen and florists sell this palm under its erroneous name of *Neanthe bella* but its correct name is *Chamaedorea elegans*. The parlor palm's tolerance to desert-like conditions, to low light intensity and resistance to below average home temperatures make it the number one house plant.

COCONUT PALM (*Cocos nucifera*). Although its original habitat is not definitely known, it probably came from the Old World tropics. It is a useful tree whose main products are copra—a source of widely used oil—and desiccated coconut and fiber. Travelers in tropical and subtropical regions have long admired the scenery created by the graceful curving, erect trunks topped by majestic crowns of glossy, feathery fronds. Many trunks reach 100 feet, yet it is recommended here as a house plant in the seedling stage.

A sprouting coconut grown in a container with half its husk exposed becomes a home conversation piece. It grows slowly and will last for several years before it outgrows its welcome as a large tree. Only an expert can pick a coconut viable for germination, so it is best to purchase one already started. Its care is simple. Keep it moist. Add fertilizer once in two months and watch for the usual insects.

PIGMY DATE PALM (*Phoenix roebelenii*). Found growing in Laos on the Mekong River in the family *Palmae*. A very graceful palm as a miniature pot plant and as a floor specimen, having many small flat leaves or fronds arising from a central crown. It is a slow grower and found to be more attractive when two or three plants are put together in a container. Good drainage must be provided in its pot, and overpotting should be avoided.

The ultimate size of *P. roebelenii* as a well-grown plant comprises 30 to 40 leaves, making a diameter of four to six feet. The leaves are borne on a trunk approximately four inches in diameter. The attained height ranges from three to five feet. It is tolerant of low temperature, excessive sun, winds and cold. It has reportedly survived a temperature drop to 18° Fahrenheit.

BUTTERFLY PALM (*Chrysalidocarpus lutescens*). It is also known as Areca palm and it belongs to the family *Palmae*. Its native habitat is Madagascar (Malagasy Republic), yet it is found growing in many places in the tropics. Its very tropical appearance, with feathery foliage arching widely from tightly clustered leaf bases, makes it an excellent decorator plant for the home, office and industrial interiors. As a floor plant, the average size obtainable is four to eight feet. It is a clustered-stem type, making it a good specimen palm. The size of the container regulates its growth. Foliage color is normally green.

Chrysalidocarpus lutescens

Phoenix roebelenii

Chamaedorea siefrizii

Rhapis excelsa

Howea belmoreana

REED PALM *(Chamaedorea siefrizii)*. Its native habitat is the Yucatan peninsula of Mexico. A tall, upright, clustered-stem palm with narrow bamboolike foliage, it is a favorite for indoor planting. Average size offered ranges from three to eight feet. It will withstand lower than normal temperatures, making it an ideal plant for tubs on patios in warmer climates.

The genus *Chamaedorea* has many other favored species. Those most desirable as house plants are listed in the table on Handling and Care of Potted Palms. Similar to *C. siefrizii* is *C. erumpens*, known as the bamboo palm. A cluster-type palm, it has bamboolike stems with thin, feathery, dark-green, recurved leaves loosely distributed from top to bottom. The average size offered is from three to nine feet.

C. cataractarum is available in two- to three-feet sizes. It is a dwarf, compact, clustered-stem type. Its featherlike, dark-green leaves originate alternately from branching stems, prostrate and forked.

Protection of the plant from direct sun should be provided, and watering is a prime consideration.

Drying of the soil ball can cause injury to small feeding roots that are characteristic of palms. Only a few palms can withstand dry soil conditions.

A test to make sure sufficient water is added is to be sure the excess water emerges from the drainage hole at the bottom.

BELMORE SENTRY PALM *(Howea belmoreana)* of the family *Palmae* has been cultivated for many years for florists' use and decoration. Formerly known under the name of Kentia, it is native to Lord Howe's Island in the South Pacific Ocean, hence the name *Howea*. Today it is cultivated by the thousands in the state of California to be used as decorator palms in the indoor-landscape business. It has thick, leathery, dark-green leaves that arch from a center axis, then droop downward with leaflets becoming slender, to pointed tips. An excellent floor plant, usually available from three to six feet tall, potted in six- to eight-inch-size containers.

The only other species of *Howea* is *H. forsterana*, referred to as the Forster sentry palm. It also comes from Lord Howe's Island. It is faster-growing and of larger proportion than *H. belmoreana*. The leaflets are not arching but flat to the center axis. A hardier palm, it will resist cool temperature, lack of strong light and some neglect.

Its rating as a favorite house plant is second only to *C. elegans*, the parlor palm. Its tolerance to below-average house temperatures, low light intensity and ability to withstand dryness makes it useful for the office and other industrial embellishment. Its water requirements, as with most palms, are on the moist side. Use as a single-stem plant or pot two and three together to make spectacular floor specimens. For potting use formula A. New plants may be started from seed in warm-temperature chambers.

LADY PALM *(Rhapis excelsa)*. A clustered-stem palm from southern China, family *Palmae*. It is much desired as a tub specimen for outdoor patios in warm countries and interior plantings everywhere. It is a very durable palm, is slow-growing and produces a dense clump. It will tolerate lower temperatures than many other palms.

Rhapis excelsa differs from a less frequently cultivated *Rhapis humilis*, which has leaf segments 1⅛ inches or more wider at the middle and broader at the tip, as compared to segments less than ¾ inches wide and narrower at the tip. *Rhapis excelsa* has much coarser leaf sheaths than *Rhapis humilis* and is more robust, with stems that can grow 12 to 15 feet high and trunks of two inches in diameter. Both plants are very popular for the home and greenhouse. As decorator plants both give a bushy bamboo effect.

Propagated by division of the clump. Stems becoming too tall or crowded can be cut out at the base to make room for new stalks to grow in.

CARE AND MAINTENANCE OF PALMS

Successful maintenance of palms, as is the case for all plants, depends on a knowledge of the individual cultural requirements. The directions for handling and care of palms are listed in the table on page 103.

LIGHT AND TEMPERATURE: Palms, accustomed to growing indoors and being moved to a patio or porch in summer, must have protection from the bright sun to prevent sun scorch. Those palms that grow in a greenhouse will benefit from unshaded glass in the winter months in cool temperate climates but must have protection of shade from the stronger sunshine in summer.

A few palms listed have proved cold-hardy as a result of habitat and experience of exposure to freezing weather for brief periods. It is concluded that these palms would be desirable for use in areas where lower temperatures exist. This includes lobbies and shopping malls.

MOISTURE: Watering is the first consideration for palms, as for other plants. As noted in the table, all palms should have moist soil. Drying of the soil ball within small containers can cause injury to the small feeder roots, which are characteristic of palms. The result is inability of the roots to supply the leaves with water. Only a few palms can withstand dry soil, as indicated in the table.

A test to make sure sufficient water is added is to see the excess water emerge from the drainage hole at the bottom of the pot. Experience will result in the application of a measured amount at regular intervals.

POTTING: A potting mixture for palms must provide good drainage, permitting aeration between waterings and letting in the oxygen that is essential for good root development. Formula A is recommended.

In the repotting of palms it is important to compact the soil very firmly around the root system. This encourages the feeder roots to penetrate into the fresh soil. A layer of drainage material in the bottom of the pot, to facilitate drainage of excess water, is essential when the potted palm is plunged inside a planter or large tub and surrounded with peat moss or other filler.

FERTILIZER: There is no special nutrient requirement for palms. A general water-soluble fertilizer applied once a month is adequate. In temperate zones, feeding should be discontinued during the cool weather and then resumed when the warm weather arrives.

INSECTS: Insect pests, unfortunately, can create a troublesome problem for indoor as well as outdoor palms. Red spider mites, mealy bugs and scale insects are the most common pests.

PRUNING: Little or no pruning is necessary for the maintenance of palms. The cutting of a cane or stem of clustered palms to thin the clumps or to reduce the height is sometimes practiced. In the natural process of growth an old leaf may turn yellow and brown and begin to droop. It can be removed by cutting rather than tearing off. Tearing the leaf sheath from the stem causes a wound, leaving an unsightly scar, and may permit fungal infection.

HANDLING AND CARE OF POTTED PALMS

Common name	Genus and species	Culture notes	Water	Temperature	Light
Fishtail palm	*Caryota mitis and *C. urens	Slightly acid potting mix.	moist	warm	high
	Chamaedorea cataractarum	Plant one or more in pot. Will tolerate lower than normal temperature.	moist (dry)	cool	low
	Chamaedorea costaricana	Retain in small pots. Will tolerate lower than normal temperature.	moist (dry)	cool	low
Parlor palm	Chamaedorea elegans	Plant one or more in a pot. Use for dish garden when small. Flowers produced when plants are one foot high.	moist (dry)	warm	low
	Chamaedorea ernesti-augusti	Requires good drainage.	moist	warm	low
Bamboo palm	Chamaedorea erumpens	Requires shade on patio.	moist	warm	low
	Chamaedorea klotzschiana	Plant one or more in a pot for effect.	moist (dry)	cool	low
	Chamaedorea seifrizii	Withstands lower than normal temperature. Ideal for outside patio in warm climates.	moist	warm (cool)	high
European fan palm	Chamaerops humilis	pH neutral potting mixture, good drainage. Suckers when young. Is a slow grower. Tolerates lower than normal temperature.	moist (dry)	warm (cool)	high
Butterfly palm	Chrysalidocarpus lutescens	Size of container regulates growth. Withstands lower than normal temperature.	moist	warm (cool)	high
Coconut palm	*Cocos nucifera (juvenile stage)	Retain in small pot to slow growth	moist (dry)	warm	low
Belmore sentry palm	Howea belmoreana	Protect from direct sun. Is slow grower. Plant three or more in a pot for effect. Withstands drafts.	moist	warm (cool)	low
Forster sentry palm	Howea forsterana	Protect from direct sun. Is faster-growing than H. belmoreana. Will resist cold, lack of light and neglect.	moist	warm (cool)	low
	Licuala grandis	Never allow potting mix to become dry. High atmospheric humidity beneficial.	moist	warm	low
Chinese fan palm	*Livistona chinensis	Is slow-growing. Avoid excessive dryness.	moist	warm (cool)	high
	*Livistona rotundifolia	Grow in small container to retain small size. Best suited for interiors.	moist	warm	low
Pigmy date palm	Phoenix roebelenii	Is a slow grower. Protect from direct sun, wind and cold. Provide good drainage in pot. Do not overpot. Neutral soil pH.	moist	warm	high
Macarthur cluster palm	*Ptychosperma macarthurii	Is a fast grower.	moist	warm	high
Broadleaf lady palm	Rhapis excelsa	Slow grower. Withstands lower than normal temperature. Usually expensive.	moist	warm (cool)	high
Slender lady palm	Rhapis humilis	Slow grower. Tolerates lower than normal temperature. Makes dense clump.	moist	warm (cool)	high
Christmas palm	*Veitchia merrillii	Avoid overpotting. Requires potting material of a neutral pH.	moist	warm (cool)	high

*Species that when young make good pot plants but will eventually outgrow containers and should be planted in large tubs or in the open ground.

Cycas revoluta

Zamia pumila

FERNS AND CYCADS

Ferns are found in their wild state all over the world. A few are native to the Arctic regions ranging southward to the equator. They grow at various elevations and number over 12,000 species. Species that grow as house plants thrive under moist conditions, moderate temperatures and are shade-loving. These are collected from tropical and subtropical areas. The species that are most widely cultivated belong to the family *Polypodiaceae*. These include, among others, Boston fern, maidenhair fern and house holly fern. These are characterized by erect underground stems having upright fronds or leaves, clustered in crowns, or by creeping stems or rhizomes with scattered leaves.

Epiphytic ferns such as the staghorns or *Platycerium, Polypodium* and *Davallia* have become very popular as house plants.

A group of importance to the commercial florist industry is of the genus *Woodwardia* and the leather-leaf fern *Polystichum adi-antiforme*. These are marketed as cut greens throughout the United States and Canada for use in wedding work and other floral decoration.

Cycads, listed here because they are non-flowering seed plants and thus related to the ferns and their allies, are an old group of so-called gymnosperms, nine genera of which grow in the tropics and subtropics. They have fernlike leaves that form a crown at the top of a stem. Male and female cones grow at the crown but on separate plants.

Table Fern *(Pteris cretica cristata)*

A member of the family *Polypodiaceae*, comes from tropical and temperate regions. A tough, useful fern for decorative purposes, it grows from six to 12 inches high. Some fronds terminate in small forks and crests. A real dwarf form of *Pteris* is *P. multifida cristata compacta* with low, dense growth habit.

LIGHT: Medium.

TEMPERATURE: Warm. Cool nights beneficial.

MOISTURE: Moist. Withstands drier atmosphere than most ferns.

PROPAGATION: Spores. Division of clump of rhizome root growth at repotting time.

POTTING: Use mix formula A. Usually needs repotting once a year.

FERTILIZER: Feed water-soluble fertilizer once every three months. Omit during winter months.

INSECTS: Scale insects.

Pteris cretica cristata

Mother Spleenwort
(Asplenium bulbiferum)

A member of the Fern family *Polypodiaceae*. Its native habitat ranges from Australia to New Zealand and into Malaysia. This species belongs to a unique group of ferns, the viviparous group that is propagated vegetatively by the offsets which germinate from bulbils produced on the upper surface of the frond. This species grows spore-bearing fronds as well.

LIGHT: Low.

TEMPERATURE: Cool.

MOISTURE: Moist. Thrives best with moist atmosphere.

PROPAGATION: Spores, bulbils or plantlets, division. See directions on viviparous propagation, page 193.

POTTING: Potting mix formula A.

FERTILIZER: Apply water-soluble type once every three months.

INSECTS: Mealy bugs and scale insects.

Asplenium bulbiferum

Nephrolepis exaltata bostoniensis

Boston Fern
(Nephrolepis exaltata bostoniensis)

An old-fashioned parlor and conservatory fern recently gaining popularity. A member of the common fern family *Polypodiaceae*, it originates in the tropical regions of both hemispheres. The species *N. exaltata*, rarely found in cultivation today, has given way to a great number of mutants or cultivars of the variety *bostoniensis*. Foliage of the Boston type is less stiff and rigid than *N. exaltata*. They exhibit much divided pinnae, as well as more delicate, wider-spreading and gracefully drooping growth habits. Some are compact dwarflike growers with finely cut foliage. Among these are 'Fluffy Ruffles' and *childsii*. Forms like *hillii*, *rooseveltii* and *whitmanii* have distinctive larger foliage.

N. cordifolia is an unusual and distinct species with root system composed of tuberous rhizomes.

LIGHT: Medium.

TEMPERATURE: Warm. Cooler nights always benefit fern growth.

MOISTURE: Moist; a requirement of almost all ferns.

PROPAGATION: Runners produce vegetative buds and develop into plantlets. Must be pinned to the soil surface. When three or more leaves develop, cut and pot up.

POTTING: Mix A. Overgrown pot-bound ferns can be divided at repotting. Select the youngest active growing clumps and use several in a pot to make good specimens. Discard oldest coarse woody clumps.

FERTILIZER: Feed spring and summer once a month with water-soluble fertilizer solution at half strength.

INSECTS: Scale insects and mealy bugs.

PRUNING: Old grayish green-brown tips or broken fronds should be removed once a year to make room for new shoots.

Asplenium nidus

Bird's-Nest Fern
(*Asplenium nidus*)

An epiphytic-type fern from Asia and Polynesia. This attractive fern produces a rosette made by its stiffly spreading, shiny green fronds of thin leathery texture, with blackish midrib and wavy margins and with black scales at the crown. The erect fronds rising from the crown produce the effect of a nest, which may be an attraction to certain species of tropical birds. Fronds of bird's-nest fern can grow to four feet long by one foot wide.

The family *Polypodiaceae* offers many ferns adaptable to home culture. Other ferns related to this genus are *A. bulbiferum* from New Zealand, Australia and Malaysia, *A. viviparum* from Mauritius. Both of these are designated as a "mother fern" because of their habit of producing bulblets that grow into plantlets. Propagation is discussed on page 191.

The epiphytic habit of bird's-nest fern will adapt to growing in drier atmospheres than those for other types.

A. nidus is an excellent plant for the outdoor patio in summer in a shady spot. Beware of slugs when outside!

LIGHT: Medium.

TEMPERATURE: Warm, with cooler nights.

MOISTURE: Moist.

PROPAGATION: Spores.

POTTING: Mix B.

FERTILIZER: Apply water-soluble type once a month in spring and summer at half strength.

INSECTS: Scale insects, mealy bugs. Snails or slugs are the most injurious. One slug alone can ruin a frond.

REMARKS: The epiphytic habit indicates caution against frequent repotting. The accumulated root system serves as a partial medium in which to grow. Do not overpot.

Platycerium vassei

Staghorn Fern

(*Platycerium vassei*)

An epiphytic fern that comes from Mozambique; other species are from tropical regions of Australia, New Guinea, Africa and the Philippines; botanically of the family *Polypodiaceae*. In their natural habitat they grow on trees. This epiphytic habit of growth renders it adaptable to growing in the home and other interior environments.

The sexual parts of the plant exist as two kinds of fronds. The sterile fronds are flat, disklike, pale green in color, and age to tan and brown at the base of the forked fronds. These serve to support the plant and accumulate organic matter that helps feed it. The forked upright or pendulous fronds are the fertile fronds that bear spores. These fronds resemble deer antlers; thus its name, Staghorn Fern.

A unique and attractive way to display and grow the Staghorn Fern is by mounting on tree fern slabs. For mounting, first place a cushion of long-fibered sphagnum moss on the slab. A tablespoonful or two of bone meal will provide some nutrition.

Tie the fern to the slab by inserting pieces of plastic-covered wire through the lower portions of sterile or basal fronds and continue through holes drilled in plaque or slab, tying at the back of tree fern slab.

LIGHT: High, exclusive of direct sunlight.

TEMPERATURE: Warm. Will tolerate cool nights.

MOISTURE: Dry. Soak about once a week, in the home.

PROPAGATION: Plantlets or "pups" sprout at the base of the plant. Pry out carefully and pot when small.

POTTING: Sphagnum moss mixed with a tablespoon of bone meal to a plant.

FERTILIZER: Feed water-soluble solution at half strength once a month during the spring and summer.

INSECTS: Scale insects.

Rabbit's-Foot Fern
(Davallia fejeensis)

Another epiphytic fern sometimes referred to as Squirrel's-Foot; comes from the Fiji Islands and belongs to the fern family *Polypodiaceae*. Its fuzzy, long-haired rhizome, one-half inch thick, creeps around the side of a pot or basket or on a ball of sphagnum moss.

LIGHT: Medium.

TEMPERATURE: Warm; cool at night.

MOISTURE: Moist. When moss or potting mixture feels dry, soak well with water.

PROPAGATION: Spores; sections of rhizomes.

POTTING: Balls of sphagnum moss, long-fiber type. Mix B if pot-grown.

FERTILIZER: Feed once a month in spring and summer with water-soluble solution at half strength.

INSECTS: Scale insects, sometimes mealy bugs.

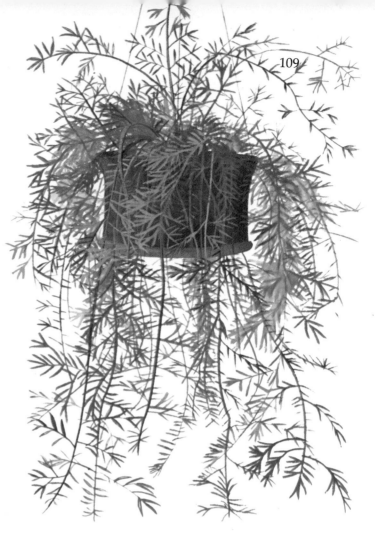

Asparagus densiflorus sprengeri

Asparagus Fern
(Asparagus densiflorus sprengeri)

A plant, not a fern, belonging to the Lily family, *Liliaceae*. It originates from West Africa and will thrive under the most adverse conditions. An easy-to-grow house plant, commonly grown by nurserymen and florists. The pendulous growth originating from tuberous roots consists of many branching sprays with light-green needles. Mature plants will often produce small, fragrant flowers, followed by bright-red berries.

LIGHT: Medium.

TEMPERATURE: Warm. Will grow at cool as well.

MOISTURE: Dry. Young plants require moist conditions.

PROPAGATION: Seed and division.

POTTING: Mix B

INSECTS: Mealy bugs.

Davallia fejeensis

Hare's-Foot Fern
(Polypodium aureum)

An excellent epiphytic fern for culture in the home or other interior environments but not often used. A native of tropical America belonging to the fern family *Polypodiaceae*. Its common name Hare's-Foot distinguishes it from Squirrel's-Foot by its very stout creeping rhizomes covered with bright rusty-brown hairlike scales. A few horticultural forms are cultivated, one of which, a sport, is known as *P. aureum mandaianum*. It possesses beautiful crested wavy pinnae or leaves of bluish-green color.

LIGHT: Medium, exclusive of direct sunlight.

TEMPERATURE: Warm; cool in winter.

MOISTURE: Moist. Can go for a week between waterings.

PROPAGATION: Division of the rhizomes.

POTTING: Mix B.

FERTILIZER: Apply water-soluble solution once a month in summer at half recommended strength.

INSECTS: Usually free.

Maidenhair
(Adiantum cuneatum)

From Brazil, a member of the family *Polypodiaceae*. Maidenhair is an old greenhouse favorite found growing in the moist atmosphere under greenhouse benches. It survives best as a house plant in the environment of a terrarium. It grows six to 15 inches tall.

LIGHT: Medium.

TEMPERATURE: Warm. Move outdoors in summer for cooler night temperature.

MOISTURE: Always moist. Humid atmosphere.

PROPAGATION: Division. Repot in late winter, cutting fronds back to the base and dividing clumps of roots.

POTTING: Use potting mix formula A.

FERTILIZER: Feed six months after potting with water-soluble fertilizer. Repeat application in three months. Omit feeding in winter.

INSECTS: Check for hard-to-see brown scale on brownish-color stems of fronds.

Polypodium aureum

Adiantum cuneatum

Holly or Fishtail Fern
(Cyrtomium falcatum)

A tough house fern able to withstand dry atmosphere and a low light intensity. A member of the fern family *Polypodiaceae,* it is found growing in scattered areas of Japan, China and also in some parts of South Africa and Polynesia.

LIGHT: Medium

TEMPERATURE: Warm.

MOISTURE: Moist. Tolerates dry atmosphere, but ball of potting material must be kept moist.

PROPAGATION: Spores. Division of the crown when more than one appears.

POTTING: Mix A. Firm soil when repotting to encourage rooting at the crown. Do not bury crown when potting.

FERTILIZER: Feed once every two months with water-soluble fertilizer at half recommended strength.

INSECTS: Scale insects, mealy bugs.

Silver Table Fern
(Pteris ensiformis victoriae)

Also known as Victoria fern, it is of the family *Polypodiaceae.* A genus of ferns grown as greenhouse ferns and as house plants for use in dish gardens and terrariums.

An attractive cultivar from Belgium is *P. ensiformis evergemiensis,* which is smaller and more vigorous than *victoriae*.

LIGHT: Medium.

TEMPERATURE: Warm. Cool nights are beneficial.

MOISTURE: Moist.

PROPAGATION: When ferns are in need of repotting, a division of the clump will yield new plants. Also by spores. See the section on how to grow spores, page 194.

POTTING: Repotting is usually necessary once a year or whenever plants become crowded in the pot.

FERTILIZER: Feed pot-bound plants once every two to three months except in winter.

INSECTS: Scale insects.

Cyrtomium falcatum

Pteris ensiformis victoriae

BROMELIADS

The pineapple family, with its 1,800-odd species, is found growing in the American tropics. The botanists identify it as the *Bromeliaceae* family, others know the group as Bromeliads. They vary in form from a delicious tropical fruit, the pineapple *Ananas comosus*, to Spanish moss *Tillandsia usneoides*, which grows as a festoon from live-oak trees in the southern United States. Many of the species used as indoor plants are described as having rosettes of leaves arranged in cuplike forms. Most of them hold water in their tightly furled leaves.

Bromeliads are much in demand as accent plants by interior decorators for modern decor. The varieties illustrated, *Aechmea fasciata*, *Aechmea miniata discolor*, Vase Plant *Billbergia pyramidalis* and Earth Star *Cryptanthus X* 'It,' are excellent as pot or planter specimens for accent and color. Other varieties are used for tree branch and driftwood decoration.

Bromeliads are not grown for their foliage alone. Some species have very small flowers, while others have showy flamboyant blooms or leaflike bracts. The flowers last only a few days, but the colorful bracts and berries will often last for months on some varieties. Flowers and fruit may be borne on upright, arching or pendant stems.

Bromeliads can be forced into flower by the use of growth-regulator chemicals. Experiments conducted by Crop Research, U.S. Department of Agriculture, Beltsville, Maryland, and by others have established schedules for flowering. Dr. H. M. Cathey of Crop Research suggests a method for homeowner use. To cause flowering, enclose a ripening apple in an airtight plastic bag with the plant for four days. Plant will bloom in one to six months after plant and apple are removed from the bag. If plants do not respond, wait another one to two months and try again. Response depends on the plant's growth rate and its maturity; more mature plants flower more readily. Eventually most plants can be triggered into flowering.

LIGHT: High light intensity but not direct sun, which will cause leaf burn. Terrestrial kinds like *Cryptanthus* will stand as much sun as you can give them.

Special fluorescent grow lights are available that are ideal for bromeliad growing. A minimum of four parallel tubes located six to 24 inches above the plants are recommended.

TEMPERATURE: Keep bromeliads at 65° to 75° during the day and between 55° and 65°at night.

MOISTURE: Do not overwater! Some epiphytic bromeliads feed through the bases of their leaves by means of water. In nature the vaselike shape of foliage collects water and directs it to its base.

Cryptanthus zonatus

These "cups" hold and must have water at all times. The potting material that supports the plant needs water only when it is dried out. This may occur once every two or three weeks. Check cups for water weekly. Empty out and add fresh water once a month.

Cryptanthus does not hold water, and being terrestrial, needs more soil moisture. As soon as potting mix is dry, soak thoroughly.

PROPAGATION: Easily grown from seeds and offsets that form next to the parent plant. The mother plant usually dies about a year after blooming, but in the meantime the plant has put up several side shoots. When these have several leaves (which takes about four to six months), cut them off and pot on their own. Take care to remove offsets with some roots attached so young plants can get a good start.

POTTING: Use mix formula C.
(1) Put about a two-inch layer of drainage material in bottom of pot.
(2) Fill with moistened mix, leaving space on top for water.
(3) Insert offset about one to two inches deep into medium. Do not fill up over basal leaves but just over hard stubby stem that is below the green leaves.
(4) Support plant with thin sticks, if needed, until roots take hold.
(5) Water well to settle medium. Put water in cups if the species is known to need it.

FERTILIZER: Do not overfertilize! Use a complete water-soluble type at half the recommended rate. Use once a month. Empty cups a week after fertilizer application and refill with fresh water.

INSECTS: Scale insects, either black or white, may appear on leaves. They can be pushed off with fingernail or toothbrush.

Cryptanthus zonatus. This genus of bromeliad, known as Earth Stars, is a terrestrial type requiring more moisture for growing and as much sun as you can give it. *C. zonatus*, a Brazilian native, is an old-time favorite, commercially grown in large quantities. It is used as a single specimen or grown with other plants in dish gardens or similar plant groupings. The leaves are purple-bronze with golden cross bands on top and silvery ones on the underside.

Cryptanthus X 'It,' recently introduced, is grown commercially. A blazing variant of color and a slower grower than some others. A single rosette may reach 12 to 16 inches across. Bright pink along the margins of the leaf, with longitudinal pink-and-cream stripes against a center of green with pinkish overcast.

Cryptanthus X 'It'

Cryptanthus bahianus

Cryptanthus bivittatus minor

114

Aechmea miniata discolor

Billbergia pyramidalis and *Tillandsia ionantha*

Tillandsia cyanea

Vriesia

Aechmea fasciata

Cryptanthus bivittatus minor, also known as *roseo-pictus,* is from Brazil. It is a flattened, small, starlike, terrestrial rosette. It has satiny, olive-green leaves with two pale bands overcast with salmon-rose that turn coppery red in strong sunlight. Used in dish gardens and planters.

Cryptanthus bahianus from Bahia, more epiphytic than terrestrial, is a stiff succulent with harsh spines. A good plant for a basket. Its recurved leaves are apple-green, margins of which turn bronzy red in the sun.

Aechmea miniata discolor, also from Brazil, is one of the most popular because of its adaptability to home environments. The olive-green leaves have maroon-purple undersides. The brilliant flower cluster is composed of bluish-lilac blooms, followed by red-orange berries which last for several months.

Billbergia pyramidalis, from Peru, is an old-time favorite for collectors because of its dense head of lovely blue flowers with striking red bracts. The light-green glossy leaves form a perfect vase plant. This is easy to grow in the home.

Tillandsia cyanea, from Ecuador, is an excellent, compact, rosette-type of bromeliad. Its linear, channeled leaves are marked with thin brown lines. Its interesting flower—a broad spike—has clear pink bracts and large violet-blue flowers.

Tillandsia ionantha, from Mexico to Nicaragua, is spring-flowering. A tufted, miniature rosette not over two to four inches high, it has numerous overlapping, recurving, thick, fleshy, dark-gray-green leaves covered with silvery bristles. The violet flowers appear without stalks close to the rosette. The flush of red color at the center of the rosettes signals the flowering season.

Vriesias, with spectacular foliage and inflorescence, are a must for any collection. Their forms and varieties shape into a leathery rosette of bluish-green leaves marked with broad cross bands of brown or purple. The underside of the leaves is grayish with purple bands. The long, sword-shaped flower spikes have flattened, fiery-red bracts and yellow flowers that last for several months. More moisture and humidity required than for some other bromeliads.

Neoregelia carolinae tricolor

Aechmea fasciata is one of the oldest and most popular favorites in cultivation. A Brazilian native of which many forms have been cultivated. Its green leaves overcast with gray, some banded, are very attractive. The pink, thistlelike flower head contrasts with the gray of the leaves, making it a handsome specimen when in flower. The bractlike head lasts several months in color.

Neoregelia carolinae tricolor comes from Brazil and is an old favorite, in both Europe and America. Its straplike, shiny green leaves turn a brilliant coral color about the center of the rosette when the plant is ready to flower. The color lasts for the life of the rosette.

Billbergia nutans is easiest of all bromeliads to grow and to flower. The common name, Queen's Tears, describes the rose-bracted, nodding flowers, green petals edged with violet, and the tear drop forming on the stigma. Its silvery-bronze foliage forms a clustering rosette.

DRIFTWOOD ARRANGEMENTS: Many bromeliads grow naturally on trees. An intriguing way to promote their use is to fasten them as arrangements on driftwood.

Things to remember:
(1) Small plants of *Tillandsia, Aechmea* and *Billbergia* can be tied firmly to the wood and their roots and bases covered with a layer of osmunda fiber, sphagnum or sheet moss to prevent the roots from drying out.
(2) Do not use copper or galvanized wire for tying, because these metals will injure plants. Use plain iron nails or wire.
(3) Fasten plants securely in a vertical position, especially those which hold water in their cups. Tie tightly to prevent movement and breakage of the new roots as they form.
(4) A small hole drilled through the driftwood and florists' enameled wire will keep plants from twisting and turning. Plants with woody bases can be drilled for fine wire or nailing.
(5) Do not use treated wood or driftwood that does not have all of the salt leached out. Also avoid contact with zinc, copper or lead-based paints.

Billbergia nutans

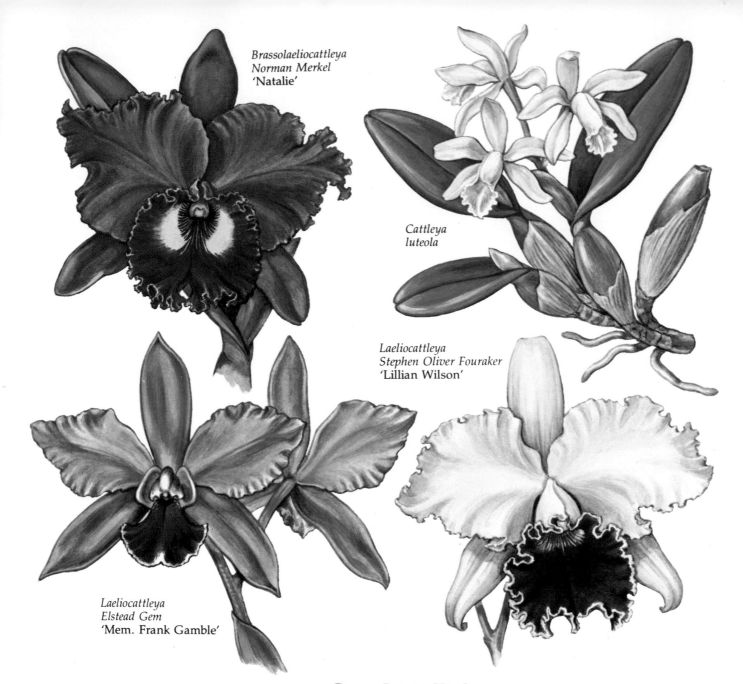

Brassolaeliocattleya
Norman Merkel
'Natalie'

Cattleya
luteola

Laeliocattleya
Stephen Oliver Fouraker
'Lillian Wilson'

Laeliocattleya
Elstead Gem
'Mem. Frank Gamble'

ORCHIDS

Orchids first achieved horticultural popularity in the early 1880s in England, where the estates of the wealthy often possessed extensive glasshouses devoted to the care of these seemingly temperamental plants. Unhelpful legends grew up around orchids, fostered by such true events as the dramatic arrival in mid-nineteenth-century London of an orchid growing on a human skull. The prices paid for orchids in these halcyon times often equaled a king's ransom.

The tide began to turn in 1859 when Sir Joseph Paxton opened the doors to his hot and muggy glasshouses to let the cool, spring breezes in. From this time onward, orchid growers attempted to duplicate natural conditions, throwing aside the old myths of intense heat and high humidity.

Since the establishment of the first orchid firm in the United States in 1896, Lager and Hurrell, orchids have been grown with increasing frequency and even greater success, either in greenhouses, on windowsills, in a Wardian case or under fluorescent lights. Today, orchids are nearly as common in the home as begonias and as easy to grow.

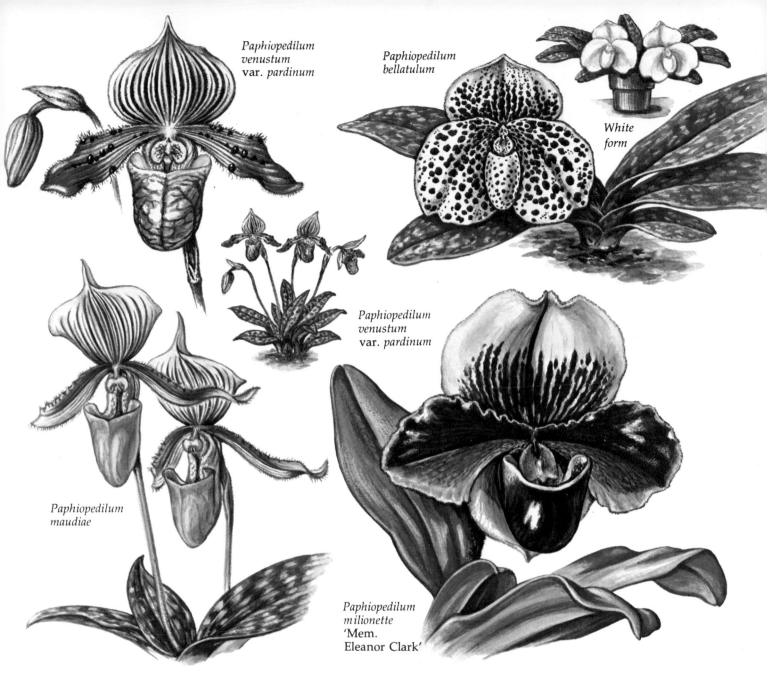

Paphiopedilum venustum var. *pardinum*

Paphiopedilum bellatulum

White form

Paphiopedilum venustum var. *pardinum*

Paphiopedilum maudiae

Paphiopedilum milionette 'Mem. Eleanor Clark'

The orchid family (*Orchidaceae*) is the largest in the plant kingdom. Over 600 genera occur in nature, with more than 30,000 species. The ease with which most orchids interbreed has produced, to date, some 60,000 artificial hybrids, many of which will thrive as house plants.

Orchids are found nearly worldwide, excluding areas of perpetual snow or arid desert. While the great majority inhabit the tropical and semitropical areas of the world, growing epiphytically on rocks and trees, open to the winds, rain and sunlight, other lovely orchids can be found in the temperate regions, growing terrestrially, on the ground.

The corsage orchid, *Cattleya*, is one of many genera found throughout Central and South America, from the sea-level banks of the Amazon River in Brazil to the cool, wind-swept mountain ranges of Costa Rica, Colombia and Ecuador. The Asiatic lands of India, Burma, Ceylon and the islands of New Guinea and New Caledonia possess many *Paphiopedilum* species, while the Philippines are the home of the "Moth Orchid," *Phalaenopsis*. Orchids even flourish on the Serengeti plains of Africa or in the vast hinterlands of Australia, and some 200 species exist in North America, including the pink "Lady's slipper," *Cypripedium*, growing in the pinewoods of the Northeast.

Orchids as House Plants: Orchids can no longer be considered difficult to grow, provided that certain basic principles are followed (pages 122–23). While the variety of shapes and colors may initially bewilder the home grower, he should make his first plant purchases from among the species and hybrids within the genera illustrated in the text: *Paphiopedilum, Phalaenopsis, Cattleya, Miltonia* and *Oncidium*. Orchid plants may be obtained from numerous nurseries at a reasonable cost today.

The following orchids have all been flowered repeatedly under home conditions by orchid growers everywhere. All require low to medium light intensities and a predominantly inter- mediate temperature range, as described on pages 122–23, with a 40–50 percent relative humidity. Maintain the proper humidity in a windowsill collection by placing plants on a wire-mesh platform above a bed of pebbles kept continually wet. The evaporation of the water will create a suitable microclimate, particularly if a small, oscillating fan blows across the surface of the water. Ventilation is equally important. Orchids should have fresh air on all but the coldest of days. Avoid extreme hot or cold drafts directly on the plants.

A large, fluorescent light set-up—a plant cart or benches built in the cellar or study—can duplicate greenhouse conditions. Enclose the entire area in clear plastic sheeting and install a small home humidifier.

ORCHIDS FOR HOME CULTURE

Kind	Color	Temperature	Light	Time of Bloom
Brassia caudata	yellow-green	intermediate	medium	fall
Brassolaeliocattleya hybrids	rose, pink, purple	intermediate	medium	various
Cattleya mossiae	lavender	intermediate	medium	Easter
Cattleya luteola	yellow, greenish-yellow	intermediate	medium	various
Sophrolaeliocattleya hybrids	lavender to red	intermediate	medium	various
Laeliocattleya hybrids	lavender, orange, yellow	intermediate	medium	various
Brassocattleya hybrids	lavender, green, pink	intermediate	medium	various
Cycnoches chlorochilon	lime-green, yellow	intermediate	medium	spring
Gastrochilus dasypogon	yellow, dotted red	intermediate	medium	various
Haemaria discolor	white flowers, lovely velvet-green leaves with gold veining	intermediate–warm	low–medium	winter
Miltonia spectabilis	white, purple	intermediate–cool	low–medium	spring
Miltonia vexillaria	pink	intermediate	medium	spring
Miltonia hybrids	white, pink, red, yellow	intermediate	medium	spring
Oncidium cheirophorum	yellow	intermediate–cool	low–medium	winter
Oncidium ornithorhynchum	pink	intermediate	medium	winter
Oncidium varicosum	yellow	intermediate	medium	winter
Oncidium hybrids	yellow, brown, orange, reddish	intermediate	medium	various
Paphiopedilum insigne	yellow, brown, reddish	intermediate	medium	various
Paphiopedilum callosum	green, purple, white	intermediate–cool	low–medium	winter
Paphiopedilum hybrids	all colors save blue	intermediate–cool	low–medium	various
Phalaenopsis amabilis	white	intermediate–warm	low–medium	various
Phalaenopsis lueddemanniana	white, purple	intermediate–warm	low–medium	various
Phalaenopsis schilleriana	pink	intermediate–warm	low–medium	winter
Phalaenopsis stuartiana	white, dotted brown	intermediate–warm	low–medium	spring
Phalaenopsis hybrids	white, pink, yellow	intermediate–warm	low–medium	various

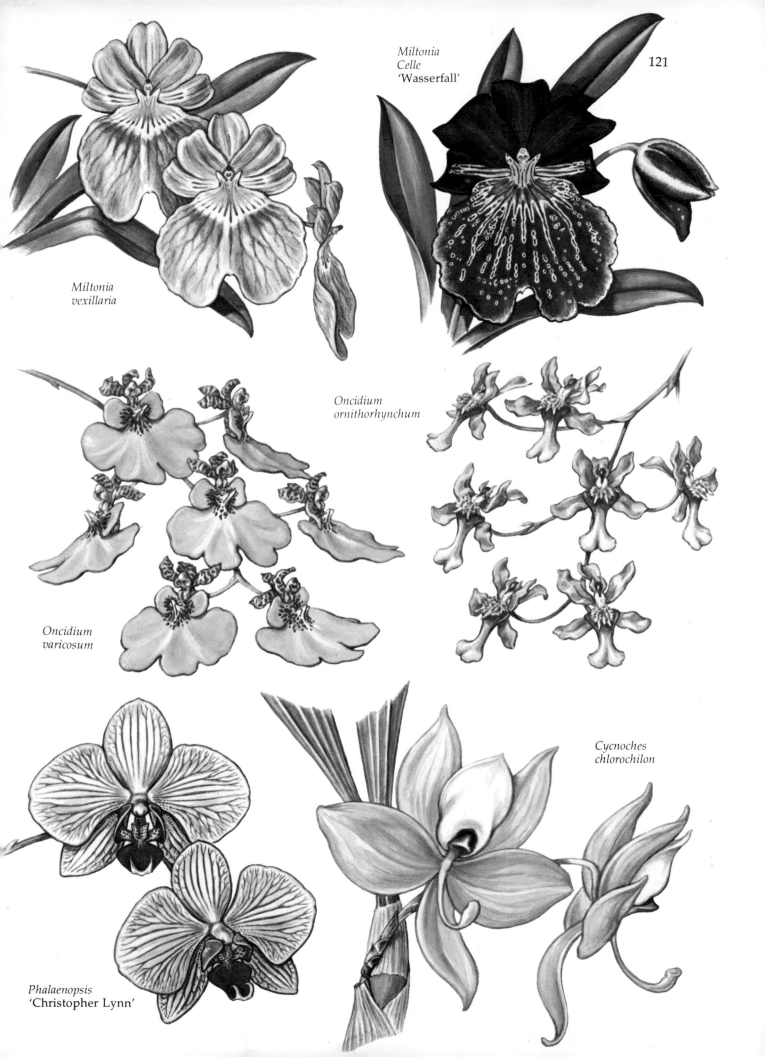

Miltonia
vexillaria

Miltonia
Celle
'Wasserfall'

Oncidium
ornithorhynchum

Oncidium
varicosum

Cycnoches
chlorochilon

Phalaenopsis
'Christopher Lynn'

Phalaenopsis schilleriana

Phalaenopsis amabilis

LIGHT: Diffused, indirect sunlight is essential for orchids. Any window exposure except directly north will be suitable. The main light categories are: *high*—nearly direct sunlight; *medium*—early morning or late afternoon sunlight; *low*—shaded conditions. Orchids also flower successfully under a bank of four 40-watt fluorescent tubes. Summer your orchids out of doors, in relatively shaded conditions, if possible.

TEMPERATURE: The main temperature ranges are *warm*—75° day, 65° night; *intermediate*—70° day, 60° night; *cool*—65° day, 55° night. A five- to 10-degree drop in temperature at night is critical for good flowering. Many orchids, however, will grow well in more than one temperature range.

MOISTURE: Most orchids are epiphytes; their roots, in nature, are quickly dried by the winds. Such orchids as *Cattleya*, *Oncidium* and *Miltonia* should approach dryness prior to rewatering. Terrestrial orchids such as *Paphiopedilum* or moisture-loving ones such as *Phalaenopsis* require some moisture at all times at their roots. This does not mean a soggy medium!

PROPAGATION: Orchids may be started from seed, using the asymbiotic culture method (without fungus fertilization) in an agar medium in a sterile environment. However because special equipment is required, this method is not usually practiced by home growers. Most orchids take four to six years from seed before they reach flowering size. Orchids may also be divided, as shown in the illustrations. Keep all cutting tools sterile by flaming after each cut.

Certain orchids may also produce "keikis" or offsets, which may be potted once they have produced their own root system.

POTTING: Various potting media are available at greenhouse supply firms. Fir bark in varying grades is used, often in combination with perlite and sphagnum moss. The dense roots of Osmunda fern may also be used, but water sparingly.

Orchids should be repotted when the old medium has decayed, when the newest growth reaches outside the pot, or if the root system is unhealthy. Repot while the orchid is in active growth, usually as it is producing a new set of roots.

Clay or plastic pots are used for most orchids, although some species may grow better on cork or tree fern slabs:

FERTILIZER: Though nutrient requirements vary within the orchid family, most orchids require less fertilizer than other plants. A water-soluble fertilizer that balances the nitrogen, phosphorus and potassium and has trace elements, applied in dilute solution once a month, is adequate for home culture. Orchids in active vegetative growth utilize fertilizer; those in a dormant or resting stage require none. Apply all fertilizers sparingly.

INSECTS: Orchids, like other plants, have their share of insect pests, even in the home. The rare attacks of fungus or of mealy bugs, aphids or scale insects, can be remedied with a combination spray of Benlate (fungicide) and Malathion (insecticide). Use all pesticides and fungicides with extreme caution.

REMARKS: In summation, give most orchids good but diffused light, water them well but do not permit the medium to become soggy, and provide a five- to ten-degree drop in temperature at night. Orchids are normally very vigorous plants and will flourish with a minimum of care.

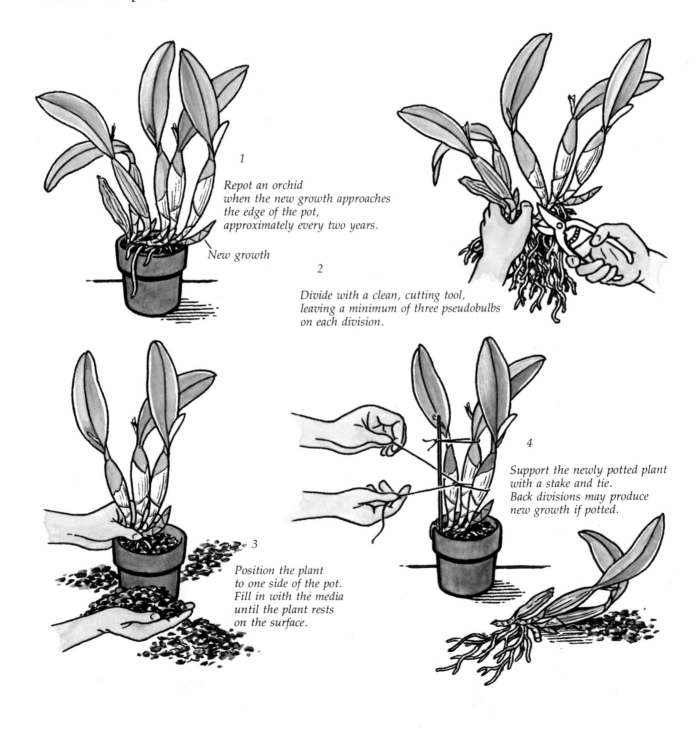

1

Repot an orchid when the new growth approaches the edge of the pot, approximately every two years.

New growth

2

Divide with a clean, cutting tool, leaving a minimum of three pseudobulbs on each division.

3

Position the plant to one side of the pot. Fill in with the media until the plant rests on the surface.

4

Support the newly potted plant with a stake and tie. Back divisions may produce new growth if potted.

Punica granatum nana

FRUIT BEARING PLANTS

Dwarf Pomegranate
(Punica granatum nana)

A dwarf form of the pomegranate tree native to the Mediterranean region. It is a conversation piece for pot-plant culture in the home. The family *Punicaceae* is small, possessing only one genus and two species. *P. granatum* is cultivated in warmer climates for its ornamental edible fruits. The species bears fruits as large as an orange.

LIGHT: Very high; direct sunlight beneficial, especially in winter.

TEMPERATURE: Warm, but cool during semi-dormancy period, which occurs in winter.

MOISTURE: Moist, with good drainage. Dry during semirest.

PROPAGATION: Seeds and cuttings.

POTTING: Mix A.

FERTILIZER: Apply water-soluble fertilizer once a month in summer at half strength.

INSECTS: Mealy bugs and spider mites.

PRUNING: Occasional trimming to make desirable shape.

REMARKS: A deciduous tree by nature, it will drop some leaves in winter, at which time less frequent watering is needed.

Calamondin Orange
(*Citrus mitis*)

An ornamental pot-plant orange cultivated and popularized as the miniature orange plant. It is a member of the rue family, which is known botanically as *Rutaceae.* A most attractive plant in containers, it bears flowers followed by bright orange fruits that last for months afterward. Flowers and fruits often occur together. It is offered at holiday time and used as a gift plant. Though it is really a sour orange and not good for eating, the skin and flesh nonetheless make good marmalade.

Usually citrus plants do not make good plants for home culture indoors. Their need for sunshine in order to grow into a healthy plant is a characteristic not to be overlooked.

Citrus meyeri, a semidwarf, almost thornless, has very fragrant flowers and produces lemons of table quality the year round.

LIGHT: Very high. Full sun, especially in winter, or very high under fluorescent lights. Should be grown out of doors in summer for benefit of direct sun.

TEMPERATURE: Warm; does not grow well below 55°.

MOISTURE: Moist; good drainage important. Roots are injured if grown in compacted water-saturated mix.

PROPAGATION: Cuttings. Plants from seeds are slow to fruit.

POTTING: Mix B with acid-soil reaction. Small, purchased plants in two-inch pots should be shifted to a six-inch pot as soon as possible. Use of plastic pots best to avoid frequent drying out.

FERTILIZER: Apply water-soluble fertilizer at half strength once a month when growth is apparent. Omit fertilizer after pruning until new shoot growth occurs.

INSECTS: Red spider mites. Will cause foliage and leaf drop.

PRUNING: Potted citrus become leggy in the home due to inadequate light. Plants may be pruned back to two-thirds size to encourage bushiness.

REMARKS: Occasional sink-spraying of leaves gets rid of dust and helps prevent infestation.

Citrus mitis

Avocado *(Persea americana)*

The alligator pear. A tropical fruit, its native habitats are the warmest parts of North and South America. For residents of temperate regions, it is a "fun" plant to grow. After you have enjoyed eating its delicious fruit, you can grow an avocado tree from the seed.

LIGHT: High. Place the potted avocado where it will get several hours of sunlight or artificial light each day.

TEMPERATURE: Warm.

MOISTURE: Moist. Always water plant with tepid water.

PROPAGATION: From seed. Wash the seed in warm water to remove all of the pulp. Cut off the pointed end of the seed and insert the broad end into a water-filled jar. To support, press three toothpicks into the top of the seed. Add enough warm water to cover about half an inch of the seed. Place the glass out of direct sun, adding water to compensate for evaporation. A mature seed should sprout in two to six weeks. When the main stem is six to eight inches high cut it back to about half size. This forces branches to form. When the roots are good and thick and the stem is leafed out, it is ready for potting. As you move the plant to the pot from its jar of water take care not to injure the root system.

POTTING: Put in rich, peaty potting mixture, like mix A. Leave the seed half exposed in the mix when planted. Use a pot that is 10 inches in diameter. When the plant is 15 inches high, place a small stake in the pot and tie the stalk to it for support.

FERTILIZER: Apply a water-soluble fertilizer solution once a month.

INSECTS: Red spider mites, mealy bugs, aphids and scale insects.

REMARKS: It is doubtful that your avocado plant will flower and produce fruit. Grow it for its leafy treelike appearance. When the plant becomes pot-bound shift it to a larger pot. This will keep it growing. Shape the plant by pruning the branches. If it gets too tall, prune it back to a desirable height. Its response to your tender loving care will delight and amaze you.

Persea americana

Ananas comosus

Pineapple *(Ananas comosus)*

The pineapple comes from tropical America. The experience of tasting a fresh pineapple is a treat many people look forward to. Amateur gardeners find the fun of growing this tropical fruit a challenge.

PROPAGATION: When buying a pineapple to start a plant choose one that has a deep orange color and a strong pineapple fragrance. If slicing for food preparation, cut off the top with about one inch of the fruit attached. Then cut away the meaty part, being careful not to injure the stem at the center. Set it aside to dry for a couple of days. When dried, suspend in a glass of water so that one-half inch of water covers the base of the stem. In a few weeks roots will appear and it should be potted in a mix. Add just enough mix to cover the base of the plant. Use potting mix B. Alternatively, set the top in a small pot of sand and keep warm and humid. Transfer to mix B when rooted.

FLOWERING AND FRUITING: Do not be disappointed if the first top does not root. Any time after two years it should be old enough to flower.

Ethylene, the well-known pollutant gas, when released in the crown area of the plant will trigger flowering.

To encourage flowering, ethylene gas can be produced as follows:

Step 1. If your plant appears healthy, producing new leaves, put it in a polyethylene bag and also put in two or three apples. The apples give off ethylene. Use good apples that you can eat afterward. Close the bag and set it aside in indirect light for four or five days.

Step 2. Open the bag, check the plant for water. If the treatment worked, you should be able to see some red color in the center of the leaf rosette and new leaf growth. Small rows of buds will appear and will grow into a pineapple.

LIGHT: Very high. Place plant in a sunny window.

TEMPERATURE: Warm.

MOISTURE: Water only enough to keep potting mix barely moist for a few weeks. When roots are established, keep mixture moist.

FERTILIZER: Apply a water-soluble plant food once a month.

128

Citrus limon 'Ponderosa'

Coffea arabica

Ponderosa Lemon
(*Citrus limon* 'Ponderosa')

'Ponderosa' is a curiosity, grown for ornamental rather than for food value. A member of the family *Rutaceae,* it is listed as a Maryland hybrid of 1887. It bears huge fruits with a thick coarse skin. Individual fruits weighing two pounds each are not unusual; they are not of table quality. The main crop is produced in winter.

LIGHT: Very high. Does best as an outdoor plant in warm regions.

TEMPERATURE: Warm. Outdoor temperatures below 40° are likely to be harmful.

MOISTURE: Moist.

PROPAGATION: Cuttings.

POTTING: Formula B. When repotting, take care not to disturb roots.

FERTILIZER: Water-soluble type every two months to established plants.

INSECTS: Spider mites and scale insects.

PRUNING: Potted plants become leggy. To control, prune heavily by cutting entire top back.

Coffee *(Coffea arabica)*

The well-known breakfast beverage of peoples around the world. It is a member of the family *Rubiaceae.* The original species came from Ethiopia and Angola. It is known for its shiny dark-green foliage on willowy branches. The flowers are pure white, fragrant and borne in clusters in the axils of the leaves. Half-inch brilliant crimson berries with a sweet pulp develop after flowering.

LIGHT: Very high.

TEMPERATURE: Warm. Cool temperature essential for flowering and fruiting.

PROPAGATION: Seeds; also cuttings, with difficulty.

POTTING: Potting mix formula B. Shift seedlings to larger pots to provide room for root growth.

FERTILIZER: Water-soluble fertilizer once a month for mature plants.

INSECTS: Mealy bugs and spider mites.

PRUNING: Prune out top growth.

Eriobotrya japonica

Chinese Loquat
(Eriobotrya japonica)

A member of the rose family and relative of the apple. Outdoor trees produce a pear-shaped fruit, yellow to orange in color, one to three inches long. The fruit is eaten fresh or may be used in the making of jelly, preserves, pies and the like. Loquat jelly is of superior quality. Outdoors the tree grows 20 to 30 feet tall, but it is much favored as an interior decorator's plant of tree-sized proportions. Its height and shape are easily controlled by pruning. It may also be used as a patio container plant for shady spots in the summer. It can be espalier-trained for indoors or out.

Its attraction lies in its big, leathery, crisp leaves which are stoutly veined and netted, measuring six to eight inches in length and two to four inches in width. The leaves are glossy green above, with rust-colored wool beneath. Flowering takes place in fall, but when pruned to control growth it may lose its potential for flowers and fruits.

LIGHT: Very high. Plants moved to patio in summer; need shade from direct sun.

TEMPERATURE: Cool.

MOISTURE: Moist.

PROPAGATION: By seeds, air layering and grafting.

POTTING: Potting mix formula Λ.

FERTILIZER: Established plants need feeding with a water-soluble fertilizer once a month.

INSECTS: Aphids, red spider mites, and scale insects.

PRUNING: Prune to shape and control growth for ornamental purposes.

Musa acuminata
'Dwarf Cavendish'

Dwarf Banana

(Musa acuminata 'Dwarf Cavendish')

The Cavendish is of Chinese origin and a member of the family *Musaceae*. It is a stout-stemmed dwarf type that reaches a height of five to seven feet at maturity. Fruit production is entirely possible when given good culture indoors. The fruits are six to eight inches long and weigh four to five ounces. They are of good quality, and if harvested seven to 14 days before ripening, hung by the bunch in a shady, cool place, they will develop flavor and nutritive value as completely as if allowed to ripen on the plant. Cut the bunch down when the individual fruits are well rounded in cross-section, including a portion of the stem to facilitate handling. The terminal flower buds should be cut off at the same time.

LIGHT: Very high.

TEMPERATURE: Warm.

MOISTURE: Moist.

PROPAGATION: By divisions of the underground rhizome. Each division should contain two buds. Or by suckers detached from base of parent stem. Take suckers when two to eight months old.

POTTING: Potting mix formula A. Use tubs for final containers at least 18 to 36 inches wide. A large container is necessary to feed a plant sufficiently for flower production and fruiting. Bury rhizome sections and suckers six to eight inches deep.

FERTILIZER: Bananas are gross feeders. Apply water-soluble fertilizer solution once a month. The development of fruit depends on a constant supply of nutrients.

INSECTS: Red spider mites.

REMARKS: Fourteen months from planting a good-sized sucker to flowering.

Ficus carica

Common Fig *(Ficus carica)*

Of the family *Moraceae* and native to western Asia, whence it undoubtedly spread into the Mediterranean region. A related species of the genera of ornamentals used as house plants, namely *Ficus benjamina, Ficus elastica decora* and *Ficus lyrata*. It is used as a pot plant in shopping malls and also in the home. Its aesthetic value comes from its artistic habit of growth and its large mulberry leaf shapes. A decorator's dream plant in every way; a very effective plant for patio growing. Potted specimens growing outdoors in frigid winter climates can be moved inside an entryway or garage for protection and dormant storage. Because it is a deciduous tree it will normally drop its leaves once a year.

For outdoor culture in sheltered locations trees are bent to the ground and covered with several inches of earth, plus a mulch, to avoid the effects of freezing and thawing. Stems are sometimes wrapped with insulation cloth before severe cold arrives. Figs may survive temperatures to 10° F. before branches will freeze.

Common figs bear fruits on one-year-old stems in the axils of the leaves.

LIGHT: Very high.

TEMPERATURE: Warm; cool for winter storage and dormancy.

MOISTURE: Moist. Dry during storage.

PROPAGATION: Cuttings, air layering.

POTTING: Mix formula A.

FERTILIZER: Once a month during growth.

INSECTS: Mealy bugs, red spider mites.

PRUNING: To create desired shape.

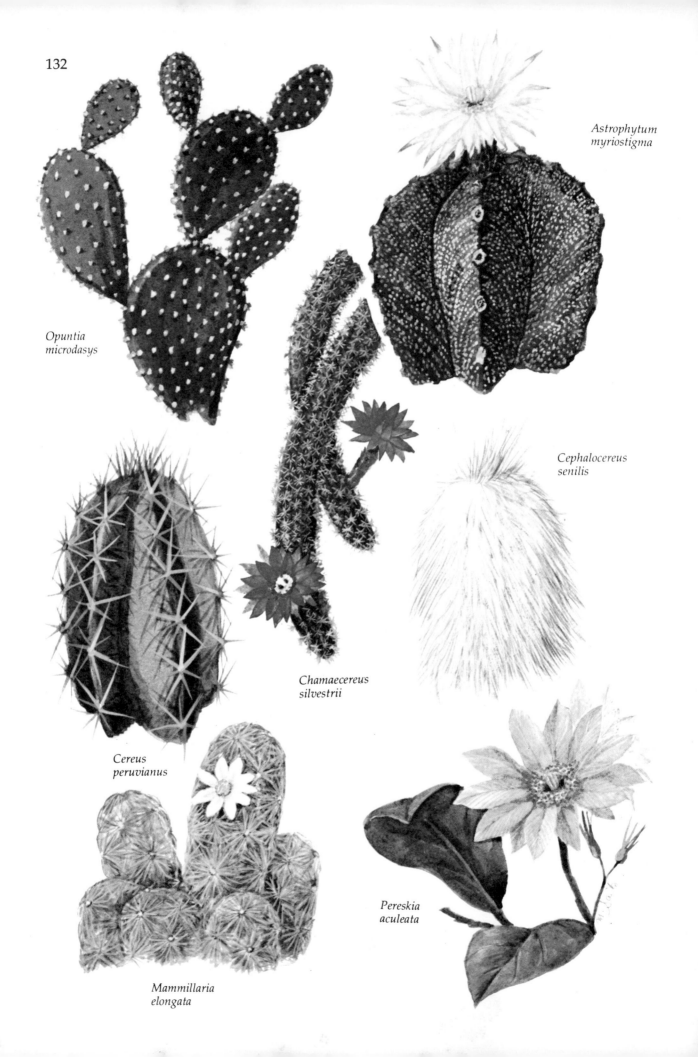

132

Opuntia microdasys

Astrophytum myriostigma

Cephalocereus senilis

Chamaecereus silvestrii

Cereus peruvianus

Mammillaria elongata

Pereskia aculeata

CACTI AND SUCCULENTS

CACTI (from the Greek word *kaktos*, meaning spiny plant) are succulentlike plants belonging to only one family—*Cactaceae*. The family is large; it includes about 2,000 species, all being perennials with fleshy growth and most without leaves (the exception is *Pereskia aculeata* and its closely related species). If any leaves are produced during the growth stage, they soon fall off. Most cactus plants have spines, although there are a few without them. The fruit is a one-celled berry with many seeds. Another characteristic of botanical significance is the areole, which is a specially modified bud from which shoots and flowers can emerge; it usually bears hairs, bristles, spines or wool.

Some well-known cacti are illustrated. Bunny Ears (*Opuntia microdasys*) is an old favorite; the flattened oval stems known as pods are dotted with areoles covered with golden-yellow glochids (barbed bristles). It is a plant to be handled with caution because the tufts of glochids stick to the skin at the slightest touch. The growing of all species of *Opuntia* is illegal in Australia because of the damage wrought by *O. ficus-indica.*

Old Man Cactus (*Cephalocereus senilis*) is a venerable cactus with snow-white hairs, and it is one of the favorites. It grows very slowly and may reach 20 feet in 100 years. Found growing on the dry hillsides of Mexico, it is called *Cabeza de Viejo*, or Old Man's Head. It is nocturnally flowering.

Peanut cactus (*Chamaecereus silvestrii*) is easy to grow, likes some moisture and sun or partial shade. Flowers in spring and produces many stems in a season.

Bishop's Cap (*Astrophytum myriostigma*) is a popular, spineless, easy-to-grow type. Flowers freely all summer long. Takes sun or semishade. Requires some moisture.

Golden Star (*Mammillaria elongata*) is a fast-growing cactus, producing many stems in one season. Each plant is a bright mosaic of golden and harmless spines.

Barbados Gooseberry (*Pereskia aculeata*) is grown like a shrub in pots. Occasionally it needs a pruning to restrain its vinelike branching. Glossy-leaved branches with showy pink, lemon-scented flowers, *Pereskias* are living examples of nonsucculent primitive cacti from which the succulent spiny types evolved.

Hedge Cactus (*Cereus peruvianus*) is possibly native to Brazil and Argentina. Typical columnar upright branching shows near the base. Young branches with six to eight flat ribs are light green and change to blue with age. It has needlelike spines in starlike clusters of five to ten at areoles. Nocturnal flowering. Branch cuttings root easily.

SUCCULENTS. What is a succulent? The term applies to plants differing from cacti in that they have juicy, fleshy, soft and thickened leaves, stems and tubers. Succulent plants come from arid or semiarid climates. Such climates influence the evolution of plants and bring about physiological structural changes, thus creating reduction of body surfaces, modification of stomata and shallow-rooting habit. These characteristics are important to limit water loss from the plant. Such changes thus have provided plants with structures specifically adapted to survive long periods of drought. It is these resistant qualities that classify them as succulents.

Succulent types of plants are found in many families. Among them are *Aizoaceae, Amaryllidaceae, Agavaceae, Asclepiadaceae, Bromeliaceae, Compositae, Crassulaceae, Euphorbiaceae, Lilaceae,* and *Portulacaceae.*

Some well-known succulents:

Panda Plant (*Kalanchoe tomentosa*) is an elegant plant, its leaves covered with soft silvery plush, stained at margins with red-brown. It likes a fertile mix, some sun and moisture. Propagated by leaf cuttings.

Jellybean plant (*Sedum pachyphyllum*) has round, club-shaped leaves with red tips and yellow flowers. Each leaf provides a new plant for propagation purposes.

Lithops dorotheae

Aloe variegata

Gasteria verrucosa

Kalanchoe tomentosa

Sedum pachyphyllum

Sempervivum tectorum

Mother-in-Law's Tongue (*Gasteria verrucosa*) is a large genus of more than 50 species native to South Africa. *G. verrucosa* is one of the best known, with leaves of about six inches long, in opposite rows. The surface of the leaf is roughened, with small, crowded tubercles, giving the leaves a distinct gray appearance. Propagation by leaf-cutting section.

Partridge-breasted Aloe (*Aloe variegata*) requires special culture for successful growing. For potting, cover loose potting mix with one inch of pebbles and merely firm plant down, taking care to keep base of rosette of leaves above potting mix. When watering, keep moisture off crown of plant. Never permit soil to stay wet. Give plenty of sun. Propagated by offsets only.

Hen-and-Chickens (*Sempervivum tectorum*) is so called because of the miniature rosettes sprouting from the base of the larger plant. Easily propagated by removing rosettes and potting.

Stone Plant (*Lithops dorotheae*) is an amazing replica of pebbles and small stones. Since it is without spines, to protect it from being eaten by animals it resembles a group of stones. Provide good drainage, giving no moisture in winter. Grow at a temperature above 50° and provide fresh air and some sun when possible. Be sure to let potting mix dry out before each watering.

Culture of cacti and succulents

LIGHT AND AIR: For successful growth and coloration of cacti and succulent plants, fresh air by means of ventilation and plentiful sunlight are most important. If natural daylight is not available, fluorescent or "grow" lights may be substituted. At least 1,000 footcandles of light energy for a 14-hour period are required.

Some succulent plants will take low light or partial shade. Among these are the orchid cactus, *gasteria* and *haworthia*.

Cacti thrive when grown in a sunny place. A warm, sunny, south window is the best location.

TEMPERATURE: Warm temperature is conducive to growth. However, during the winter months a rest period should be provided for by cool temperature conditions: 50° to 60° is desirable. The rest period at this temperature may last for one or more months, depending on the species. The plants will give an indication as to this duration by the appearance of new shoot growth, thus calling for a warmer temperature and more frequent watering.

MOISTURE: Too much water is the main cause of fatality in succulent plants. The amount of water depends on time of year, temperature, age of plant and the species. During winter or dormant period, plants should be kept as dry as possible and temperature kept at 50° to 60°. Resist temptation to water. If one wishes the plant to flower, this dormant period is most important.

PROPAGATION: Cacti and other succulents may be grown by seed, cuttings, budding and grafting. Succulents are among the easiest plants to be propagated by cuttings. A good rooting mixture is peat moss and perlite or sand. It is important that cuttings be allowed to heal over before being set in mixture. This may take several days or weeks.

POTTING: Use mix C. Transplant or repot *only* in the spring, using small pots. Cacti and other succulents do not grow in pure sand as is sometimes thought. Even in arid desert regions there is much decomposed vegetation that, with the rains, becomes available as food.

FERTILIZER: Generally, cacti and succulents are not demanding in their food or fertilizer requirements. However, more healthy and vigorous plants are produced when properly supplied with nutrients.

A water-soluble type of fertilizer applied once every two months at half strength in summer is beneficial. A dry garden fertilizer or a controlled-release type applied once in the spring will give like results. *Do not apply any fertilizer in the winter.*

INSECTS AND DISEASES: Cacti and succulents are susceptible to root rot, black spot, root mealy bugs, scale insects, mealy bugs, red spider mites, aphids, and nematodes.

REMARKS: In warm weather, it is good to take plants outside. A gravel bed or wire mesh should support them.

Do not put aloes, haworthias or any small cacti outside in strong sunlight in the summer unless protection by a roof is provided to keep off direct sunshine and rains.

Snake Plant or Mother-in-Law's Tongue
(*Sansevieria trifasciata laurentii*)

From the Congo, of the family *Agavaceae*, it has the reputation of being one of the toughest house plants of all. It will survive under the most adverse conditions of low light and dryness, though not extreme cold. The variety *laurentii* is more desired because of its stiff, sword-shaped, yellow-margined leaves.

S. trifasciata is similar in growth habit but has zigzag gray markings.

S. trifasciata hahnii, a sport of the above (U.S. patent 1941), is known as "Bird's-nest sansevieria." It is different in habit, forming a low-spreading growth with leaves slightly reflexed, cross-banded with lighter green. It suckers freely from the base.

LIGHT: All intensities of light.

TEMPERATURE: Cool to warm.

MOISTURE: Dry.

PROPAGATION: Division of clump. Sectional leaf cuttings. Exception: *S. trifasciata laurentii* reverts back to green form; therefore, use division of clump method.

POTTING: Mix B. Repot only when pot-bound.

FERTILIZER: Water-soluble or slow-release feeding only once in three to four months.

INSECTS: Mealy bugs.

Sansevieria trifasciata hahnii

Sansevieria trifasciata laurentii

Jade Plant *(Crassula argentea)*

Of the family *Crassulaceae* from South Africa, the largest-growing *Crassula*. In mild climates and in its native home it may attain a height of eight to 12 feet. It is better known as a smaller plant today grown more extensively for dish gardens and as a pot plant than any of the other succulent plants. When given good cultural conditions it will flower in midwinter. Its flowers are a dainty pink, turning white with age. The leaves are a glossy jade-green, thick and fleshy, rounded on the top side, flat on the underside, and turn reddish along the edges in the sun. *C. argentea minima* is of more compact growing habit; its dark green leaves turn red at the apex when grown in the sun.

Another species, *C. arborescens*, is a large-leaved, shrubby species, even more attractive than *C. argentea*. Its leaves are silvery with a red margin marked with tiny spots.

LIGHT: Very high.

TEMPERATURE: Cool, best for growing and flowering.

MOISTURE: Dry; more moisture than cacti.

PROPAGATION: Leaf and terminal cuttings. Let cutting dry overnight before inserting into medium. Apply little moisture during rooting period.

POTTING: Mix formula C. Repot in spring. Do so only when pot-bound. Use three-quarter size pots. Do not overpot.

FERTILIZER: Apply water-soluble fertilizer once every two months in summer only.

INSECTS: Mealy bugs.

PRUNING: Sometimes needed to attain a shapely plant.

Crassula argentea

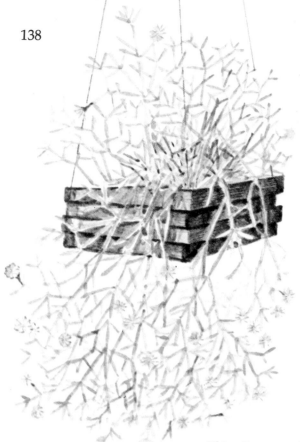

Rhipsalis cereuscula

Rice Cactus *(Rhipsalis cereuscula)*

An epiphytic type of cactus found growing from Uruguay to Brazil. It grows in crotches of trees, forming erect clumps. The pencil-sized stems and branches are crowned by short-angled twigs that carry tiny bristles in the areoles. Pink to white flowers are produced at the top of branches. Fruits develop looking like the white berries of mistletoe, which is characteristic of most *Rhipsalis*. A related species is the mistletoe cactus, *R. cassutha*, which grows on trees and rock cliffs and hangs downward as far as 3 feet or more. The cream-colored flowers are followed by mistletoelike fruits.

LIGHT: Very high.

TEMPERATURE: Warm.

MOISTURE: Dry.

PROPAGATION: Stem cuttings; seeds.

POTTING: A mixture of sphagnum moss and perlite (50-50) plus fertilizer.

FERTILIZER: Monthly application of water-soluble fertilizer in summer.

INSECTS: Mealy bugs.

Crown-of-Thorns
(Euphorbia milii; Euphorbia splendens)

Of the family *Euphorbiaceae*, it is identified by its milky sap. *E. milii* is a spiny shrub with thick spiny stems and tiny oval-shaped leaves of bright green that are shed in winter. In spite of the loss of leaves, flowers continue to develop to some extent all winter. Leaves appear on the plants again in spring.

To keep rampant growth of its stout spiny stems under control it can be trained to a trellis.

LIGHT: Very high.

TEMPERATURE: Cool.

MOISTURE: Moist, but allowed to dry between soakings.

PROPAGATION: Cuttings, allowed to dry overnight before inserting.

POTTING: Potting mix formula B.

FERTILIZER: Apply water-soluble fertilizer once every two months except in winter.

INSECTS: Mealy bugs and red spider mites.

PRUNING: To control undesirable branching.

Euphorbia milii

Epiphyllum oxypetalum

Night-Blooming Cereus
(Epiphyllum oxypetalum)

It belongs to an epiphytic group of cacti that climb into trees by means of aerial roots. They are not parasitic, because they use the tree for support only. *Epiphyllums* are found growing throughout Mexico, Central America and into Brazil. They are very easy to grow and look best when supported by stakes or a trellis, rather than being left to pursue their rampant growth habit. *E. oxypetalum*, also called Queen of the Night, is the best night-blooming species for home culture. Flowering takes place through summer and autumn. Its large, fragrant white flowers measure six inches or more across. Flowers start to open early evening and close when the sun rises. Flowers de-velop from areoles along the margin of the flattened stemlike leaf. True leaves are lack-ing. Fruits develop after flowering and are edible. Flowering takes place from growth made the previous summer season, not on present year's wood.

LIGHT: Very high; direct sun part of the day.

TEMPERATURE: Cool place of 50° for winter.

MOISTURE: Dry. Dry in winter when stored cool. Water when surface of soil is dry.

PROPAGATION: Cuttings.

POTTING: Potting formula C. Do not overpot.

FERTILIZER: Feed established plants once a month in summer. Omit in winter.

INSECTS: Mealy bugs.

PRUNING: Undesirable growth may be pruned and new plants started from cuttings.

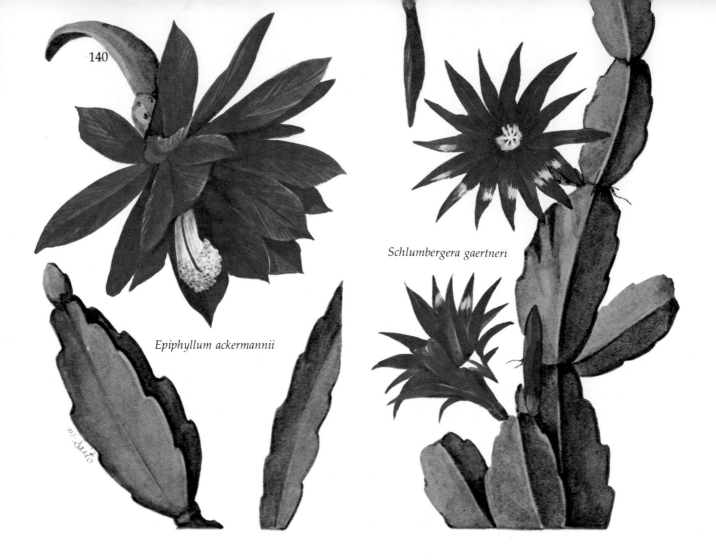

140

Schlumbergera gaertneri

Epiphyllum ackermannii

ORCHID CACTUS (*Epiphyllum ackermannii*) is found growing naturally in tropical America and Mexico at an altitude of 6,000 to 8,000 feet. Its huge, glowing red blossoms are like water lilies and measure as much as ten inches in diameter. Their flowering period extends from early spring into summer. Its branches are usually flattened, sometimes three-angled. Hybridizers have created many cultivars with glowing satiny petals that display a rainbowlike iridescence. Its vivid and clear colors are shining reds of all shades, scarlet to deep crimson, as well as bright pinks, salmon, orange, snowy white, white and gold. More beautiful, if possible, are the bicolors with scarlet outer petals and radiant violet throats.

A hint for culture: Orchid cacti are found wild in tropical forests and not on dry, hot deserts. They are usually found growing as epiphytes in trees.

EASTER CACTUS (*Schlumbergera gaertneri*) The species *gaertneri* is a tree dweller, an epiphytic Brazilian cactus with stiff, spreading branches of long flattened joints, dull green in color, with purplish margins; the end joints have a tendency to droop and have a few bristlelike hairs. The flowers are tubular with radiating petals, two to three inches in length, dark red in color, and appear in spring. A variety, *S. gaertneri makoyana*, known as Cat's Whiskers, has bluish-green branches and purplish margins with yellowish-brown whiskerlike bristles at the tips. Starlike light orange-red flowers occur in spring.

Like the *Epiphyllum*, these plants do not resemble the cactus. They also come from the same tropical forests in which one finds orchids and bromeliads growing side by side. Culture is similar to methods used for orchids and bromeliads.

Schlumbergera truncata

Schlumbergera bridgesii

THANKSGIVING or CRAB CACTUS (*Schlumbergera truncata*) differs from the Christmas cactus in that the margins of the joints are saw-toothed, the teeth point forward, and the anthers are yellowish. Flowers are usually orange, but hybrids come in various shades of color. Flowering occurs earlier than for Christmas cactus, appearing to be less dependent on critical cool temperatures and short days.

The plants are propagated by taking cuttings consisting of two or three joints and placing them in pots of sphagnum moss for rooting. Water is withheld until rooting occurs or signs of wilting appear. When established as rooted plants, resume practice of feeding.

The plants respond to simple cleft and scion grafting on *Selenicereus* stock. Growth is much more rapid, and standards or treelike forms are developed.

CHRISTMAS or CRAB'S CLAW CACTUS (*Schlumbergera bridgesii*). Formerly known as *Epiphyllum truncatum* and also as *Zygocactus truncatus*, it is correctly identified by taxonomists as *S. bridgesii*.

The Christmas cactus has jointed stems that are flattened and leaflike, with rounded teeth on the margins, and four- to six-angled or winged, purplish anthers. Growers of cactus list color variations including whites and shades of pink, red and orange.

The Crab's Claw Cactus is classified as a short-day plant for flowering—that is, its flowering is usually assured when short days of nine hours occur normally or are induced by positioning the plant in a dark closet and when the night temperature drops to 60° or below. Exposure to this combination of factors for a period of about five weeks will bring flowers in ten to 12 weeks from the start of these culture conditions.

142

Tulipa gesneriana

Hyacinthus orientalis

Crocus species

Muscari armeniacum

GROWING BULBS

The revival of forcing hardy bulbs or tender tropical bulbs, corms or tubers takes its place among current ideas for indoor gardeners. A most rewarding experience is to bring flowers into your home during the winter months.

Three classes of bulbs for winter flowering:

1. *Hardy types* are daffodils and hyacinths, which can be forced for Christmas, and crocuses, hyacinths and tulips for later forcing. Also included with this group is lily-of-the-valley.

2. *Half-hardy bulbs* that grow at cool but not freezing temperatures include freesias, ixias and ornithogalums. Temperature requirements of these bulbs are difficult to manipulate in the home, so these should be left for nurserymen to grow.

3. *Tender tropical or subtropical bulbs* such as amaryllis, veltheimias and caladiums (for their foliage) are easily handled by the home gardener.

TULIP (*Tulipa gesneriana*). This is the most common of the lily family. It originated in the Mediterranean region, in Asia and Japan. Early flowering and extremely dwarf species are from the species *T. suaveolens*. Many other species and varieties are grown in gardens. For best results choose single-flowered early varieties from catalogues. Pot five or six bulbs in a five-inch bulb pan. The outside bulbs in the pan are set with the flat side to the inside wall so that the first leaf developed will hang over the edge of the pan. Store the potted bulbs at 46° to 48°. Plants started in September to October will flower in January and February. The storage period usually runs eight to ten weeks. After storage grow as cool as possible.

CROCUS (*Crocus vernus*; hybrids). A vari-colored early-flowering bulb, the crocus is one of the first harbingers of spring. Original species came from Europe, and it belongs to the iris family. Like hyacinths, crocus bulbs will grow in water. Specially designed vases of crystal glass about 3½ inches tall have a cuplike depression for holding one bulb so that the base of the bulb sets just above the water. Once started, keep in a cool, dark place for roots to develop. Then bring into a well-lighted room to flower. Crocus pots looking like so-called strawberry jars are also ideal for starting crocus bulbs. Most all varieties of crocus can be forced. Plant in shallow containers so that the top of the bulb is just covered with a mix. Store at 48° to 50° for eight to ten weeks and force at a cool temperature for flowering. Bulbs of the autumn-flowering crocus, *Colchicum autumnale*, which belongs to the lily family, are purchased for planting in the fall and can be forced. Place in a container without potting medium or moisture, supporting bulb with pebbles or sand. After flowering, the bulbs are planted permanently in the ground.

HYACINTH (*Hyacinthus orientalis*). This plant belongs to the lily family and is a native of Syria, Asia Minor and Greece. Roman hyacinths are of the variety *albus* and are cultured mainly for forcing. So-called prepared hyacinths are used for forcing. Specially designed hyacinth glasses hold a hyacinth bulb so that the base of the bulb is at the water level for rooting. No storage is needed as for other bulbs. However, starting at a cool 60° in the dark to promote rooting is beneficial. Hyacinth bulbs treated for forcing in pots are started in the early autumn. Normally three large bulbs are planted in a six-inch bulb pan. Fill with mix so that the necks of the bulbs are just showing. Store at 48° to 55° for about ten weeks.

GRAPE HYACINTH (*Muscari armeniacum*). The simplest of all bulbs to force. Save a few bulbs out of your autumn planting and plant in a shallow pot, using any good potting soil, in late autumn. Move to a cool place, 40° to 50°, for at least two months. Water about once a week until foliage sprouts. Then move to a sunny window and enjoy a bit of blue sky in your home.

*Narcissus
pseudo-narcissus*

*Narcissus tazetta
papyraceus*

*Convallaria
majalis*

DAFFODIL *(Narcissus pseudo-narcissus)*. The large trumpet type with the common yellow color is one of the first of spring flowers to appear as cut flowers in flower shops or supermarkets. Bulbs for forcing are sold in early autumn as pre-cooled early flowering varieties. 'King Alfred,' 'Beersheba' and 'Rembrandt' are a few of the good varieties. Miniature daffodils are also available for forcing, are much smaller and are preferred by many gardeners.

For forcing, select double-nosed bulbs with undamaged tips. Using mix B, place five or six bulbs in a five- or six-inch bulb pan or azalea pot. Set bulbs so that the tips of bulbs are one inch below the rim of the pot. Fill with mix to that level. Potting time in the

Northern Hemisphere is September to December, the earlier the better. Store pots of bulbs for six to eight weeks. Remove from storage when roots come through the drainage hole at the bottom of the pot and when the tops have started to grow. When first removed from storage, place in a cool basement window or spare room. When shoot growth has taken on green color move to a forcing temperature of about 60°. High light and cool temperatures are then essential for producing a good quality flowering plant.

PAPER-WHITE NARCISSUS *(Narcissus tazetta papyraceus)*. A tropical bulb originating from the Canary Islands; a member of the amaryllis family. Bulbs are available in autumn from garden stores and flower shops, are ready to pot and grow to flowering. No cool storage treatment is required. The best temperature for quality is 50° to 60°, but they will flower at living-room temperature. Bulbs can be planted every two weeks to give a succession of bloom. Plant the bulbs in shallow dishes, filling to the neck of the bulbs with pebbles, florists' shredded styrofoam or other water-holding material. Store at room temperature before planting. Flowering will occur in four to six weeks. The later the time of starting, the shorter the time for flowering. Other varieties available are the Golden Paper-white narcissus, *N.* 'Soleil d'Or,' and the Chinese sacred lily, *N. tazetta polyanthos*.

LILY-OF-THE-VALLEY (*Convallaria majalis*). This is favored everywhere for its sweetly fragrant, dainty flowers in the spring of the year. A member of the lily family, it is native to Europe, East Asia and North America. It can be forced into flower at any time of the year. The "pips" prepared by specialists by cold-storage treatment can be purchased ready to flower at most any time of the year. Purchased pips are planted in sphagnum moss and kept well supplied with water. Closely spaced in the container, they can be forced at a temperature of 75° to 80° in low light intensity until flower stems are well started. Flowering takes place in high light, as is the case for Paper-white narcissus. Approximate time for forcing to flowering is 21 days.

General Cultural directions

LIGHT: High light intensity is desirable for final stages of flowering bulbous plants. Full sunlight is beneficial for paper-white narcissus and for lily-of-the-valley.

TEMPERATURE: Storage temperatures averaging 48° are generally recommended for most bulbs. Fluctuation can be expected where a controlled-temperature room is not available. A discussion of outdoor storage is included under "Remarks." An exception to low-temperature storage is for *prepared* hyacinths and crocuses that are placed at 60° for a short time for root formation. The paper-white narcissus requires no storage at low temperature.

MOISTURE: Moist. *Never drying out* is a must for bulb culture. Be sure all bulbs are thoroughly watered after potting, during storage and thereafter. Pots of bulbs placed in a cold basement or garage can be wrapped in black polyethylene to keep them moist and provide darkness.

POTTING: Bulbs for forcing have enough stored food to bring them into flower. Generally, fertilizing is not needed. Thus the requirement of a potting medium is for support and to retain moisture. A mix containing soil, peat and sand or a mixture of peat and perlite in equal parts will answer the potting requirements. Packaged mixes may need the addition of perlite or sand to give them better drainage. It is emphasized that good moisture retention of the mix is important for the storage and forcing period.

INSECTS: Aphids on tulips can be troublesome.

REMARKS: The provision of storage where an adequate temperature can be maintained is an obstacle to home forcing of bulbs. Outdoor storage can be provided in a cold frame, a pit or trench in the ground. Another method is the above-ground arrangement (see illustration).

Soil temperatures for the first few weeks during the time bulbs are buried outside may be 50° to 55°, which is conducive to root growth. It is expected that a drop to 45° will take place and, eventually, possibly to 32° to 35°. The temperature should not go below 32°. The moisture content of mix for potted bulbs should be checked before freezing weather sets in. A sheet of polyethylene may be added to give additional protection. A snow cover is excellent insulation.

BULB PLANTING PROCEDURE

1. Fill the container to within 1¼ to 1½ inches of the top of pot with loose, slightly moist planting medium.

2. Place the bulbs gently on top of the soil mix. The bulbs should never be pushed into the pot or flat since this compacts medium directly beneath the root plate.

3. Cover the bulbs with the planting medium up to about one-eight to one-fourth inch below the top of the container. This is done so that watering will have to drain through, not flow over the sides. The planted containers are then labeled and placed in the storage location.

DISH GARDENS

A dish garden is like a garden in miniature, and has become popular as an indoor gardening activity, particularly among those who live in city dwellings. Combinations of small tropical foliage plants, of woodland plants and of desert plants in varieties of form, color and texture are planted in containers to make dish gardens. A well-planted garden uses the principles of good floral design and compares with a pleasing arrangement of cut flowers and foliage.

Choice of container. The size of the container in relation to the size of the plants is considered. The container must be at least three inches deep and not more than eight inches high and should hold enough potting mixture for three to four or more plants.

Ceramic containers of dark or dull colors are more desirable than light colors. Containers made of brass, copper, pewter, iron and glass are used. Metal containers should be coated with plastic on the inside or lined with polyethylene (polythene) sheeting to prevent corrosion of the metal by nutrient salts contained in the potting mix. Ceramic containers depicting frogs, turkeys, Santa Claus, and all sorts of creations are available.

Selection of plants. It is logical that plants of tropical origin be chosen for dish gardens because they are best adapted to today's interiors with modern heating and lighting.

Only a few of the plant materials used for dish gardens are really dwarf varieties. The plants used together in a dish garden should have the same water requirements—that is, "moist" or "dry." It is foolish to think that cactus or peperomia will survive when planted in the same dish with ferns.

Dish-garden plants should be fairly slow-growing types. This qualification limits selection. Plants may be purchased or selected from the woodland. Plants purchased growing in 1½–2½-inch pots are best for transplanting to an area as small as a dish garden.

Use plants of different heights and colors to avoid massing of green foliage. Create a center of interest by the use of ceramic figurines, ducks, birds, lichen-covered rock, pieces of driftwood or shelf fungi.

In general, there are three different dish-garden types: 1) tropical gardens, 2) desert gardens, 3) woodland gardens.

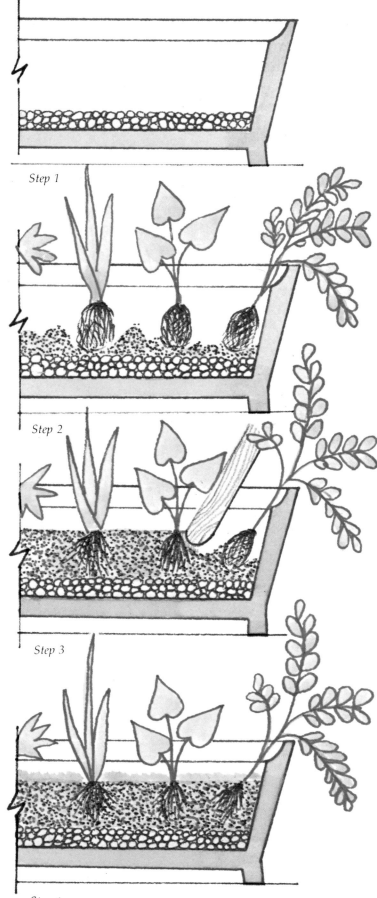

Planting the dish garden. The potting mixture for dish gardens is found under heading for potting mixes.

Steps to follow in planting the gardens

Step 1. Place a one-half to one-inch layer of small pebbles or aquarium gravel in the bottom of the container for drainage.

Step 2. Arrange the plants for landscape effect.

Step 3. Fill between the plants with the potting mix. Firm the mixture about the plants with a blunt stick. Allow one-half inch below the rim for catching water.

Step 4. A top dressing for "ground cover" may be used. Sheet moss, florist wood moss or marble chips are suitable. However, it is difficult to watch the moisture content of the mix when these materials are used.

Watering the dish gardens. The tropical and woodland plants will need to be checked for water at least twice a week. Because there are several plants in one container, water is used up faster than with one plant in a pot.

Desert plants will need water less frequently. Check for water every two to three weeks.

DO NOT FORGET: If there is no drainage hole in the bottom of the container, there is danger of *overwatering.*

An efficient method of watering is to submerge the container in a bucket of water. When air bubbles stop appearing, remove. If plant is overwatered, place the dish on its side for about 20 minutes for excess water to drain off.

The finger-touch method for checking moisture content described in the chapter on moisture, page 176, may be used here also.

Dish-garden planters need optimum light conditions exclusive of direct sunlight and a temperature of normal living rooms.

If foliage wilts after planting, spray with atomizer or place planter in a large polyethylene bag for a day or two until plants recover from transplanting. Supplemental lighting with a table lamp will prolong the plant life of a dish garden. Control growth if necessary by occasional pruning or a soft pinch.

Step 1

Step 2

Step 3

Step 4

SELECTED PLANTS FOR DISH GARDENS

Listing of plants for these gardens is by groups that have similar growth requirements and thus go together. Any group of plants may be planted together to make a single garden or used in combination, if desired.

Plants for tropical gardens (Culture requirements are moist soil and medium light).

GROUP 1

Chinese evergreen—*Aglaonema modestum*
Gold-dust dracaena—*Dracaena godseffiana* 'Florida Beauty'
Heart-leaved philodendron—*Philodendron scandens* subsp. *oxycardium*

GROUP 2

Parlor palm—*Chamaedorea elegans*
Marble-leaf pothos—*Pothos aureus* 'Marble Queen'
Pteris fern—*Pteris cretica albolineata*
Ardisia—*Ardisia crispa*

GROUP 3

Euonymus—*Euonymus japonicus medio-pictus*
English ivy—*Hedera helix* 'Hahn's Self-branching'
False holly—*Osmanthus heterophylla variegatus*
Piggyback plant—*Tolmiea menziesii*

GROUP 4

Variegated mock orange—*Pittosporum tobira variegata*
Dwarf kangaroo vine—*Cissus antarctica minor*
Boxwood—*Buxus microphylla japonica*

GROUP 5

Parlor palm—*Chamaedorea elegans*
Arrowhead vine—*Syngonium podophyllum*
Pink fittonia—*Fittonia verschaffeltii*
Ardisia—*Ardisia crispa*

GROUP 6

Sander's dracaena—*Dracaena sanderiana*
Natal plum—*Carissa grandiflora*
'Bonsai'
English ivy—*Hedera helix* 'Maple Queen'
Chinese evergreen—*Aglaonema commutatum*
var. *maculatum*
Devil's ivy—*Epipremnum aureum*
(*Scindapsus aureus*)

GROUP 7

Sander's Dracaena—*Dracaena sanderiana*
Mother-in-Law's Tongue—*Sansevieria*
'Golden Hahnii'
Earth Star—*Cryptanthus* 'It'
Heart-Leaved philodendron—*Philodendron*
scandens subsp.
oxycardium

GROUP 8

Mother-in-Law's Tongue—*Sansevieria*
trifasciata laurentii
English Ivy—*Hedera helix*
'Hahn's Self-branching'
Peperomia—*Peperomia floridana*
Gold-Dust Dracaena—*Dracaena godseffiana*

GROUP 9

Mother-in-Law's Tongue—*Sansevieria*
trifasciata
Buddhist Pine—*Podocarpus macrophyllus*
maki
Prayer Plant—*Maranta kerchoveana*
Aluminum Plant—*Pilea cadierei*
English Ivy—*Hedera helix* 'Needle Point'

GROUP 10

Asparagus Fern—*Asparagus plumosus*
Coral Berry—*Ardisia crispa*
Parlor Palm—*Chamaedorea elegans*
English Ivy—*Hedera helix* 'Jubilee'

GROUP 11

Euonymus—*Euonymus radicans gracilis*
Peperomia—*Peperomia floridana*
Pink Fittonia—*Fittonia verschaffeltii*
Baby's Tears—*Helxine soleirolii*

GROUP 12

Chinese Evergreen—*Aglaonema modestum*
Umbrella Plant—*Cyperus alternifolius*
gracilis
Table Fern—*Pteris ensiformis victoriae*
Devil's Ivy—*Epipremnum aureum*

DESERT GARDENS

Desert gardens are planted in attractive shallow ceramic containers and in glass, such as terrariums. The author identifies glass containers of cacti and succulents as "desertariums." In this glass treatment no cover is used as with terrariums. Cacti can be combined with a few species of succulents such as the liliaceous *Haworthia*. Haworthias are small rosette-forming plants that resemble century plants and agaves of the American desert. Sedums and kalanchoes are to be avoided, for they tend to become "leggy."

Cacti can be arranged to represent really effective desert scenes by following examples of pictures in popular magazines. Use of a miniature Mexican or a thatched hut and burro figurines may be added to complete the picture. Well-placed stones to represent boulders and mountains are really the only accessories needed in cactus-planted "desertariums."

For planting, drainage is the most important consideration. Place gravel or sand to the thickness of one inch at the bottom of the container. Add potting mix (refer to potting mix formula C, page 180) to the center in a pile and line the glass with a shell-like thickness of sand. Continue to add mix and sand liner alternately until the desired planting depth is attained. Colored sand may be used in a process called "sand casting" to create rainbow effects.

Choose small plants or slow-growing types from the list on page 151. For handling, to prevent picking up spines with the fingers, use a strip of brown wrapping paper to grasp the plant. After planting tamp mix with a dowel to settle plant in place. When planting is completed, cover surface with a layer of sand or fine gravel. Gravel that is used for fish aquariums may be found in pet shops. An assortment of colors is available, if desired. Gravel at the base of plants keeps the stems dry and also helps to prevent rot diseases.

Finally, clean glass inside and out. Use a small brush to remove dirt or gravel that adheres to plants. Carefully moisten the garden by measuring a tablespoonful or two of water to each plant. Size of the plant will determine amount. Plants that have been bruised in planting should not be watered for three or four days.

A watering once a month usually supplies enough water for plants in a desert garden.

An alternate method of planting is suggested. When the container is large enough, the cactus plants in clay pots may be left in their pots and plunged into the medium; cover the rims so they are not visible. This avoids root disturbance that could cause a weak plant to be lost.

Plants for Desert Gardens

Group 1
  Variegated Wax Plant— *Hoya carnosa variegata*
  Peperomia—*Peperomia floridana*
  Variegated Snake Plant—*Sansevieria trifasciata laurentii*
  Jade Plant—*Crassula argentea*

Group 2
  Umbrella Tree (seedling)—*Schefflera actinophylla*
  Moses-in-the-Cradle—*Rhoeo spathacea*
  Spotted Gasteria—*Gasteria maculata*
  Jade Plant—*Crassula argentea*

Group 3
  Hen-and-Chickens—*Sempervivum tectorum*
  Zebra Haworthia—*Haworthia fasciata*
  Bird's-Nest Sansevieria—*Sansevieria trifasciata hahnii*
  Star Flower—*Stapelia variegata*

Group 4
  Any species resembling cactus—*Euphorbia*
  Variegated Peperomia—*Peperomia scandens variegata*
  Sansevieria—*Sansevieria trifasciata*
  Wax Plant—*Hoya carnosa* (any variety)

1. *Dracaena sanderiana*

2. *Pilea cadierei*

3. *Podocarpus macrophyllus maki*

4. *Saintpaulia*

5. *Selaginella kraussiana brownii*

6. *Chamaedorea elegans*

TERRARIUMS

What is a terrarium? *Terra* comes from the Latin meaning *earth* and *-arium* is borrowed from *aquarium*, which is a home for aquatic plants and fishes. Put together, we have a home for land creatures or plants. The forerunner of the terrarium was a glass box, called a Wardian Case. It was devised by Dr. N.B. Ward (1791–1868) and used by plant collectors to protect plants from adverse environmental conditions during transportation by sea.

When a terrarium is carefully planted the enclosure becomes a balanced ecological system comparable to a well-balanced fish aquarium.

Containers

The true terrarium is made of glass or plastic, a container of any shape or size, with the opening covered by a loose-fitting lid for ventilation. The most important requirement is transparency of the container (with no color tint). Glass is preferred to plastic because it does not scratch easily and will not discolor, as do some plastics.

Many designs have been invented. Old fish bowls, water jugs, humidors, large goblets and even glass-top coffee tables are used as terrarium containers. Expensive leaded glass and artfully designed wall hangers have invaded the terrarium market.

Planting design

Terrarium planters can be attractive and interesting when designed to reproduce a miniature landscape. The same principles of design used to create an outdoor garden are followed. Do not crowd plantings. Create open areas suggesting meadows. Build hills, low spots and grottoes. Install natural rock coral and driftwood for naturalistic effect. Use coarse white sand or natural-color aquarium gravel to simulate beaches or garden paths. Pieces of mirror or clam shells may be placed to imitate pools of water.

Miniature figurines of animals, birds and sets of Japanese houses, lanterns and bridges are available.

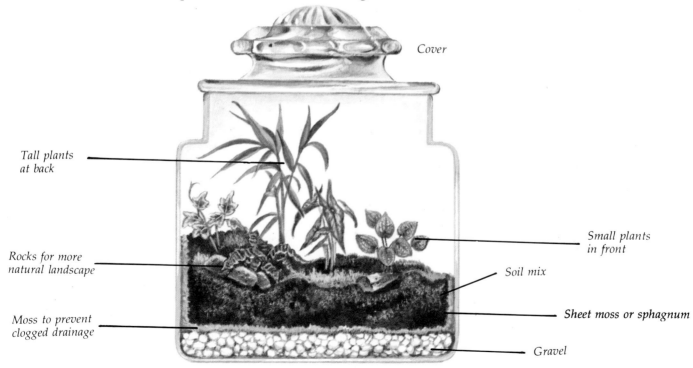

Cover

Tall plants at back

Rocks for more natural landscape

Moss to prevent clogged drainage

Small plants in front

Soil mix

Sheet moss or sphagnum

Gravel

A glass-covered aquarium used as a terrarium

Plant selection

A large variety of plants have been grown in terrariums. Some species have proven satisfactory, but a greater number have not adapted to the environment of the terrarium.

Plants selected survive under like environmental conditions and are subdivided into: 1) tall or treelike, 2) medium or shrublike, 3) low or ground cover and 4) flowering plants.

The plants are selected because of their slow growth habit. However, in the ideal environment of a terrarium they will grow and eventually crowd the container. Pruning directions are suggested under the section on "Maintenance."

Purchased plants for transplanting should not be larger than 2¼-inch pot size for small terrariums. Plants growing in nutrient blocks of peat moss are ideal. Well-rooted cuttings transplant into terrariums without difficulty.

IMPORTANT: Carefully inspect all plant material for evidence of disease and insects. If in doubt, treat with appropriate spray.

A planting mix formula is suggested in the chapter on potting soil formulas.

Drainage material

A fine grade of aquarium gravel is placed in the bottom of the container to serve as a well and to help avoid the error of overwatering.

Granulated charcoal (aquarium grade) may be added to a planting mix but is not necessary. It is recommended as an additive to mixes using garden soil as a component.

Add the planting mix and drainage material to a terrarium container, as outlined in the section on how to plant.

Plants for Terrariums

A. *Tall (treelike)*
Variegated aglaonema—*Aglaonema commutatum maculatum*
Parlor palm—*Chameadorea elegans*
Dwarf umbrella plant—*Cyperus alternifolius gracilis*
Sander's dracaena—*Dracaena sanderiana*
Dwarf winter creeper—*Euonymus fortunei radicans gracilis (variegatus)*
Classic myrtle—*Myrtus communis microphylla*
Chinese podocarpus—*Podocarpus macrophyllus maki*

B. *Medium (shrublike)*
Dwarf Japanese
sweet flag—*Acorus gramineus pusillus*
White-striped Japanese sweet flag—*Acorus gramineus variegatus*
Maidenhair fern—*Adiantum cuneatum*
Dwarf asparagus fern—*Asparagus plumosus nanus*
Mother fern (plantlets)—*Asplenium bulbiferum*
Dwarf natal plum—*Carissa* 'Bonsai'
Dwarf natal plum—*Carissa grandiflora* 'Boxwood Beauty'
Gold-dust dracaena—*Dracaena godseffiiana*
Red-nerved fittonia—*Fittonia verschaffeltii*
Silver-nerved fittonia—*Fittonia verschaffeltii argyroneura*
English ivy—*Hedera helix* 'Jubilee'
English ivy—*Hedera helix* 'Needlepoint'
English ivy—*Hedera helix* 'Pixie'

Prayer plant—*Maranta leuconeura kerchoveana*
Spurge—*Pachysandra terminalis*
Variegated spurge—*Pachysandra terminalis variegata*
Hare's-foot fern—*Polypodium aureum undulatum*
Hedge fern—*Polystichum setiferum*
Dwarf serissa—*Serissa foetida variegata*

C. *Low (ground cover)*
Creeping fig—*Ficus pumila (F. repens minima)*
Gill-over-the-ground—*Nepeta hederacea variegata*
Creeping pilea—*Pilea depressa*
Panamiga (Friendship plant)—*Pilea involucrata*
Dwarf club moss—*Selaginella kraussiana brownii*
Spreading club moss—*Selaginella kraussiana*
Creeping selaginella—*Selaginella uncinata*

D. *Flowering plants*
Miniature eyelash begonia—*Begonia boweri*
Dwarf begonia—*Begonia* 'China Doll'
Dwarf begonia—*Begonia ficicola*
Dwarf begonia—*Begonia* 'Rajah'
Miniature gloxinia—*Sinningia pusilla*
Miniature gloxinia—*Sinningia* 'Baby Doll'
Miniature gloxinia—*Sinningia* 'White Sprite'
Dwarf African violets—*Saintpaulia* (dwarf varieties, cultivars)

Cryptanthus X 'It'

How to plant

Step 1. Wash all containers aseptically clean to prevent the growth of molds and fungi. Clorox, Jeyes Fluid or a proprietary fungicide are suitable sterilizing agents.

Step 2. For a first-class job, line the inside wall of the glass with a thin layer of sheet moss to hide the planting mix. Sheet moss can be purchased from a florist or garden shop. Dyed florist moss is to be avoided.

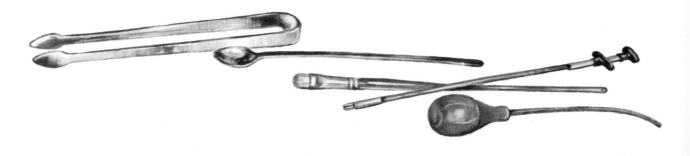

Step 3. Place drainage material in bottom and add mix according to chart. Design or lay out surface of the mix. Make hills, valleys and pathways.

Step 4. Select plants, giving thought to height and texture. Choose figurines and accessories that adapt to them.

Step 5. Dig holes with a spoon and plant as you would out of doors. Backfill each plant and pack mix with a one-half-inch wooden rod. Lightly water each plant with a syringe, wash bottle or bulb baster.

Step 6. Position accessories simultaneously with plants to complete landscape.

Step 7. When planting job is completed tamp surface to make firm.

Step 8. Cover exposed planting mix with moss, if desired. Cover some areas with gravel for paths and beach scenes. Mosses help hold moisture.

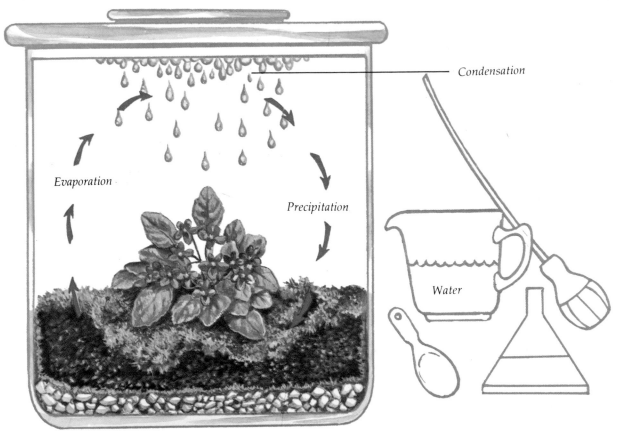

Condensation

Evaporation

Precipitation

Water

Watering and ventilation

When the right amount of water is added to a terrarium, a rain cycle is established. It is a natural thing for tiny droplets of water to form on the inside of the glass.

When the tiny droplets are no longer in evidence, additional water may be needed.

Look at the moss liner for dryness. Remove a section of moss and check the surface mix for dryness. If water is needed, add water a tablespoonful at a time until you see moisture in the gravel or on the moss.

A heavy condensation of water or fog on the inside of the glass indicates an overbalance of moisture. A drop in temperature will cause fogging of the glass. To remedy this, wipe out the excess moisture. Leave the top off overnight or longer and replace when the glass is dry.

Some manufactured containers have a built-in ventilating system that helps prevent fogging.

MAINTENANCE AND CARE

LIGHT: Bright light near a window or a table lamp is the best location. *Do not* put your terrarium in *direct sunlight*; the sun's rays can actually burn your plants.

TEMPERATURE: Generally, plants in a terrarium are tropical and will do best at 65° to 75°.

PRUNING: A program of pruning should start at planting time. The fast-growing plants such as *euonymus, fittonia* and English ivy can be soft-pinched at the growing tip. This will slow growth and encourage branching. In the ideal environment plants will grow and crowd the container. Periodically, snip off the top or side branches with sharp scissors. Cut back to just above a node or leaf joint.

DISEASES AND INSECTS: Use of clean containers, clean plants and sterilized planting mixes minimizes troubles.

Aerosol sprays recommended for insect control under the sections "Insects" and "Diseases" will take care of most problems.

*Various containers
used as terrariums*

TERRARIUM TOOLS: Designed by the home operator, they include long-handled iced-tea spoons, stiff wire hooks (from coat hangers), funnel, wooden dowels and a long-handled artist's paintbrush. A bulb baster or a laboratory wash bottle is useful for applying water to the plants of the terrarium.

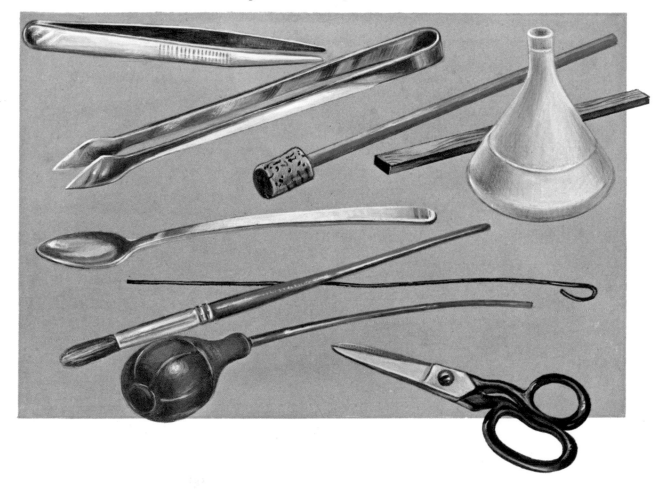

160

Literati

Group planting

Rock planting

Informal upright

Broom

Cascade

Upright

Slanting

Multiple trunk

Miniatures

BONSAI

Bonsai (pronounced **bone-sigh***) is a Japanese art of growing miniature trees in small-sized containers. To achieve traditional bonsai, one combines a sense of art with a knowledge of horticulture. The ultimate goal is to produce a miniature specimen that possesses all of the characteristics of a mature specimen growing in a naturalistic setting.*

The art of bonsai originated in China and was later developed by the Japanese. Old Japanese garden books of the seventeenth and eighteenth centuries illustrate and describe bonsai. Wild trees dwarfed in nature were first used. When a supply became difficult to obtain, Japanese gardeners began to culture more readily available plant materials.

Standards and rules governing shape and design were set by Japanese horticulturists, and, through the years, guidelines for classic bonsai styles have been established.

American bonsai developed with a much freer concept of growing dwarfed plants as miniatures and the use of many tropical plants as well as some hardy varieties. Thus indoor cultivation of bonsai came about.

In comparison, the Japanese use hardy conifers and deciduous trees and shrubs; and, because of cultural requirements, the plant specimens are grown outdoors most of the year. These are brought indoors for a short period for display but returned to the outdoor environment for year-round survival.

Selection of plant material

Tropical trees, shrubs and some vines can be trained to grow as bonsai. The culture directions for growing each particular plant must be followed for successful results. The application of principles of design and culture of bonsai is essential to achieve a miniature plant. The tropical bonsai must be kept indoors unless outdoor temperatures fill the plant's requirements. In northern climates with cold winters, plants will benefit from outdoor culture on the patio in summer.

Some characteristics to look for in choosing plant material for training are: 1) small leaved, 2) short internodes (distance between leaves), 3) attractive bark, 4) stoutness of main stalk, 5) a habit of branching for good twig formation, and 6) all parts of plant in scale.

For a beginning, purchase healthy young plants from a two-and-a-half-inch to a four-inch pot size. Larger potted specimen plants may be used if desired. Check to see that the plant has a healthy root system and is free from insects and disease.

Choose a basic style

Decide on the final shape you wish to create before you start. Use one of the styles illustrated. Work with a single trunk as your basic design. This is simplest and best for a beginning.

The five basic styles are: 1) formal upright, 2) informal upright, 3) slanting, 4) cascade and 5) semicascade. These are determined by the over-all shape of the tree and the

Good tools make work easier

*The art of bonsai employs
the choice of a compatible container*

direction or angle the trunk slants away from the main axis.

The formal upright style is the basis for all bonsai forms. It is easiest to develop because it avoids the necessity for wiring and bending. In this form the tree has an erect leader with horizontal branches. There should be a lower branch extending farther out from the trunk than the others. Two of the lowest branches should come forward to the front side, with one set higher than the other. There should be a single branch at the back, extending between the two forward branches, to give the tree depth. Trim off small branches too close to the trunk or presenting clutter at the base.

Pot up specimen of formal upright style in an oval or rectangular container, placing the plant about a third of the distance from one end.

The informal upright style is similar to the formal upright style but with the top bending toward the front. This gives an illusion of motion and displays more informality. Glance down on the tree from above. If the angle is not correct, the tree may be lifted and the root ball reset to provide the correct angle. Trim branches to give proper balance.

Select an oval or rectangular container and place the plant a third of the distance from the end.

The slanting style places the trunk at a more acute angle than does either of the previous styles. The lowest branch should spread in the direction opposite to which the trunk slants, with the top bending forward slightly. Lower branches arranged in groups of three should start at a distance of one third of the way up the trunk. Slanting trees have the look of trees in nature which have been bent by prevailing winds. Prune out small branches to display distinctive placement of groups of branches.

Plant this style in the center of a round or square container.

The cascade style is representative of a natural tree grown over a cliff edge or down an embankment. Plant in a container a branch or branches with most of the foliage hanging below the surface of the soil. This style should be displayed on the edge of a table or on a shelf.

This type takes longer to train than do the others. Train so that an uppermost branch is vertical and the remainder extends forward and downward. A round or hexagonal and deep container is used for this style.

The semicascade style has a main trunk that extends away from the container and drops downward but not below the pot, as does the cascade style. Most of the branches are trained toward the front, with the shorter branches left closer to the trunk. This style looks best planted in a low hexagonal or round container that is shallower than the pot used for the cascade style.

Other style variations according to size, how planted, number of trees, number of trunks, root system, etc, are: *Miniature bonsai (under six inches); rock planting; twin planting; literati; driftwood; broom style; group planting (forest); multiple trunk; windswept; sinuous.*

Containers for bonsai

The style of the bonsai plant usually determines the pot. This is the first consideration and must be decided on. Generally containers come in round, oval, hexagonal, square and rectangular shapes; shapes usually come in sets of three sizes. The color of the container should harmonize with the color of the foliage, mostly earthy colors of dark brown, dark red, dark purple, gray and black. Evergreen conifers are usually grown in dull white or brown containers; colorful fruit or flowering plants in green, tan or white. Having better moisture retention, glazed containers are best for indoor bonsai.

The container should be just large enough to accommodate the root system after careful pruning has been done.

Training

When planting your bonsai, keep in mind your chosen theme and how it will look in the container. Like people, plants have a "best profile." Decide which is the front of the tree and then shape it. Branches should look balanced and exhibit a floating habit. Branches should not crisscross. Look down from above to make sure an upper branch does not overshadow a lower branch. Next in procedure is the basic and timely operation of pruning, nipping or pinching and wiring. For this procedure basic tools are needed: a pair of hook-and-blade pruning shears, a narrow garden trowel, blunt sticks (dowels), a pair of sturdy wire cutters and copper wire of various sizes, as well as a small watering can.

Pruning to control growth, to remove dead-wood, to remove crisscrossed branches and excess foliage is accomplished first. Prune to encourage branches to grow toward open space. Do not do all of the pruning at one time. Do it as undesirable shoots develop.

Nipping or pinching is a continuous process with tropical bonsai plants. Pinch back new growth or thin out before it becomes too thick.

Wiring is the final step. Copper wire is used because it is flexible. No. 8, the heaviest, is used for the main trunk, while No. 16, the smallest, is used for soft branches. Start wiring from the lowest point and work upward. Anchor the wire by pushing end into soil. Wire loosely. After limbs to be bent are wired, bend by hand to the desired angle or direction. Wires may have to remain in place for a year before removal.

Potting and repotting

Fast-growing trees like weeping fig, citrus or hibiscus will need repotting and root pruning at least twice a year; slower-growing types like classic myrtle and jade plant only once a year. The plant should be carefully removed from its container and an inch or more of surface soil of the ball removed. Loosened roots are trimmed back to the ball of soil. Thin out thick root masses. Heavy roots supporting top branching should be saved to establish a balance of physiological relationship.

Potting media and fertilizer recommendations coincide with those for potted house plants. Soilless mixtures are good bonsai mixes. Fertilizer is necessary to maintain the good health of the plants. It is recommended that a feeding of water-soluble type be applied during the active growth months of spring and summer. Feed once a month at half strength. Omit feeding for the month following a repotting operation. An application of slow-release type fertilizer in spring and fall is ample.

Watering, as with all cultural directions, is even more critical with bonsai than other house plants. Most tropical bonsai will require daily watering, depending on house temperature and exposure to light. When outdoors in summer on the patio, watering twice a day may be necessary. The succulent types like jade plant will need less frequent waterings. Bonsai-trained tropicals in small, shallow containers are naturally going to take more water than other house plants.

Cascade

Semicascade

Semicascade

Formal upright

Slanting

TROPICAL PLANTS FOR TRAINING

Acacia—*Acacia baileyana*

Aralia—*Polyscias balfouriana*
    Polyscias fruticosa
    Polyscias guilfoylei

Birds-eye Bush—*Ochna multiflora*

Camellia—*Camellia japonica*
    Camellia sasanqua

Cape Jasmine—*Gardenia jasminoides radicans*
    Gardenia jasminoides

Cherry, Surinam—*Eugenia uniflora*

Citrus (Calamondin, Kumquat, Lemon,
  Lime, Orange and Tangerine)—*Citrus* species

Cypress, Arizona—*Cupressus arizonica*

Cypress, Monterey—*Cupressus macrocarpa*

Fig, Mistletoe—*Ficus diversifolia*

Herb, Elfin—*Cuphea hyssopifolia*

Hibiscus—*Hibiscus rosa-sinensis cooperi*

Holly, Miniature—*Malpighia coccigera*

Jacaranda—*Jacaranda acutifolia*

Jade Plant—*Crassula* species

Jasmine—*Jasminum parkeri*

Jasmine, Orange—*Murraya exotica*

Jasmine, Star—*Trachelospermum jasminoides*

Laurel, Indian—*Ficus retusa*

Myrtle, Classic—*Myrtus communis*

Oak, Cork—*Quercus suber*

Oak, Indoor—*Nicodemia diversifolia*

Oak, Silk—*Grevillea robusta*

Olive, Common—*Olea europaea*

Orchid Tree—*Bauhinia variegata*

Pepper Tree, Brazilian—*Schinus terebinthifolius*

Pepper Tree, California—*Schinus molle*

Pink Shower—*Cassia grandis*

Pistachio, Chinese—*Pistachio chinensis*

Plum, Natal—*Carissa grandiflora*

Poinciana, Royal—*Delonix regia*

Pomegranate, Dwarf—*Punica granatum nana*

Popinac, White—*Leucaena glauca*

Powderpuff Tree—*Calliandra surinamensis*

Sago Palm—*Cycas revoluta*

Serissa—*Serissa foetida*

Shower Tree—*Cassia eremophila*

Weeping Fig—*Ficus benjamina*

RAPID-GROWING TROPICAL TREES

Brazilian Pepper—*Schinus terebinthifolius*

Jacaranda—*Jacaranda acutifolia*

Kafir Plum—*Harpephyllum caffrum*

Pink Shower—*Cassia grandis*

Powderpuff Tree—*Calliandra surinamensis*

Weeping Fig—*Ficus benjamina*

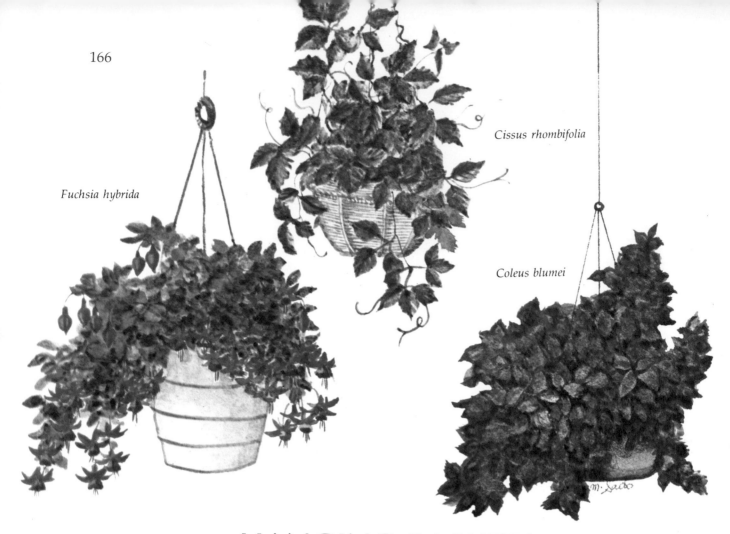

Fuchsia hybrida

Cissus rhombifolia

Coleus blumei

HANGING BASKETS

Many plants have a trailing or climbing habit of growth that is difficult to control when a container rests on a table or even on a bench in a greenhouse. In recent years the renewed interest in cultivating plants in hanging containers has solved this problem.

Lists of plants now include species that have never before been tried as hanging plants. Flowering annuals, perennials, foliage, herbs and even vegetables are used now. How convenient to have a hanging basket of ripe tomatoes within reach from your kitchen window!

The selection of plants for containers may be based on personal preference, yet there are plants which, because of growth character and ease of handling, make better specimens than others for hanging baskets.

Containers

How does one select? Any type of hanging basket will do. However, the weight of the basket, its size, color and proper provision for watering and drainage should be considered. A basket of open-weave construction is desirable because it is light in weight and durable. This kind may be lined with black plastic, burlap fiber or long-fibered sphagnum moss. Wire baskets can be lined with the same materials. Similarly, in the lightweight classification are containers made of plastic and styrofoam. Color also is a consideration. Green, tan or white are attractive with plants bearing brightly colored flowers or fruit. Brown, gray or terra cotta look best with most foliage plants.

Watering

To take care of the watering/drainage/drip problem, it is practical and efficient to move the container to the kitchen sink for a copious watering. Add water until it flows freely from the drainage hole at the bottom. Sau-

Begonia tuberhybrida pendula flore pleno

Nephrolepis exaltata bostoniensis

Bougainvillea glabra

cers clamped or permanently fastened to the bottom serve to catch drip only after watering, not irrigation water. A cork plug may be inserted into the drainage hole to stop after-drip. Plants left at the sink overnight will have ceased all dripping by the next morning. Baskets that are lined with a porous material such as sphagnum moss are best irrigated by submersion in a pail of water. When air bubbles cease at the surface, the container may be lifted for draining.

Supports for containers

Various methods for hanging containers are provided by link chain, nylon cord and an arrangement of uniquely designed fiber knotted into a harnesslike support known as macramé. Macramé may be used to give support to clay pots that can be lifted out easily for a watering. Wire pot hangers used by orchid growers simply clamp onto the rims of clay pots and serve as convenient hangers for plants on the patio.

Other culture

The same rules for culture of potted plants apply to hanging plants. Flowering plants and cacti can take advantage of sunlight if hung from a window casing. Care must be given to foliage thus exposed by moving out of direct sun in spring and summer.

Bougainvillea, not ordinarily grown in the house, will survive in a sunny window and usually rewards its owner with brightly colored flower bracts. Pruning or cutting back long shoots of bougainvillea in summer will control growth for hanging-basket culture. Other rank-growing vines will need cutting back and pinching to control growth and promote bushiness. Three plants set together will provide a quick display in a container of full dimension. Potting mixes recommended are suitable for hanging plants as well as potted specimens.

When plants are watered they should be inspected for insect pests and, if these are found, treated as recommended in the chapters on insects and diseases (pages 200–203).

PATIO PLANTING

Most house plants are benefited by a "vacation" outdoors on the patio in summer. The outdoor environment offers optimum light, cooler night temperatures and fresh air, which results in healthier, more normal-looking plants by autumn.

Cultural needs of plants growing outdoors become more critical than for inside growing. To maintain healthier, attractive plants requires more attention to watering, fertilizing and insect and disease control.

Containers

When house plants are moved outside they should be set into beds of peat moss or sunk into oversized containers that are decorative or are designed to enhance the architecture of the building or patio structure.

Placing the potted plant within a larger tub or container of peat moss prevents the plant from being toppled over by wind or stray animals. Less frequent watering is accomplished by this arrangement.

A "pot-within-a-pot" method for patio culture is described in "Pots and Potting," page 184.

Tubs are generally made of redwood, cypress or cedar. Some are fashioned from fiber glass. All tubs should have a drainage hole from three-fourths to one inch in diameter. Tubs must stand on feet or cleats to facilitate drainage of water. The size and height of the plant should determine the shape of the container. For example, a square tub may be used for an azalea and a taller or round tub for palms or podocarpus.

Watering

More water will be needed when plants are outside because of the bright light or direct sun and the warmer temperatures of midsummer. Air movement also contributes to drying out. A simple way to water is to wait until the surface of the potting medium becomes slightly dry. Then add water until it comes out at the base of the container. Never let the potting mixture become so dry that it pulls away from the sides of the container. When heavy rains have created a moist situation, watering is needed less frequently.

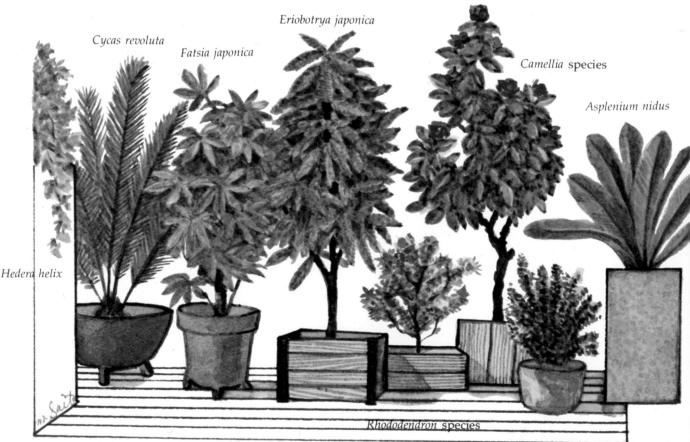

Hedera helix

Cycas revoluta

Fatsia japonica

Eriobotrya japonica

Camellia species

Asplenium nidus

Rhododendron species

Buxus sempervirens

Fertilizer

Apply a complete type of fertilizer one month after repotting. Subsequent feedings with a water-soluble fertilizer solution each month while outside are beneficial. If a slow-release type of fertilizer is used, only one application will be necessary.

Repotting

The time when plants are moved to an outdoor patio is a good time to repot or move to a larger container.

Conditioning

Caution is advised regarding the moving of tender plants outside. Do not move plants until the danger of freezing temperatures (32° or lower) is past. Tender plants that have been growing in low-light intensity should be exposed gradually to brighter outdoor light conditions. Brown blotches will appear on foliage if exposed to direct sun. Place the plants in the shade of the roof, under a tree, or provide lath shade to pre-vent such damage. Most house plants will survive very well without direct sunlight, but flowering species like the geranium, petunia and *Begonia semperflorens* do better in some sunshine.

A few plants for patio growing (to be moved inside for the winter):

Azalea (florists' type)—*Rhododendron* species
Camellia—*Camellia* species
Citrus—*Citrus* species
Coleus—*Coleus blumei* cultivars
Common (English) Boxwood—*Buxus semper-virens*
Fuchsia—*Fuchsia hybrida*
Geranium (zonal)—*Pelargonium X hortorum*
Ivy—*Hedera helix*
Japanese Fatsia—*Fatsia japonica*
Japanese Pittosporum—*Pittosporum tobira*
Japanese Privet—*Ligustrum japonicum*
Loquat—*Eriobotrya japonica*
Petunia—*Petunia hybrida*
Sago Palm—*Cycas revoluta*
Tuberous-rooted Begonia—*Begonia tuberhybrida*
Vinca Vine—*Vinca major variegata*
Wax Begonia—*Begonia semperflorens* and hybrids

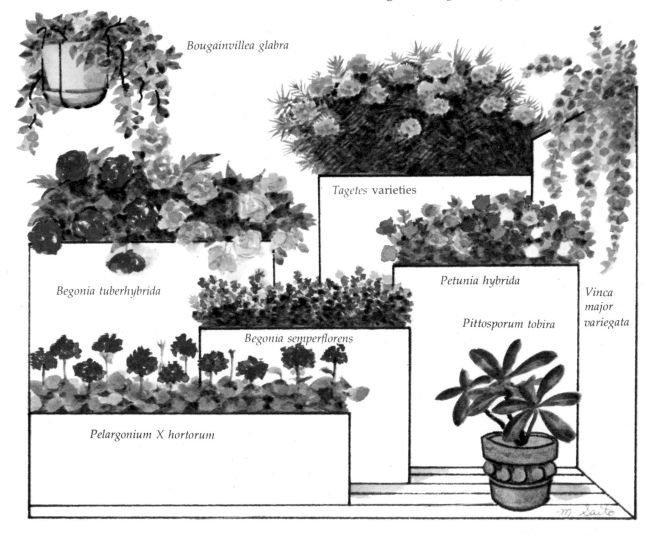

Bougainvillea glabra

Tagetes varieties

Begonia tuberhybrida

Petunia hybrida

Vinca major variegata

Pittosporum tobira

Begonia semperflorens

Pelargonium X hortorum

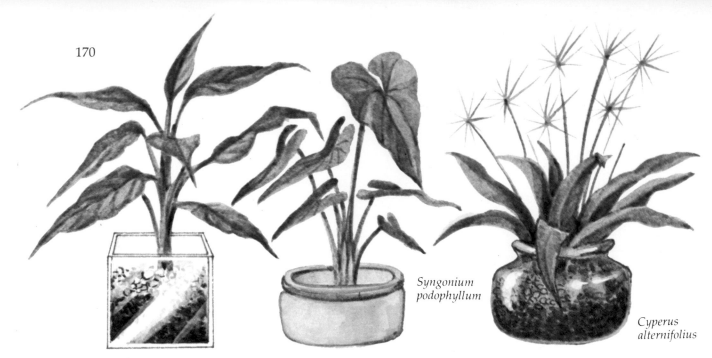

*Aglaonema
modestum*

*Syngonium
podophyllum*

*Cyperus
alternifolius*

PLANTS IN WATER

An old-fashioned yet practical method of starting plants in a tumbler of water or a bottle is still in use today.

A sophisticated and interesting development of this practice is "miniature water gardens" or "bottle gardening."

Any plant that roots easily in water may be cultured and adapted to a landscaped, attractive-looking water garden. Many plants have embryonic root systems at each node on the stem. When separated from the parent plant and placed in water, they develop roots in a short time.

Plants started in water survive better when transplanted to a water garden than do those transplanted from soil.

Planting media

Washed gravel, coarse sand, sea shells (washed) or pearl chips (as used in aquariums) will serve as support to the rooted plants. Charcoal granules purchased from a pet shop and added to the medium will keep the water "sweet-smelling."

Plant food

A water-soluble fertilizer diluted to one-fourth the strength indicated on the package will serve as needed nutrition.

How to plant

Step 1. Choose the container and wash it with soap and water to discourage the growth of bacteria.

Step 2. Place a small quantity of support material in the bottom of the container; add one or two tablespoons of charcoal. Arrange the gravel so that it supports the plants.

Step 3. Prepare fertilizer water in a separate vessel and add to half the depth of the gravel base. Maintaining a shallow amount of solution allows for the oxygen supply necessary for rooting and for healthy plant growth.

Step 4. Install landscape features such as figurines, pieces of driftwood, bridges, rocks and other objects of interest.

Maintenance and care

Experience will teach you how often to add clear water to maintain the proper water level.

Change the water-fertilizer solution once a month to help prevent salinity problems and the growth of algae.

Take the container of plants to the kitchen sink, tip and drain, holding your opened hand as a screen for the gravel base.

Plants for Miniature Water Gardens

Arrowhead Plant—*Syngonium podophyllum*
Chinese Evergreen—*Aglaonema modestum*
Coleus—*Coleus blumei*
Corn Plant—*Dracaena fragrans massangeana*
Croton—*Codiaeum variegatum pictum*
Devil's Ivy—*Epipremnum aureum*
Dumb Cane—*Dieffenbachia picta*
Dwarf Umbrella Plant—*Cyperus alternifolius gracilis*
English Ivy—*Hedera helix* varieties
Hurricane or Swiss-Cheese Plant—*Monstera deliciosa,* seedlings
Jade Plant—*Crassula argentea*
Japanese Sweet Flag—*Acorus gramineus*
Malaysian Dracaena—*Pleomele reflexa*
Moses-in-the-Cradle—*Rhoeo spathacea*
Painted Drop Tongue—*Aglaonema crispum*
Parlor Ivy—*Philodendron scandens* subsp. *oxycardium*
Sander's Dracaena—*Dracaena sanderiana*
Silver Evergreen—*Aglaonema commutatum maculatum*
Spathe Flower—*Spathiphyllum 'Clevelandii'*
Swedish Ivy—*Plectranthus australis*
Ti Plant—*Cordyline terminalis*
Umbrella Plant—*Cyperus alternifolius*
Variegated Screw-Pine—*Pandanus veitchii*
Variegated Wandering Jew—*Tradescantia fluminensis variegata*
Wandering Jew—*Zebrina pendula*

Tradescantia fluminensis variegata

Senecio mikanioides

Chlorophytum comosum vittatum

Cyperus alternifolius

Aglaonema modestum

HOW TO GROW HOUSE PLANTS

The use of plants in the home or the landscape dates back to Egyptian times. Trees were grown in large containers carved from rock. One of the earliest reports of nursery practices dates back to 3,500 years ago when frankincense trees were transplanted in containers from the Somali coast, to be grown in the gardens of Europe.

Today, tropical plants large and small from the jungles near the equator are cultured and conditioned by nursery men for growth in our homes and offices. They are adaptable to living-room temperatures of 65° to 85° Fahrenheit. Some plants prefer 55° to 70°, as in the cool lobby or entryway.

Flowering plants and cacti prefer sunny locations and can be grown on the sun porch or window sill, while others, such as palms and ferns, prefer the low light areas of a room corner. Plants like *cyperus* and *spathiphyllum* find a pool in a solarium duplicates their native habitat along the banks of a tropical stream.

Light

There are three major environmental factors that limit the growth and well-being of

General Electric Model 214

plants: light, temperature and moisture. The foremost of these is light.

The importance of adequate light cannot be overemphasized for growing indoor plants. A plant's survival depends on available water and nutrients, proper temperature and energy. House plants derive energy from some source of light. That light is the most critical of the house plant's needs. Sun is the dominating natural source of light, yet many of our foliage plants that come from our shaded jungle habitats will survive in the dimly lit interiors of our homes and public buildings. When light is transmitted to the leaf of a plant it energizes the chloroplasts which in turn convert to chemical energy. In the process energy is used to combine carbon dioxide from the air with water in the cells to form carbohydrates (starches and sugars) and oxygen. This is the food manufacturing process called photosynthesis. The carbohydrates produced are translocated throughout the plant to grow leaves, stems and roots.

Where light is very poor or nonexistent there would be no photosynthesis, no production of carbohydrates and consequently no growth, and eventually the plant dies.

Hence, there are three important light factors that affect the survival of plants: 1) *intensity*, 2) *quality* and 3) *duration*.

Intensity

Intensity is the controlling factor of food manufacturing; with more light, more food is produced. Many of our foliage house plants, being natives of our tropical rain forests, are injured (sunburned) when placed in full sun. Thus, it is necessary to know the light requirements of your plants. Adequate light is often available near windows. Where a natural light source is not enough, it must be supplemented with artificial light or the plant must be grown in artificial light alone.

The intensity of light is measured in several ways. Horticulturists measure indoor light in terms of footcandles. A footcandle is a unit of illumination on a surface that is one foot from a uniform point source of light of one candle and equal to one lumen per square foot. It can be measured with a direct reading meter such as General Electric model 214. The new type 214 pocket light meter has three scales: 10 to 50, 50-250 and 200-1000 footcandles. Scale selection is made by a three-position switch located on the side of the meter. Readings from 20 to 50 fc and from 100 to 250 fc are accurate within plus or minus 10 percent; all other readings within plus or minus 15 percent. The new pocket model is color and cosine corrected. Meter is available through General Electric lamp distributors and lamp sales offices.

Light intensity readings are taken at the plant level. When light intensity is known one can increase or decrease the lighting to meet a plant's requirements.

Quality

The quality of light is the second important factor. This is measured in millimicrons or angstrom units (10 angstrom units = 1 millimicron). Growth response in plants is due primarily to red and blue wavelengths of light. Incandescent bulbs produce a larger proportion of red light spectrum while fluorescent lights produce predominantly blue. These factors are important when growing plants under artificial light alone. Most plants will flower under fluorescent lighting using cool white or a combination of cool white and warm white. Horticultural tubes are in use which supply both red and blue in a wide spectrum. For maintenance of foliage, cool white light gives the highest intensity that is beneficial.

Duration

Duration of light is a measurement of the total number of footcandles of light received. This is the product of the intensity reading of footcandles times the number of hours light strikes the plant. The longer the time the plant receives light, the more food is produced. When plants are grown in low light areas they should be lighted for longer periods to counteract low light intensity.

Most plants will maintain fairly well with twelve to fourteen hours daily of artificial light intensity in footcandle requirements of a species.

A portable light cart for starting and growing plants

174

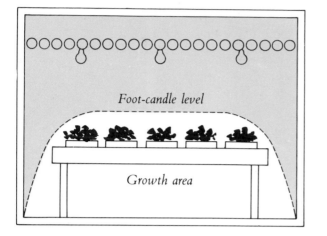

With lamps mounted crosswise over bench, footcandle level drops off at ends, where light is absorbed by walls.

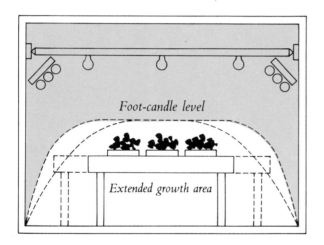

With lamps mounted lengthwise over bench, light falls off at ends. Extra rows of lamps near the walls provide more uniform lighting and increased growing area.

Supplemental plant lighting

Additional light is often desirable and necessary to bring the light requirements up to the preferred footcandle reading. This can be supplied from either fluorescent fixtures of various design or incandescent sources. Other introductions of light may be scheduled. A plant on an end table receiving light from a large window can be rotated a quarter turn a month or at each watering.

REFERENCE: Plant Growth Lighting: Bulletin TP 127 General Electric Co.

This maintains well-developed leaves on all sides. Plants moved from low to high light areas and vice versa will benefit likewise. Plants may be left for a month without harm, then exchanged to their former location. Plants can be moved to a table or floor lamp for supplementary evening lighting. Incandescent floods or reflector spots may be installed for supplementary lighting. Distance from plants is considered because of heating effects. A 150-watt flood lamp is placed not less than four feet from the plant. A 150-watt spotlight must be at least eight feet from the foliage.

Light levels for house plants

The following list of light levels is expressed as readings in footcandles and as approximate light source locations in a building. Light references listed under culture of individual species are corresponding terms of **low, medium, high** and **very high**.

150-watt floodlamp placed at least four feet from foliage

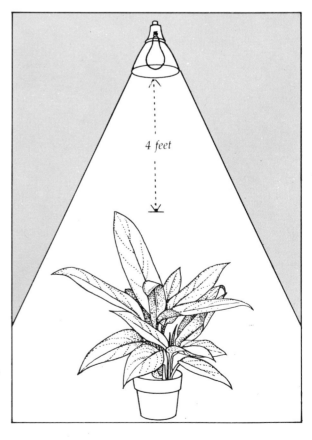

4 feet

Low—A minimum light level of 25 foot-candles and a preferred level of 75-200 footcandles (locations more than eight feet from large windows with no direct light).

Medium—A minimum of 75-100 foot-candles and a preferred level of 200-500 footcandles (an average well-lighted area four to eight feet from large window).

High—A minimum of 200 footcandles and a preferred level of 500 footcandles (areas within four feet of a large window facing south, east or west).

Very high—A minimum of 1,000 foot-candles and a preferred level of over 1,000 footcandles (on or at a sunny window sill facing south).

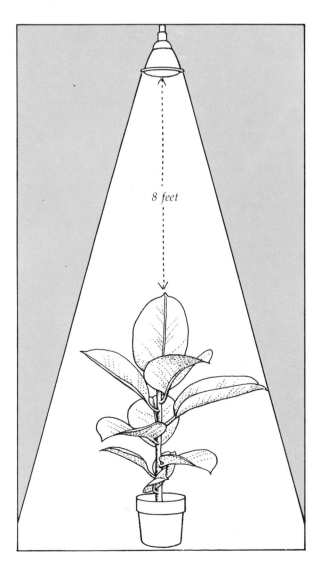

Temperature

Tropical plants, because of their geographical locations, are thought by some to require high temperatures. Many of our best house plants grow at high altitudes and thrive best with cooler minimum temperatures of 45° to 50° F., while plants growing in lower elevations grow best at 75° to 85°.

Desert plants accustomed to hot, bright days thrive best with cooler nights. When the physiology of the plant is understood, we realize that the cooler temperatures of our living quarters are beneficial for plants. Cool nights are needed for the translocation of manufactured sugars from the leaves to the roots and other growing parts.

It is a practice of commercial growers to set the night temperature of their greenhouses to run 10° Fahrenheit lower than day temperature.

In most situations, the temperatures cannot be changed and the plants must be happy with existing temperatures. In general, we find there are two ranges of temperature in our interior environments, **cool** and **warm**.

Warm we define as 75° Fahrenheit, with variations from 60° to 85°. These conditions are found in our homes and offices.

Cool we define as 60° Fahrenheit, with variations from 50° to 70°. Such conditions are found in lobbies and enclosed sun porches.

For the purpose of general reference and classification of the plant's requirements in this book, we will indicate the temperatures as follows:

Warm: day, 70° to 85° Fahrenheit
night, 60° to 65°

Cool: day, 60° to 70° Fahrenheit
night, 50° to 55°

Degrees Fahrenheit to degrees Celsius (Centigrade) conversion factor: $(°F. - 32) \times 5/9 = °C$.

150-watt spotlamp placed at least eight feet from foliage

WATERING HOUSE PLANTS

Overwatering is the greatest cause of plant problems. Many plants are lost because of overwatering. A plant's roots require air as well as water. Saturated soils exclude oxygen, causing the roots to rot. The plant is no longer able to take up nourishment.

Underwatering or drying out of the plant can be almost as serious. It is easier to detect this problem, because the leaves wilt readily. When the soil becomes too dry, the roots are injured and can no longer take up water. This occurs because the nutrient level becomes concentrated or too high and a burning effect upon the roots takes place. Free water must always be present to keep the nutrients dissolved for uptake by the plant.

It is not easy to decide how much to water or how often. Some plants like palms and ferns must never dry out, while peperomias and wax plants require a drier soil. Plants like *cyperus* and *acorus* need a constantly wet soil. It can be safely stated that all plants need moisture of varying degrees.

The moisture requirements also depend on the soil mixture, the porosity of the pot, the temperature of the room and the kind and amount of light it receives.

For a practical solution and for the purpose of classification of a plant's need for water in the text, the following terms will be used:

Wet indicates plants will probably need water every other day. These plants must have a constant supply of water in the growing medium at all times. One occasion of drying out usually means damage to the leaves. Example of plants needing wet soil are *cyperus* and *acorus*.

Moist indicates plants probably need watering every three to six days. Example: palms and ferns. These kinds of plants have a fine root system that is severely injured if the soil dries out. The surface soil should not become dry between waterings.

Dry indicates plants probably need watering every eight to fourteen days. These kinds of plants have coarse roots which are adapted to dry conditions. As a result they grow slower, thus delaying the development of plant parts. The surface soil layer should always feel dry before watering. Examples are peperomia, *hoya*, cacti and succulents.

The finger test

An old rule of thumb that has withstood the test of time is: *Water when the surface of the soil feels dry to the touch*. If you have any doubt, go a little further and dig into the top a half inch. If it is dry, by all means apply water. Consider your plant's moisture requirements. Is it in the **wet**, **moist** or **dry** group? If in doubt, let it go another day. Another factor to remember is that modern soilless potting mixes are designed to drain well in a short time, allowing air to come in and yet retaining enough moisture to support plant growth.

Close observation and some note-keeping will help. Mark the calendar and put on a measured amount. A little record-keeping will in time reveal how often and how much. Experience is still the best teacher. Many home gardeners find that most of their plants need water once a week. When a regular frequency is established, most plants will acclimate to it. Above all, when you water fill the pot to the rim.

The type of container will affect the matter of watering. Containers with drainage holes at the bottom are watered until the excess water drains out and away. If a saucer is provided, this drainage water is discarded because few plants can sit in water continuously. Containers without drainage holes must have a layer of gravel in the bottom to collect excess water. To check these containers lay them on their sides in a sink so the excess can run out.

Many plants die as a result of a wet, soggy potting soil condition.

PLANTS FOR INTERIOR DECORATION

Most homeowners or apartment dwellers are pleased to have a plant growing indoors; it is a challenge to select a specific plant that can contribute to the decorative scheme of the room. The chart on the next two pages lists many plants suitable for decorating the home or office. You will find on these lists the common name of the plants, their scientific names, and the sizes of the mature plants, as well as the water and light requirements of each listing. This will assist in the selection of useful plants that will add interest, color, and charm to your home.

Small or table plants are suitable for placement on a table, chest or windowsill. Many of these smaller plants are adaptable to use in terrariums, dish gardens and hanging baskets. Table or desk plants are available in four-inch to eight-inch pot sizes. These are often used singly but can be set into a planter box to simulate a planted-out effect.

Floor plants are those plants available from two to six feet tall. They are used as individual specimens or in planter groups.

Tall plants are designated as tree plants. Some grow with a single trunk and may be grouped in a container to produce a multiple stemmed specimen. Tree plants are available from a minimum of four feet to a maximum of ceiling height. Tall plants may need to be air-layered or trimmed to maintain desired heights.

Sleek modern rooms with bold severe spaces call for plants that are dramatic. Specimen plants of tree or floor size can be used as living sculpture silhouetted against a wall.

Table-sized plants should be used singly or in groups to make an interesting arrangement. These groupings may be flowering plants, green plants, ferns or cacti. Just one beautiful begonia, orchid or bromeliad may be startling in its simplicity. Use table plants in place of, or in combination with other small accents such as books, figurines and porcelains to liven up the decor. An occasional change of plants, particularly those that are in flower, gives an added sparkle to any room.

In conventional or traditional settings, plants should be used as accessories rather than as features. Study the period of the room and select and arrange the plants in the spirit of the room. Palms, Java fig and rubber plant provide form and bulk which are often useful in dramatic groupings or room dividers. Corn plant, dragon tree, hurricane plant or Norfolk Island pine are used as floor plants and provide colorful accents.

PLANTS FOR INTERIOR LANDSCAPING

Common Name	Botanical Name	Mature Size	Light Level	Water Requirement
African Violet	*Saintpaulia* species	table plant	high	moist
Aglaonema	*Aglaonema* 'White Rajah'	table plant	low	moist
Asparagus Fern	*Asparagus densiflorus sprengeri*	table plant	medium	moist
Bamboo Palm	*Chamaedorea erumpens*	tree, floor, table plant	low	moist
Begonias	*Begonia* species and hybrids	table plant	high	moist
Belmore Palm	*Howea belmoreana*	tree, floor plant	low	moist
Boston Fern	*Nephrolepis exaltata bostoniensis*	table plant	medium	moist
Bromeliads (many species)		table plant	medium	moist
Calamondin Orange	*Citrus mitis*	table plant	high	dry
Cast-Iron Plant	*Aspidistra elatior*	table, floor plant	low	dry
Chinese Evergreen	*Aglaonema commutatum*	table plant	low	moist
Coleus	*Coleus blumei*	table plant	very high	moist
Corn Plant	*Dracaena fragrans massangeana*	floor, table plant	low	wet
Devil's Ivy	*Epipremnum aureum* (*Pothos aureus*)	table plant	medium	dry
Dragon Tree	*Dracaena marginata*	tree, floor plant	medium	wet
Dumb Cane	*Dieffenbachia amoena*	floor, table plant	medium	moist
Dumb Cane	*Dieffenbachia exotica*	table plant	medium	moist
Dwarf Date Palm	*Phoenix roebelenii*	floor, table plant	medium	wet
English Ivy	*Hedera helix*	table plant	medium	moist
False Aralia	*Dizygotheca elegantissima*	floor, table plant	high	moist
Fiddle-leaf Fig	*Ficus lyrata*	tree, floor plant	medium	moist
Flame Violet	*Episcia cupreata*	table plant	very high	wet
Geranium	*Pelargonium* hybrids and cultivars	table plant	very high	dry
Gloxinia	*Sinningia* species and cultivars	table plant	very high	wet

Grape Ivy	*Cissus rhombifolia*	table plant	medium	moist
Green Dracaena	*Dracaena deremensis*	floor, table plant	medium	wet
Green Pleomele	*Pleomele reflexa*	floor plant	medium	wet
Hurricane Plant	*Monstera deliciosa*	floor plant	high	moist
India Laurel	*Ficus microcarpa (retusa nitida)*	tree	medium	moist
Jade Plant	*Crassula argentea*	table plant	very high	dry
Japanese Loquat	*Eriobotrya japonica*	tree	very high	moist
Kangaroo Vine	*Cissus antarctica*	table plant	high	moist
Lady Palm	*Rhapis excelsa*	tree, floor plant	medium	wet
Mock Orange	*Pittosporum tobira*	floor, table plant	high	dry
Norfolk Island Pine	*Araucaria heterophylla*	tree, floor table plant	high	moist
Orchids (many species)		table plant	very high	moist/dry
Parlor Palm	*Chamaedorea elegans*	floor, table plant	low	moist
Impatiens	*Impatiens wallerana*	table plant	medium	moist
Peperomia	*Peperomia caperata*	table plant	medium	dry
Peuter Plant	*Aglaonema roebelinii*	table plant	low	moist
Philodendron, Common	*Philodendron scandens* **subsp.** *oxycardium*	table plant	low	dry
Philodendron, Self-heading	*Philodendron* hybrids	floor, table plant	medium	moist
Philodendron	*Philodendron selloum*	floor plant	low	dry
Podocarpus	*Podocarpus macrophyllus maki*	tree, floor, table plant	high	moist
Prayer Plant	*Maranta leuconeura kerchoveana*	table plant	medium	moist
Rubber Plant	*Ficus elastica decora*	tree, floor, table plant	medium	moist
Umbrella Plant	*Schefflera actinophylla*	tree, floor, table plant	high	dry
Wax Plant	*Hoya carnosa*	table plant	medium	dry
Weeping Java Fig	*Ficus benjamina exotica*	tree	medium	moist
White Flag	*Spathiphyllum* 'Mauna Loa'	table plant	medium	moist
White-striped Dracaena	*Dracaena deremensis warneckei*	table plant	medium	dry

The temperature requirements of plants listed are generally those of room temperature: 60° to 75° Fahrenheit at night and 65° to 85° during the day. Any differences are cited in the comments on individual plants. Temperatures of up to 10° lower than the limits set here are tolerated for short periods.

POTTING-SOIL FORMULAS

FORMULA A

For those plants that need a growing medium with high moisture-retention characteristics. Plants having a fine root system are included in this group. Recommended for the following plants and others of similar culture: African violet; *aglaonema; aphelandra; begonia; cyperus; dracaena;* fern; *ficus;* helxine; palm; *spathiphyllum; tolmiea.*

Material

Sphagnum peat moss ....two parts
Vermiculite or soil ....one part
Perlite or sand ....one part

*Fertilizer ingredients
for four quarts of mix**

Garden fertilizer ....two teaspoons
    (5-10-5, or 6-12-6, or 10-10-10)
Superphosphate ....two teaspoons
Ground limestone ....three teaspoons

Four quarts equal two six-inch standard-size pots. All ingredients are measured in level teaspoonfuls.

FORMULA B

For general potting. For plants that require good drainage and aeration but must not dry out completely between watering. Use for the following plants and for others with similar requirements: *Achimenes; aeschynanthus; cordyline; columnea; dieffenbachia; episcia; hoya; monstera; nephthytis; philodendron; pandanus; peperomia.*

Material

Sphagnum peat moss ....one part
Vermiculite or soil ....one part
Perlite or sand ....one part

*Fertilizer ingredients
for four quarts of mix*

Garden fertilizer ....two teaspoons
    (5-10-5, or 6-12-6, or 10-10-10)
Superphosphate ....two teaspoons
Ground limestone ....three teaspoons

FORMULA C

For desertlike plants and some succulent plants with a root system that will withstand periods of dryness between watering. Plants having coarse tubers or rhizomatous roots are in this category. Following are recommended and others with similar culture requirements: *Aloe; astrophytum;* bromeliads; *cereus; crassula; gasteria; kalanchoe; lithops; mammillaria; opuntia; sedum; sempervivum.*

Material

Sphagnum peat moss ....two parts
Perlite (coarse) ....one part
Sand (coarse) ....one part

*Fertilizer ingredients
for four quarts of mix*

Garden fertilizer ....two teaspoons
    (5-10-5, or 6-12-6, or 10-10-10)
*Superphosphate ....two teaspoons
Ground limestone ....three teaspoons

When mixing for cactus, use two teaspoons of bone meal instead of superphosphate.

FORMULA D

For seed sowing.

Material

Sphagnum peat moss ....one part
(screened with a one-fourth-inch mesh sieve)
Vermiculite ....one part

*Fertilizer ingredients
for four quarts of mix*

Ammonium nitrate...........one teaspoon
Superphosphate ....two teaspoons
Ground limestone ....three teaspoons

Alternatively, one can use some of the wide range of proprietary potting soils or seed-sowing mixes. In Britain the John Innes potting and seed-growing composts can be recommended, or any of the all-peat formulations.

Soilless mixtures are recommended for house plants. Garden soil formerly used in potting mixtures for plant growing is becoming scarce. Its composition varies with each source, and it usually needs sterilization to get rid of weed seeds, disease and insects.

Soilless mixes can be purchased from garden stores and plant shops. The mixes come in packages of assorted sizes and are packed in polyethylene (polythene) bags for convenient storage. They are mixed with nutrients, ready for use. Some are formulated for foliage plants, for African violets, for cacti, for other plants and for seed sowing.

Hints for home mixing:
1. *Peat moss should be moistened two to three days before mixing.*
2. *Peat moss and other ingredients should be thoroughly mixed together.*
3. *Fertilizer nutrients should be carefully measured and mixed together.*
4. *All materials should be spread on a clean surface and turned with a scoop shovel. The pile should be turned at least five times to ensure thorough mixing.*
5. *Mixes may be stored for future use in polyethylene bags or plastic trash cans with covers.*

Fertilizer Quantities for Large Amounts of Mixes

Material	For one bushel	For one cubic yard
Ammonium nitrate	3 tablespoons	2 pounds
Garden fertilizer (5-10-5, or 6-12-6, or 10-10-10)	6 tablespoons	5 pounds
Superphosphate (0-20-0)	2 tablespoons	2 pounds
Ground limestone	10 tablespoons	10 pounds
Bone meal	2 tablespoons	5 pounds
*Potassium nitrate (13-0-44)	2½ tablespoons	1 pound
or		
*Calcium nitrate (15.5-0-0)	2½ tablespoons	1½ pounds
*Fritted trace elements	½ teaspoon	2 ounces

*Add these fertilizer ingredients to soilless mixes (without soil) in addition to garden fertilizers, superphosphate and ground limestone. Dolemite limestone, containing magnesium, is preferred to ground limestone if available. Use at the same rate.

METRIC SYSTEM CONVERSION GUIDE

Dry material weight
1 ounce (avoirdupois) = 28.4 grams (gm)
1 pound (lb) = 453.6 grams

Volume
1 bushel (bu) = 1.24 cubic feet = 35.2 liters
1 cubic yard = 27.5 bushels = 765 liters

Capacity
1 dry quart = 0.908 liters

Length
1 inch = 2.54 centimeters (cm)
1 foot = 0.31 meters (m)

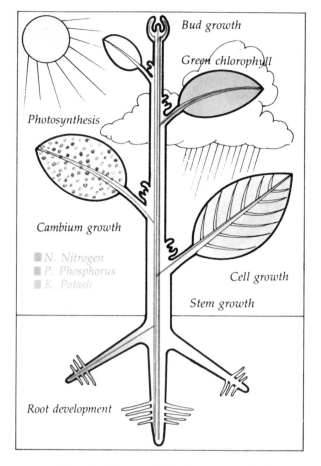

Bud growth

Green chlorophyll

Photosynthesis

Cambium growth

■ *N. Nitrogen*
■ *P. Phosphorus*
■ *K. Potash*

Cell growth

Stem growth

Root development

The role of plant food for the growing plant

FERTILIZERS

"N.P.K." stands for the *major* plant nutrients used by growing plants. "N" is for nitrogen, which makes green color and growth. "P" is for phosphorus, which gives the plant sturdy growth, and "K" is for potash, which furnishes energy for over-all plant development.

There are also *minor* elements, numbering about fifteen in all. These include chemicals like iron, magnesium, boron, zinc, etc.

A package of fertilizer marked 5-10-5 expresses the percentage of each of the major elements, i.e., 5 percent nitrogen, 10 percent phosphorus and 5 percent potash.

Minor elements are usually included in most fertilizer formulas and may not be indicated by chemical names or percentages.

Water-soluble forms of plant food are the most common and convenient to use for house plants, such as a 20-20-20 formula. They are sold as a powder, liquid or in tablet form. It is important to follow the manufacturer's directions for mixing. But apply only at one half the rate recommended.

Dry-granular garden type, such as a 5-10-5, 6-12-6 or 10-10-10.

Controlled-release fertilizer such as Osmocote (14-14-14 or 18-9-9), MagAmp (7-40-6) or Peters (14-7-7) are favored by commercial plant growers, and some brands are now available in consumer-size packages. These formulas are designed so that one application will last from four to ten months, depending on formulation.

Water-soluble type: Potted plants growing in soilless potting mixes need more frequent applications than plants growing in potting mixtures containing soil. The design of soilless mixes affords better drainage and aeration, requiring more frequent watering, which results in faster leaching or loss of nutrients.

Artificially lighted plants may be fertilized once a month with a *water-soluble fertilizer;* plants under normal indoor light conditions, every two months. These are general recommendations. For individual plant recommendation, refer to culture.

Dry-granular type: Apply once every four months regardless of light conditions. Use at the following rates of application:

A scant one third teaspoon per four-inch pot

One level teaspoon per six-inch pot

One level tablespoon per eight-inch pot

Controlled-release type: Read the recommendations on the package before using. Where light intensity is high or a greenhouse is used for growing, it may be necessary to supplement with a water-soluble type.

A fertilizer is not a cure-all for plant trouble or a substitute for problems of water or light. An overdose of fertilizer or an application too often will damage or kill your plant.

If in doubt—DON'T FERTILIZE.

PRUNING, TRAINING AND CLEANING

Pruning: Prune, trim, pinch—any way to accomplish the desirable shape for your plant. Judiciously exercising one of these techniques gives your plant the characteristics which are typical of its variety.

Pruning will remedy stretching for light, promote branching and provide cuttings for starting more plants.

Prune to remove large sections if necessary, to maintain shape and desirable height. Prune to remove dead branches and diseased parts. Most plants produce new growth by being cut back to six or eight inches from the soil to get rid of legginess.

Plants not prunable are single-stem palms; cluster-type palms are pruned by removing tallest shoots from the base of the plant, if necessary.

Pinch to remove the very tip of the shoot. This will control height and induce branching. Pinch the tips with the fingernails or with scissors. Pinch just above a leaf joint or node. Start when plants are young, not over six inches tall, and pinch regularly as growth progresses.

Plants that branch naturally, such as African violet, Boston fern, gloxinia and watermelon peperomia, require no pinching. Aluminum plant, geranium, coleus, fuchsia and tuberous begonia are pinched occasionally because they will grow into a single stem without a pinch.

Disbudding of side buds on flowering plants increases the size of the main flower buds. This technique is used to produce show material for exhibitions. Tuberous begonia responds well to this practice. Pinch out the buds as soon as they are large enough to handle.

Disbranching, like disbudding or pinching, removes side branches of flowering plants like geranium and fuchsia. It is used to train plants to a single trunk or tree specimen. These are called "standards." An example illustrated in this book is classic myrtle. Plants are started from cuttings and allowed to grow until they reach the desired height. The trunk is formed by a periodic removal of side branches.

Training plants is another technique used for climbing plants and for developing shapes. Philodendron, ivy, *scindapsus, hoya,* passion vine and others need support or special treatment to display their normal growth habits. The support should be inconspicuous and of such design as maintains the plant in its natural shape. Some of the materials used are cork bark, driftwood and tree fern, which are suitable for foliage types like philodendron. Trellises made of wire, steel rods or green vinyl-covered fencing are used for climbing vines and bulbous plants like the glory lily.

Shape plants by rotating from time to time. Plants will grow to be one-sided if light falls on one side of a plant continuously. Start practice when plants are small.

Cleaning: Good housekeeping means dust-free, insect-free and even disease-free plants. Cleaning plants removes the dust. Pick up dead leaves, check for insects, trim off diseased leaves or stems to produce healthy plants.

Wash foliage: Don't use milk, olive oil or liquid wax for cleaning foliage. These substances leave an oily deposit on the leaf which then collects dust and, if used on the under side, may clog the breathing pores.

Use a sink spray or bathtub shower with warm water. In summer take outdoors and use the garden hose and a fine-nozzle spray, or let the rain bathe the plant.

A generally safe recommendation is to use a few drops of a dishwashing detergent in warm water with a soft sponge to remove the dust. Holding a leaf in hand and carefully sponging the under side of the leaf helps control red spider mites.

When to repot

In winter, house plants slow down in growth and appear to be dormant. This is due to the reduction in light intensity and the shorter days. Because of these conditions, spring and early summer, when growth is resumed, are times to repot.

Plants growing under artificial lights for twelve to sixteen hours a day are in a condition of active growth and may be repotted when needed.

A plant should be repotted to a larger-size pot when its roots form a close mesh surrounding the ball of potting mix. This is referred to as a pot-bound condition.

A plant also may be repotted when it appears unhealthy. Repotting is done to replace the potting mix to improve drainage and aeration.

Shifting seedlings from small pots to the next larger size will assure continuation of growth.

How to repot

STEP 1. To remove the plant, place your fingers on the soil surface, grasp the pot with the other hand, turn to inverted position and jolt the rim against the edge of a workbench until the plant slips free of the pot.

STEP 2. Remove a thin layer of surface soil at top of ball. Loosen roots at bottom and break away drainage material. If roots are excessively coiled, trim away about one third of roots at bottom. When roots are heavily meshed on the sides of the ball, lightly cut vertically by shallow slashes in three places with a sharp knife. This will encourage branching of roots which will grow into the fresh media.

STEP 3. The pot size chosen should permit one-half inch or more space between the ball and the inside wall of the pot. The larger the pot the more space for potting mix. If a large amount of mix is removed, you can repot in the same size or smaller pot, although normally you would shift to the next larger size.

When new clay pots are used, soak in water for a day or so before use.

For pots with a drainage hole, place a few pieces of broken crock over the hole, starting with the six-inch size. A crock for smaller pots is not needed. If there is no drainage hole, follow the procedure of building a well as discussed on page 187.

STEP 4. Accomplish the repotting job by back-filling with the mix, tamping with a potting stick to prevent air-pockets.

Set the plant low enough so that the finished surface is lower than the rim of the pot in order to hold ample water.

Surface space for water:

Pot size	Depth of space
3-inch	¼ inch
4-inch	½ inch
5-, 6-, 7-inch	¾ inch
8-inch	1¼ inch
9-, 10-, 12-inch	1½ inch

A clay pot may be installed inside a larger decorator-type container. A well to catch excess drainage water is constructed in the bottom of the larger container. The depth of the drainage material is determined by the location of the pot rim at the top. It should set just below the rim of the larger container. The space between the walls of the two containers is filled with peat or sphagnum moss.

Water is applied to the moss and seeps through the clay pot to give the plant a constant supply of water, but a limited amount which will restrain the growth of the plant.

Choosing pot size: The question is—"Do I use a shallow pot, a three-quarter size or a standard-size pot?" Clay pots are made in shallow pans, used for small bulbs and creeping plants; three-quarter size for bulbs, ferns, etc.; and the standard size for general potting. A pot's size is designated as the diameter of its top rim.

The character of the root system determines the depth of the pot used. Where roots run to the bottom of the ball, it is evident that a standard-size pot is required. If the roots are few and congregate in the upper soil mass, use a shallow container.

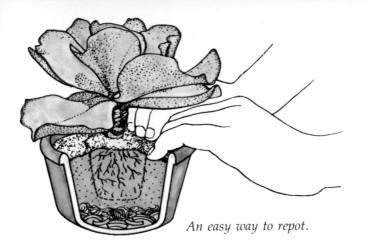

An easy way to repot.

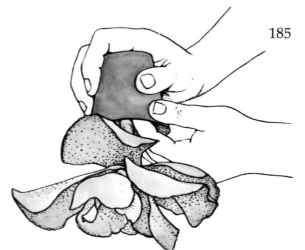

Step 1. *To remove plant from pot, place your fingers on the soil surface, invert and jolt rim against edge of table until plant slips free of the pot.*

Step 2. *Trim away one third of roots if excessively coiled.*

Step 3. *For pots with a drainage hole, place a few pieces of broken crock over the hole.*

Step 4. *Accomplish repotting by backfilling with the mix, firming with a potting stick to prevent air pockets.*

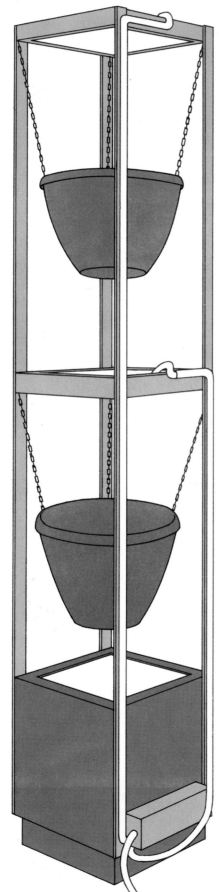

*A light rack
for hanging baskets*

POTS

Kinds of pots

Clay pots, plastic pots, ceramic containers, polystyrene and glass vessels provide receptacles for growing house plants.

Clay pots come in sizes ranging from a thimble to fourteen inches in diameter, or even larger if you don't mind the cost. Clay pots are preferred by many because the porosity of the clay allows air to move in and out.

Plastic is popular because the plants do not dry out so rapidly, thus cutting down on the need to water frequently. When a well-drained and aerated mix is used, plants do as well in plastic as in clay.

Saucers made of plastic or rubber are placed under pots to catch runoff of water.

Driftwood for growing epiphytic type and other plants

Creative designs of plant containers vary in form, color, texture and basic material. For interiors, select a type best suited to your decor.

Ceramic, polystyrene and fiberglass containers usually are without drainage holes. A "well" must be constructed to receive the drainage water. To do this, put one-half inch or more gravel (the larger the pot, the more gravel needed) in the bottom. Cover the gravel with a layer of long-fibered sphagnum moss to prevent filtration of the potting mix. The mix should be placed on top of this.

Other growing structures: Tree-fern slab and cork bark are practical supports for orchids, bromeliads and epiphytic ferns. These plants are tied to the supports, using a cushion of sphagnum moss for moisture.

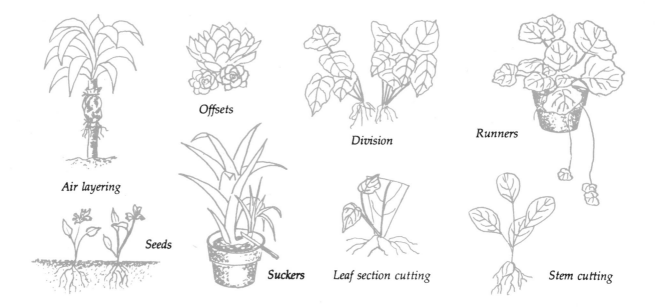

Air layering

Offsets

Division

Runners

Seeds

Suckers

Leaf section cutting

Stem cutting

STARTING NEW PLANTS

Methods of Propagation

Starting of new plants from older plants is called propagation. In many species new plants are started from seed. Seed, however, is not always viable, and since seed plants do not always resemble their parents, it is desirable to propagate by other means—namely, cuttings. Other methods also used for starting house plants include division, runners and suckers, air layering and a more skillful operation, grafting and budding.

Cuttings are selected from healthy plants free from insects, disease and nutritional problems. Plants in flower are generally not used because blossoming may inhibit rooting. The best time to take cuttings is spring and summer. Take cuttings from plants growing under artificial lights at any time of the year.

Rooting media: Choose a medium that will provide good drainage and aeration with good water-holding capacity. For general use a good grade of sand will serve well. Excellent media are perlite, a volcanic ash, and vermiculite, an expanded mica, sold under the name of Terralite.

Propagation structures: A clay or plastic pot or tray made of styrofoam or plastic that will hold about three inches of medium is suitable. Enclosing the container within a polyethylene bag will prevent loss of moisture and facilitate watering care. The cover may be removed in a week or left on until cuttings are rooted.

Planting and watering: When cuttings are prepared, stick two to three inches deep into the rooting medium and press firmly. Water well and keep moist but not saturated. The main problem is to keep the cuttings from wilting.

Chemical aids: Chemicals known as growth regulators or rooting hormones are used to hasten the rooting of hard-to-root plants. Cuttings from plants such as English ivy, *acuba* and citrus will root better if so treated. Softwood cuttings of coleus, geranium, begonia and others should not be treated. Great care should be used to follow the directions of the manufacturer.

Care after rooting: When roots have formed one-fourth to one inch long, the cutting is ready for potting. After potting ample water is needed to keep the plant from wilting.

Terminal cuttings

Consists of terminal growing point of the stem with one or more nodes below. Sectional cuttings use a portion of the stem with two or more nodes without the terminal growing point. Examples: coleus, ivy, peperomia, philodendron and begonia. Make a cutting three to six inches long, using a sharp knife. Cut through the stem below a node or leaf joint. Trim off one or two leaves from the bottom of the cutting and insert in the rooting medium. The more leaves left on the top portion, the more surface for food manufacture.

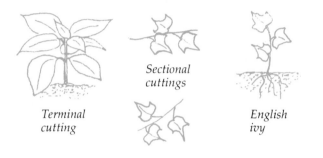

Terminal
cutting

Sectional
cuttings

English
ivy

Leaf cuttings

Consists of one leaf only, used for propagating rex begonia, *sedum* and *sansevieria*.

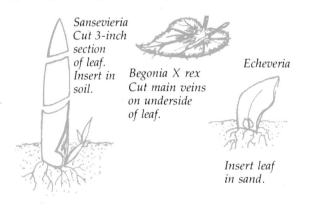

Sansevieria
Cut 3-inch
section
of leaf.
Insert in
soil.

Begonia X rex
Cut main veins
on underside
of leaf.

Echeveria

Insert leaf
in sand.

Leaf-petiole cuttings

Use a stem with leaf attached for starting plants of tuberous-rooted begonias, gloxinia, peperomia and African violet.

Peperomia
root in soil

African violet
root in water

Leaf-bud cuttings

Consists of a piece of stem and one or more nodes for propagation of English ivy, wax plant, *nephthytis,* philodendron, German ivy and *cissus* vine.

Philodendron

New plant

Leaf sectioning

Leaf sectioning is a method used mainly to start new plants from large-leaved fibrous begonias and peperomias

Select large, healthy, mature leaves, not the oldest ones. Cut off a leaf from a plant and remove the stalk or petiole. Make pie-shaped pieces of the leaf. With a sharp knife cut from the main center vein, but between the radiating leaf veins, to the outer edge of the leaf. Sections of leaf root best if a piece of a large vein remains attached to the pointed end of the pie-shaped section.

Insert the sections to a depth of half an inch (pointed end down) into the potting medium. Place at 45° angle and give support by positioning a wooden plant label at the back side. This will help excess moisture to drain from leaf and prevent the leaf section from collapsing on the moist medium.

A new plantlet will develop at the base of the cutting when two or three leaves have formed. Pot and cut away the old leaf, which is no longer needed.

Begonia X rex leaf

Plant in moist atmosphere.

Cut wedge-shaped leaf
sections with
part of the
large vein.

Sand or peat

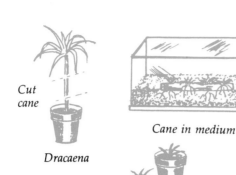

Cut
cane

Dracaena

Cane in medium

When rooted
remove from cane
and pot.

Cane cuttings

A method of cutting leafless stems or canes of tall, leggy plants like dracaenas, *dieffenbachia* and *cordyline* into four- to six-inch stem sections for rooting. Cut canes and dry overnight to callus the ends. The next day place them on a propagation medium horizontally and cover to keep moist. Buds or "eyes" on the canes will sprout in one to two months, producing roots. The cane may be planted upright or cuttings removed and planted to develop into plants with their own roots.

Fern

Cut or gently
pull apart rootstalk
or rhizome.

Division

Division is the separation of the crown of the plant into one or more growing points. To accomplish this, remove the plant from the pot and cut through the root stalk or rhizome of the plant. It is advisable to leave more than one growing point to a plant. Pot and water thoroughly. Kinds which are

started by division are cast-iron plant, *Cyperus*, piggyback, spider plant, fern and others.

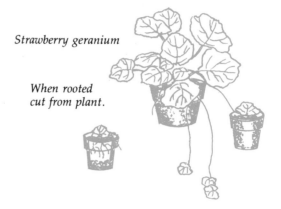

Strawberry geranium

When rooted
cut from plant.

Runners

Runners are vinelike cords originating from the base of the main plant. These cords or stems usually have nodes with the ability to root and produce a new plant. The strawberry geranium, *episcia* and Boston fern are some of the house plants that have runners producing plantlets. These plantlets can be cut off and potted like a cutting or rooted in a pot of mix alongside the parent plant while attached. When rooted, it is cut from the parent plant and shifted to a larger pot when needed.

Hen and chickens

Twist or slightly
pull offset,
then pot.

Offsets

Offsets are similar to runners, but, instead of the new plants occurring on vinelike stems, they are produced close to the base of the parent plant. Hen-and-chickens of the rock garden is an example. Century plant, aloes and screw-pine are some house plants that make offsets that are used for starting new plants. A twist or slight pull removes offsets, which then become new plants when potted.

Suckers

Suckers are secondary growth that originates from ground level or below, from adventitious roots or underground rhizomes. As an example, bromeliads produce these growths which can be cut or broken off, then potted to grow as normal plants. Staghorn fern produces suckerlike growths alongside and close to basal female fronds.

Sucker growth should be of a good size, with some mature leaves or stems, when it is separated from the parent plant. It is likewise desirable to have a few roots in evidence at the base of the section.

Bromeliad

*Cut or break off
sucker at base of plant.*

Root in peat moss, then pot.

Bulbs

There are two kinds. One type is like the hardy bulbs of narcissus and tulips, with thick layers wrapped around the bud; the other is like the Easter lily, with separate overlapping scales. Most bulbs produce tiny bulblets between scales or layers that eventually form new or offset bulbs. A method of using separated scales is also used. Most plant people purchase new bulbs, like the amaryllis, and grow them year after year rather than take the time and patience required for propagation, which is a slow process. Bulbous plants are also raised from seed.

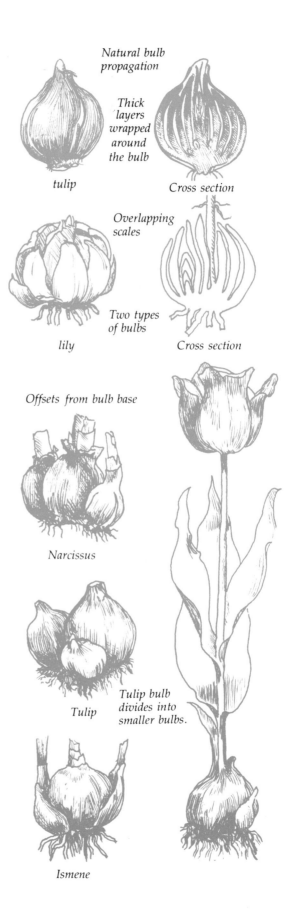

*Natural bulb
propagation*

Thick layers wrapped around the bulb

tulip

Cross section

Overlapping scales

Two types of bulbs

lily

Cross section

Offsets from bulb base

Narcissus

Tulip

Tulip bulb divides into smaller bulbs.

Ismene

Tubers

Tubers are underground roots or stems, cylindrical, oblong or rounded in shape, made up of fleshy or woody tissue. Stem tubers may bear several tiny scalelike leaves with buds or eyes capable of sprouting new plants; root tubers have buds at the crown or upper end only, where they are attached to the stem. Stored food in the tuber supports a new plant until it grows feeding roots. The potato is a common example of a stem tuber, the dahlia of a root tuber. Many house plants grow from tubers. *Caladium* can be divided by cutting the tuber into sections, each containing a bud or eye. Cut when new shoot growth occurs, which is usually in late winter or early spring. Large-sized sections make the largest plants. Cut surfaces of tubers are dried overnight and dusted with ferbam or sulfur before being potted. Glory lily is best repotted after the foliage dies down and old and new tubers are sorted out by detaching at the stem ends. New tubers showing a growing tip are best for starting. Tuberous begonias are propagated by cutting the tubers into sections at the time new shoot growth becomes apparent. Gloxinia and *rechsteineria* are started by the same method as tuberous begonia.

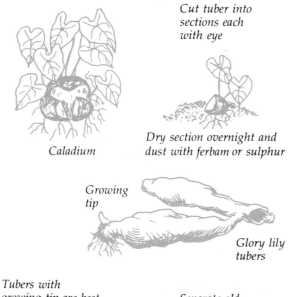

Caladium

Cut tuber into sections each with eye

Dry section overnight and dust with ferbam or sulphur

Growing tip

Glory lily tubers

Tubers with growing tip are best for starting new plant.

Separate old from new end tubers.

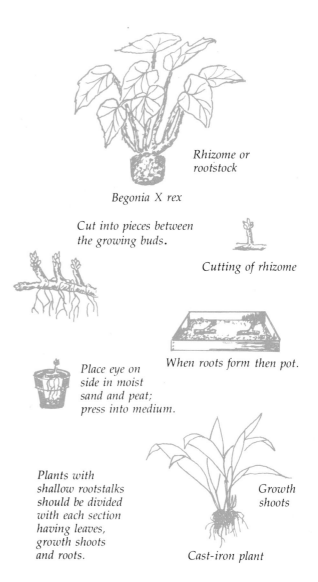

Rhizome or rootstock

Begonia X rex

Cut into pieces between the growing buds.

Cutting of rhizome

When roots form then pot.

Place eye on side in moist sand and peat; press into medium.

Plants with shallow rootstalks should be divided with each section having leaves, growth shoots and roots.

Growth shoots

Cast-iron plant

Rhizomes and propagules

A rhizome or rootstock is a thickened underground stem but is sometimes found on the surface; it consists of buds or eyes which produce shoots and grow roots to take up food. Some rhizomes are large and robust like those of Rex begonia. Others are small and scaly like those of *Achimenes*. In *Achimenes* these are sometimes found as structures in the axils of leaves; since they do not appear underground they do not fit the definition of the term *rhizome*. Instead scientists use the word *propagule*—a term used for any unspecified unit of propagation.

Methods of propagation

Germination of seeds or bulblets which are attached to the plant is one of nature's ways of starting new plants in the survival pattern. Small plants take shape and grow while attached to the parent plant. Succulents like *kalanchoe* produce plantlets along the margins of leaves. Piggyback plantlets are produced on top of the leaf blade at the petiole or stem. *Cyperus* produces plants in the axils of the leaf whorl. Small plants of *kalanchoe* are easily removed and transplanted to pots, many with roots already started. The piggyback is started from a leaf and petiole inserted in the propagation medium so that the base of the leaf is close to the medium. Roots are produced at the base of the leaf to nourish the new plantlet. When potted the old leaf is trimmed away.

Ferns are reproduced by viviparous propagation. *Asplenium viviparum, A. bulbiferum,* *Polystichum setiferum (angulare), P. aculeatum, Woodwardia radicans, W. orientalis,* commonly known as mother ferns, are capable of producing bulblets from which small plants arise. The small fern plants are found growing on the upper side of a frond, usually at the axil of the leaflet (pinnae) and rachis (stalk). To start these plantlets on their own a frond is hooked onto the surface of a tray or pot of sand and peat moss. When roots are well developed, remove to individual pots. A method used by the author is to remove the plantlet to a Jiffy 7 peat pellet. These are placed in a polyethylene bag or a glass enclosure in which humid atmosphere is maintained. In a glass case provision for a crack of air and occasional spray with an atomizer is beneficial. Growth is rapid and plantlets are ready to be transplanted to pots in about six to eight weeks. Lighting with fluorescent lights of 800 to 1,000 footcandles for 14 to 16 hours greatly accelerates growth.

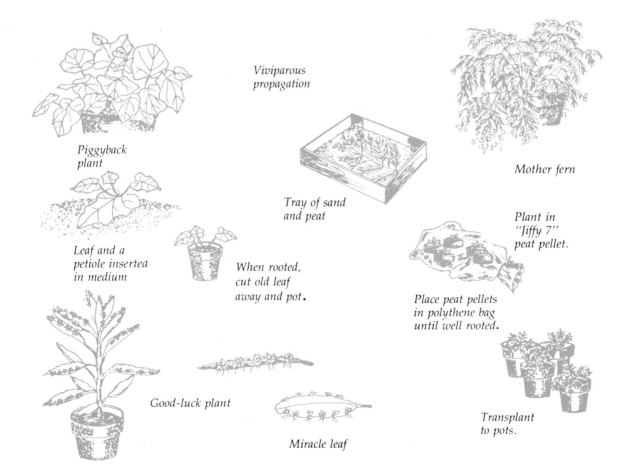

Piggyback plant

Leaf and a petiole inserted in medium

When rooted, cut old leaf away and pot.

Good-luck plant

Miracle leaf

Viviparous propagation

Tray of sand and peat

Mother fern

Plant in "Jiffy 7" peat pellet.

Place peat pellets in polythene bag until well rooted.

Transplant to pots.

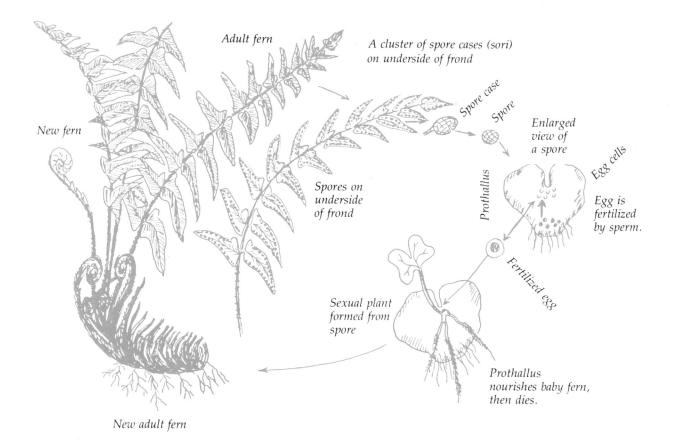

Adult fern

A cluster of spore cases (sori) on underside of frond

New fern

Spore case

Spore

Enlarged view of a spore

Spores on underside of frond

Prothallus

Egg cells

Egg is fertilized by sperm.

Fertilized egg

Sexual plant formed from spore

Prothallus nourishes baby fern, then dies.

New adult fern

Spores

Spores cause sexual reproduction in ferns. Seeds are developed by flowering plants, but ferns, mosses, lichens, fungi, algae and mushrooms depend on a microscopic organ called a spore for starting new plants. On the under side of fern fronds are found groups of orange or brown dots or lines called spore cases, which hold spores. When a spore drops into an environment of water, warm temperature, nutrients and air it grows into a small flat greenish heart-shaped plantlike structure with hairlike roots. About a year is needed for it to develop into a mature fern capable of producing spores of its own. However, this is the first of two cycles in its life cycle. This plantlike organ is called a prothallus and it bears reproductive organs on its lower surface. In the presence of a drop of moisture, male and female organs mate and the germ cell develops into the second stage, a true

fern plant. For a while the fern plant is nourished by the prothallus, which eventually dies, leaving the fern to grow as an independent plant.

Fern spores are easily collected from the under side of a frond. Careful observation with a hand lens will reveal the time when spore cases split open. When this occurs, remove the frond from the plant and place on white paper to dry. In a day or two the paper will be covered with millions of spores. For further drying and storage, place in a paper envelope and sow any time after two weeks. Early spring is excellent for sowing spores.

Several methods of sowing have been used. The important factor is sterilization of media and other utensils used. Some gardeners with access to laboratory facilities attain success using agar medium. Others use the inverted clay pot in a tray of water. Some

METHODS OF SOWING SPORES

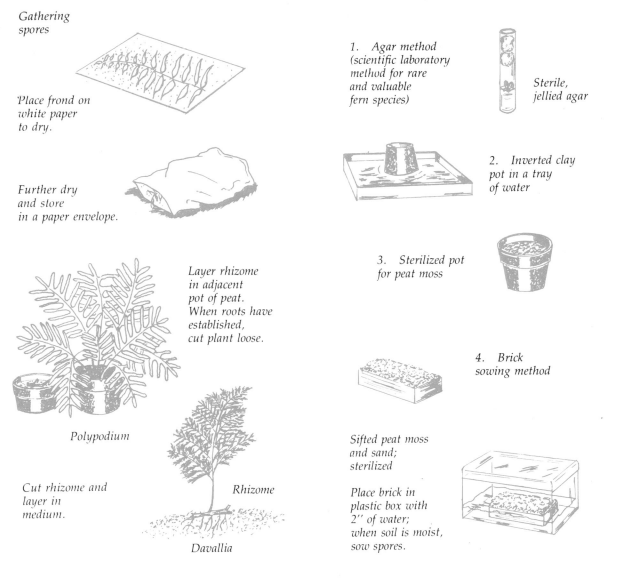

*Gathering
spores*

*Place frond on
white paper
to dry.*

*Further dry
and store
in a paper envelope.*

*Layer rhizome
in adjacent
pot of peat.
When roots have
established,
cut plant loose.*

Polypodium

*Cut rhizome and
layer in
medium.*

Rhizome

Davallia

*1.   Agar method
(scientific laboratory
method for rare
and valuable
fern species)*

*Sterile,
jellied agar*

*2.   Inverted clay
pot in a tray
of water*

*3.   Sterilized pot
for peat moss*

*4.   Brick
sowing method*

*Sifted peat moss
and sand;
sterilized*

*Place brick in
plastic box with
2" of water;
when soil is moist,
sow spores.*

sow on a sterilized pot of peat moss. A brick method is described by Arno and Irene Nehrling in their book *Propagating House Plants*. A building brick is spread on its upper surface with a layer of sifted peat moss and sand, then sterilized in an oven at 250° F. for half an hour. Place the brick in a container such as an oblong plastic food box with two inches of water added. When the sand and peat mix is moist, sow the spores on the surface. Replace cover and shade from direct light. When spores germinate and prothallia appear crack the lid to admit air and remove the shade. If fluorescent lights are available, adjust to 300 footcandles for a 16-hour period. Advance intensity to 800 or 1,000 footcandles as growth progresses. When plants are large enough to handle transplant to small, then to larger pots.

Other methods of fern propagation

Davallia and *Polypodium* are propagated by spores, but a faster process is by layering the rhizomes in adjacent pots of peat or sphagnum moss. Fasten rhizome with hairpins or tie to a ball of sphagnum moss. When roots are firmly established plant can be cut loose. Another way is by cutting rhizomes into pieces two to three inches long and laying in a propagating medium.

Air layering

A method of propagation used for hard-to-root or large-foliage plant varieties like rubber plants.

Select vigorously growing healthy shoots from pencil size up to shoots one half inch in diameter.

Remove leaves and twigs three to four inches above and below the cut to be made. The location of the cut is usually 12 to 15 inches below the top of the stem.

Two methods of making the cut are illustrated. Either one will produce satisfactory results.

(1) Make two cuts through the bark, completely encircling the twig, about one inch apart. Remove the bark between the cuts to expose the wood. Be sure the cambium, a light-green area beneath the bark, is completely removed to prevent new bark from forming.

(2) For this method, make a long slanting cut upward, about halfway through the stem. Keep the incision open by inserting a small chip of wood to prevent cambium layer of the stock from healing.

After making the cuts, enclose the exposed areas with a ball of moist sphagnum moss. Soak and squeeze the excess moisture from the ball of moss before applying to the cut. Wrap moss snugly around the twig and enclose with aluminum foil or a square of polyethylene. Tie top and bottom to prevent loss of moisture.

After roots have formed in several weeks, depending on the variety, cut just below the ball of roots and transplant to a pot. Leave moss attached but make sure moss is moist before potting. Enclose entire plant in a polyethylene bag for a week or so to insure survival.

A chemical rooting hormone has been found beneficial in hastening the rooting process for hard-to-root varieties. Only a light dusting of hormone powder need be applied to the cut surfaces.

The sphagnum ball should be checked for adequate moisture from time to time.

Besides rubber plants, species responding to the air-layering method are philodendrons, dracaenas and dieffenbachias.

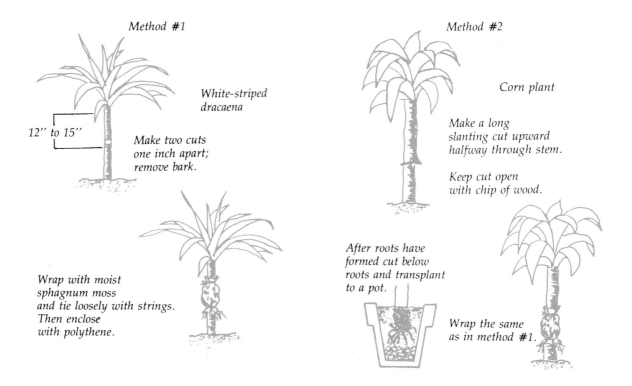

Method #1

White-striped dracaena

12″ to 15″

Make two cuts one inch apart; remove bark.

Wrap with moist sphagnum moss and tie loosely with strings. Then enclose with polythene.

Method #2

Corn plant

Make a long slanting cut upward halfway through stem.

Keep cut open with chip of wood.

After roots have formed cut below roots and transplant to a pot.

Wrap the same as in method #1.

Units:

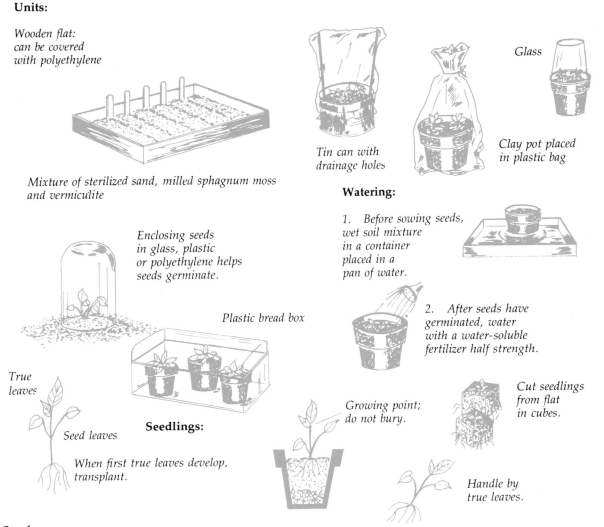

Wooden flat:
can be covered
with polyethylene

Glass

Tin can with
drainage holes

Clay pot placed
in plastic bag

Mixture of sterilized sand, milled sphagnum moss
and vermiculite

Watering:

Enclosing seeds
in glass, plastic
or polyethylene helps
seeds germinate.

1. Before sowing seeds,
wet soil mixture
in a container
placed in a
pan of water.

Plastic bread box

2. After seeds have
germinated, water
with a water-soluble
fertilizer half strength.

True
leaves

Cut seedlings
from flat
in cubes.

Seed leaves

Seedlings:

Growing point;
do not bury.

When first true leaves develop,
transplant.

Handle by
true leaves.

Seeds

Media for germination of seeds may consist of any of the following: sterilized sand, milled sphagnum moss or vermiculite. A combination of any of these may be used with good results. When the seedlings have germinated, a water-soluble fertilizer solution mixed at half strength should be used to water the medium. Nonfertilized water is used for subsequent watering.

Watering

To obtain good germination, thoroughly wet the mix by placing the container of mix to soak in a shallow pan of water. When the top of mix is moist, remove and sow the seeds. After sowing the seeds, enclose the container in a polyethylene bag until they have germinated.

Temperature and light

Place the container in a room where 65° to 70° F. can be maintained. Artificial lighting with fluorescent tubes spaced six to eight inches above seedlings should be scheduled for 14 hours a day, usually from 8:00 A.M. to 10:00 P.M.

After germination, when the first set of true leaves develops, transplant to individual pots for growing on. Seedlings should be gradually acclimated to natural light and day length over a three- to four-day period.

PLANT PROBLEMS

Many common house-plant problems are a result of faulty culture.

Common Symptom	Possible Cause	Solution
LIGHT		
Leaf wilt	Excessive heat from lights or direct sun.	Move plants farther from light source.
Foliage has a yellow color; leaves drop.	Excess light	Pull curtains for sun shield
Yellow to brown patches on leaf	Sunburn	Take out of direct sun from March to October
Weak, thin and soft growth; oldest leaves drop	Insufficient light	Increase light intensity or lengthen light period

	WATER	
Leaf wilt	Roots injured (rotting) from plant sitting in drainage water (consequent lack of oxygen) also Roots injured because of lack of water (high salt content in soil mass)	Provide drainage in bottom of pot, using crushed stone or broken pieces of crock; discard drainage water after watering Water more frequently to maintain a moist soil
Brown leaf tips, brown leaf margins	Dry atmosphere; also insufficient water	Keep potting mix moist
Leaf curl and leaf drop	Too much fertilizer, wind burn, drafts	Avoid drying out between waterings; avoid drafts

TEMPERATURE		
Weak, thin and soft growth, new leaves small; bud drop	High temperature, especially at night	Reduce night temperature by 10°
Yellow leaves, leaf drop, spots; bud drop	Low temperatures (also air pollution, gas fumes)	Increase room temperature
Rapid growth	Temperature not suitable for plant species	Check culture for recommendation

NUTRITION		
Stunted plant, leaves small, yellow-green color	Nitrogen deficiency	
Stunted plant; small leaves; leaf margins yellow, sometimes purple, sometimes gray	Phosphorus deficiency	Apply a complete fertilizer of water-soluble type, according to the manufacturer's directions on the package When deficiency is corrected, apply only at infrequent intervals; once every two to three months is recommended to maintain growth
Leaf margins yellow, then brown; lower leaves affected first, often with purplish cast	Potash deficiency	
Chlorosis or yellowing leaf between veins, with veins remaining green; young leaves affected first	Iron deficiency	Apply a chelated iron compound at manufacturer's directions

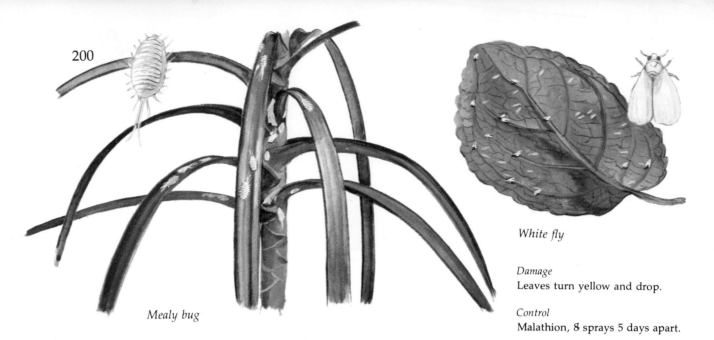

Mealy bug

White fly

Damage
Leaves turn yellow and drop.

Control
Malathion, 8 sprays 5 days apart.

Damage
Leaves turn yellow and die. Plant becomes stunted.

Control
Malathion, 2 sprays 7 to 10 days apart.

INSECTS

House-plant pests are best controlled by sprays or dips. Sprays are applied to plants with one- or two-gallon compressed-air sprayers or by hand·atomizers, such as a common pressure-spray bottle. Some plants are more difficult to wet than others. If the solution does not spread and wet the foliage, add only a few drops of a mild household detergent to one gallon of the solution.

Sprays or dips should be stirred frequently and vigorously to maintain uniform strength during application.

Recommended aerosols are very efficient and practical. Aerosols containing the ingredient Malathion in combination with Pyrethrum, Rotenone or Methoxychlor are fairly effective when used properly.

Pest aerosols for household or garden should not be used on house plants. They will burn foliage and often kill plants.

It is sometimes more practical to dip a plant. Mix the solution in a pail large enough to accommodate the plant. Turn the plant upside down, agitate to wet the stems and leaves thoroughly. A crumpled newspaper held by hand over the potting mix will prevent it from falling out.

Prevention control: Practice good housekeeping with plants. Inspect all plants and cut flowers brought into the home for "bugs." Isolate new plants for a month and look for bugs to develop.

Sterilize pots and potting mixtures to prevent infestation of soil-borne insects. Put pots and a container of potting mixture in the kitchen oven and heat to 180° for 30 minutes.

Wash foliage at least once a month to help remove mealy bugs, scale and spider mites. Soapy water used in place of pesticides is effective in removing most plant insects.

Hand-pick bugs with tweezers or toothpick when first discovered. A cotton swab dipped in rubbing alcohol will effectively kill mealy bugs and aphids on contact.

A word of caution: Pesticides used carelessly can be injurious to man, animals and plants. Always take time to read the label and follow directions. Use *only* pesticides that are labeled and carry directions for home and garden use.

SOME COMMON INSECTS OF HOUSE PLANTS	
Damage	*Control*
Aphid Sucks plant juices. New growth stunted; foliage curls. Sticky honeydew secreted that is a host to sooty-mold disease.	Malathion, 2 sprays 7 to 10 days apart
Snail *Slug* Feeds on flowers, leaves, stems and roots. Leaves a glistening trail of slime wherever it crawls.	Hand-pick at night; look under pots. Use baits containing Metaldehyde. Shallow dishes of beer near pot are partially effective
Millipede May feed on seedlings, roots, tubers, bulbs or fleshy stems of plants, but mostly eats decaying organic matter.	Eliminate hiding places and excessive organic materials. Drench soil surface with Malathion, Sevin or Diazinon
Red spider mite Yellow or brown specks on foliage; plant may become stunted and die.	Kelthane, 2 sprays 5 days apart
Scale Plant becomes yellow and slowly dies. Sticky honeydew may be present.	Malathion, 3 sprays 7 to 10 days apart

DISEASES

Some Common Diseases of House Plants

Disease	Plant
Root knot nematode disease (caused by *Meloidogyne* species)	African violet, tropical foliage plants
Leaf nematode (*Aphelenchoides* species)	African violet, peperomia, gloxinia, Rieger begonia, gardenia and tropical foliage plants
Powdery mildew (airborne fungus *Oidium* species)	African violet, begonia
Crown rot (caused by *Pythium* species)	African violet, philodendron, pothos and other tropical foliage plants
Damping-off (a complex of several diseases)	Seedlings
Leaf spot (caused by *Septoria phlytaenioides* and *Cercospora* species)	Clerodendrum
Bacterial blight (caused by *Xanthomonas pelargonii*)	Geranium
Botrytis blight (caused by airborne fungus, *Botrytis cinerea*)	Geranium, begonia, azalea
Bacterial blight (caused by *Xanthomonas begoniae*)	Begonia (Rieger begonia very sensitive)
Sooty mold (caused by fungus growth on honeydew secreted by insects)	Any plant

Overwatering, poor ventilation, use of unsterilized potting mixtures, dirty pots and failure to control insects help propagate plant diseases.

NOTE: For rates of application of recommended fungicides, follow the directions on the package.

Symptoms	Control
Infected plants appear stunted and unhealthy; wilt on warm days; root galls appear as nodules on roots	Discard infected plants and soil
Yellowish leaf spots or brownish areas that turn almost black on underside of leaf	Discard plants; control materials are unsafe for homeowners
Whitish, powdery mildew growth on surface of leaves, sometimes on petals of flowers	Spray with Karathane or Actidione
Black, wet rot that makes roots look hollow and collapse, induced by cold, wet soil	Drench soil with Truban or Dexon; sterilize potting medium (discard plants) and used pots
Pre-emergence seed decay; rot of seedling at soil line	Purchase treated seed; sterilize seed-sow medium
Small, yellow, circular or irregular spots	Spray with Captan
Limited basal rot; black die-back of growing points in older plants and ultimate wilting	Grow only in sterilized potting mixture and pots; discard sick plants
Brown rotting and blighting; fuzzy, grayish spore masses	Remove old flowers and destroy infected parts; avoid excessive moisture
Small, circular blisterlike spots on leaves; yellow-greenish spots on leaf margins and ultimate wilting	Keep water off leaves; subirrigate
Charcoal-like fungus appears as black coating on stems and leaf surfaces	To prevent, control insects

GLOSSARY

Adventitious roots are those that arise from aerial plant parts, underground stems or from relatively old roots

Areole, in cacti, a clearly defined small area that may bear felt, spines, glochids, flowers or new branches

Anther, the pollen-bearing part of the stamens

Annual, a plant that completes its life cycle in a year or less

Blade, the extended part of a leaf or petal

Bulbet, a small bulb arising in a leaf axil

Callus, a term applied to the mass of parenchyma cells that develops from and around wounded plant tissue

Calyx, the circle of floral parts, composed of sepals

Chlorosis, an abnormal plant condition in which leaves turn yellow, particularly between the veins

Clone, a group of plants derived by vegetative propagation from one original plant

Cultivar, a plant of hybrid or mutant origin that is maintained only in cultivation

Cuttings, parts of a plant, usually stems, leaves or roots, prepared and used for propagation

Deciduous, a plant or tree that sheds all of its leaves annually

Division, the portion of a plant used for propagation; also the act of preparing such a division

Dolomite, a form of limestone containing magnesium, prepared for agricultural use

Epiphyte, an air plant growing nonparasitically on another plant or elevated support

Espalier, a tree or shrub with branches trained in a flat herringbone pattern on house walls, fences or trellis; a fence or trellis upon which such a plant grows

Eye, an underdeveloped growth bud that ultimately produces a new plant or new growth; eyes at joints of a rooted cutting will produce new growth

F$_1$ first-generation progeny from hybridization or plant breeding

Flat, a shallow tray used in greenhouses to contain small pots, propagation media and to transport numbers of plants conveniently

Floret, technically a minute flower; applied to the flowers of grasses and composites (daisy family)

Forcing, hastening a plant to maturity or other usable state

Frond, a leaf, once applied to leaves of ferns but now to leaves of palms

Genus, a designation of the first part of the scientific name of a species

Glochid, a thin barbed bristle, produced in the areoles of cholla, prickly pear and other cacti

Hardy—when used in connection with temperate zone plants it means frost- or freeze-tolerant

Hybrid, a plant resulting from a cross between parents that are genetically distinct

Inferior, beneath, below; said of an ovary situated below the apparent point of attachment of stamens and perianths (sepals and petals)

Iron chelate, a chemical that is added to the soil to treat plants with iron chlorosis; a combination of iron and a complex organic substance that makes the iron already in soils more available to plants

Leaflet, a small leaf, several of which make up a compound leaf (e.g. of the ash tree)

Mutant, the result of a sudden variation in an inherited characteristic

Node, a joint where one or more leaves or other vestiges are borne on a stem

Offset, a small bulb or other portion of a plant that can be detached for propagation

Ovary, the ovule-bearing part of a pistil

Peat moss, peat formed from partial decomposition of sphagnum moss, reeds, grasses or sedges; sphagnum peat moss is considered as best for mixing with potting soils

Perlite, a mineral expanded by heating to form white-colored, very light kernels used for lightening soil

Perennial, a plant that lives more than two years

Petiole, the supporting stalk of a leaf

Pinna, the leaflet of a compound leaf, mainly of ferns; the primary divisions (pinnae) attached to the main stem or midrib of the frond

pH—the term "pH" is a measure of the degree of acidity or alkalinity of a soil. The values range from 0, which is the most acid, to 14.0, which is most alkaline. The neutral point is 7.0. Soil reaction as measured by pH is important because it has a direct relationship on the availability of nutrients for plant growth

Pinnate, refers to a compound leaf with leaflets or segments along each side of a midrib or stalk

Pips, terminal root stocks of certain flowering plants, especially lily of the valley; also seeds of certain fruits

Pistil, the unit of the female element of a flower, comprised of ovary, style and stigma

Rachis, axis, main stalk or midrib bearing pinnae of a fern or palm frond

Rhizome, a thickened underground stem that spreads by creeping

Root-bound (or pot-bound), a condition that results from a plant remaining too long in its container

Rosette, a cluster of leaves arranged in an overlapping circular pattern, somewhat like the petals of a rose

Runner, a slender stem that grows along the surface of the ground and bears young plants, such as that of the strawberry

Seed, the ripened ovule

Sphagnum, a group of mosses native to bogs; collected in whole pieces, fresh or dried; pieces of sphagnum moss are used for air layering and lining wire baskets or totems

Spore, a simple type of reproductive cell that is capable of producing a new plant; mosses and ferns reproduce by spores

Sport, a plant that shows a marked change from the parent stock; a mutation

Standard, a plant that does not naturally grow as a tree, and which is trained into a small, treelike form

Stomata, the minute orifices or pores in the epidermis of a leaf

Subirrigation, application of water to a plant by capillarity from below

Sucker, any unwanted shoot; may come from underground or the lower part of a plant

Surfactant, wetting agent that makes water wetter by lowering its surface tension, enabling water to wet soil components more quickly

Tubercle, a miniature tuber; tuberlike body or projection

Tuberous root, a thickened underground food-storage structure that is technically a root

Variety, a third word in a botanical name that indicates a variant of a species

Vermiculite, a mineral that is heated and exploded to form spongelike, lightweight kernels; useful in conditioning soils and as a medium in which to root cuttings

Whorl, three or more leaves, branches or flowers that grow in a circle from a joint or node on a stem or trunk

INDEX